REVISIONING SPIRITUALITY

REVISIONING SPIRITUALITY

Human Transformation AND THE Communal Imagination

John Markey AND
Michael Ceragioli

Paulist Press
New York / Mahwah, NJ

Cover image by Eric Tao
Cover and book design by Lynn Else

Sections of chapters 2 and 3 are adapted from John Markey, OP, Creating Communion: The Theology of the Constitutions of the Church (2003) and used by courtesy of New City Press.

Library of Congress Cataloging-in-Publication Data
Names: Markey, John J. author | Ceragioli, Michael author
Title: Revisioning spirituality: human transformation and the communal imagination / John Markey, OP, and Michael Ceragioli.
Description: New York; Mahwah, NJ: Paulist Press, [2025] | Includes index. | Summary: "This book assesses and develops the contemporary study of Christian spirituality, beginning with the story of the birth of the academic discipline in the United States in the late twentieth century"—Provided by publisher.
Identifiers: LCCN 2024060247 (print) | LCCN 2024060248 (ebook) | ISBN 9780809157747 paperback | ISBN 9780809189403 ebook
Subjects: LCSH: Spirituality—Catholic Church—History—20th century
Classification: LCC BX2350.65 .M3337 2025 (print) | LCC BX2350.65 (ebook) | DDC 248.4/82—dc23/eng/20250804
LC record available at https://lccn.loc.gov/2024060247
LC ebook record available at https://lccn.loc.gov/2024060248

ISBN 978-0-8091-5774-7 (paperback)
ISBN 978-0-8091-8940-3 (ebook)

Published by Paulist Press
997 Macarthur Boulevard
Mahwah, NJ 07430
www.paulistpress.com

Printed and bound in the
United States of America

To Ron Rolheiser
Mentor, colleague, friend

CONTENTS

ACKNOWLEDGEMENTS

IN A BOOK THAT considers the history of the discipline of Christian spirituality, it is first of all important to express gratitude for those who aided us in understanding our common task. The relationships we have forged are not merely academic. The key figures for the development of our understanding include Sandra Schneiders, Philip Sheldrake, Wendy Wright, Bernard McGinn, and, chiefly, Ron Rolheiser, who created the milieu and opportunity to bring about our collaboration on this book. We also pay respect to Donald Gelpi, whose inquiry into American pragmatism and Christianity we seek to carry forward.

We are also grateful to the Oblate School of Theology (OST), especially Sr. Sue Pontz and Scott Woodward, a community in which we have found both guides and stimulating peers. In addition to the above-mentioned figures, Dan Horan, Tim Robinson, Amy Maxey, and Cliff Knighten have helped to inform and sharpen our sense of this field of study in the collaboration and conversation we have shared at OST. The emerging pragmatist community rooted in San Antonio at the school deserves special mention: August Higgins, Nathan Garcia, Greg Zuschlag, and the Chief Pragmatist-in-Residence, Paniel Reyes Cardenas, have been indispensable in the development of the ideas presented in this text. Outside of the OST world, we have benefited tremendously from our talks with Chris Tirres and Nancy Pineda-Madrid.

On a personal level, we have each depended on the support of our families for nurturing us and our aspirations. I, John, would like to particularly thank my own family, my dear friends the Streit family, Cyd Crouse, and my Dominican community here in San Antonio, particularly Wayne Cavalier and Marcos Ramos for all the generosity and support that they have shown me during this process. I, Michael, thank my parents, Guy and Debbie, and my sister Monica for their love, steadfastness, and rare wisdom. I also thank Cathy Burzik for her kindness and encouragement during my time at OST. Finally, I thank Allie, without whom nothing would be possible.

We are especially grateful to our editor at Paulist Press, Donna Crilly, who has been a ready ear and flexible advisor along the way. We thank the whole Paulist team as well. A final special thanks to Monsignor Jeremiah McCarthy—the humble pillar of support for many in our community—for his diligent reading and editing of the text.

INTRODUCTION

Revisioning the Foundations of Christian Spirituality

ON THE BIRTHS OF ACADEMIC DISCIPLINES

THE BIRTH OF AN ACADEMIC discipline is a sign with a meaning worth unfolding. The birth of an academic discipline reveals something of the state of consciousness at the time and place of the discipline's founding, just as it signals a direction for future thought. Consider how burgeoning economic theory ran in tandem with the Industrial Age, breaking through as a study of its own with the publication of Adam Smith's *The Wealth of Nations* (first appearing, not incidentally, in 1776). So, too, the emergence of academic psychology approximately a century later in part reflected and in part ushered in a new era of the mind: the intensely self-preoccupied, conflict-ridden, and isolated form of consciousness brilliantly characterized by literary Modernists like Eliot, Woolf, and Kafka. With respect to the emergent malady of the soul, you might say that academic psychology represents *symptom*, *doctor*, and *exacerbating agent* all rolled into one: psychology is the study that indicates the depth and contours of human late modern dysfunction, that provides tools and instructions for the relief corps sent to assist, and that advances the powerful worldview that stimulates and reinforces the predicament. Indeed, Freud, the pioneer standing to psychology as Smith does to economics, combines these three features in one body of work—diagnosing a whole culture's illness in *Western Civilization and Its Discontents*, providing methods of treatment in psychoanalysis, and, in retrospect, doing as much to deepen our sense of individual isolation as to relieve it. Whether we evaluate economics or psychology, the birth of an academic discipline proves to be a sign worth unfolding.

Nevertheless, one cannot proceed far in the exploration of the birth event without encountering the resistance of conflictual interpretations: in the first place, it proves difficult to establish agreement on the publication, the organization, the discovery, or the declaration that establishes the discipline under review. And tied up with the question of the founding event is the matter of the authorities to be invoked. A certain school of psychoanalysts, for example, will not permit you to begin counting psychology's birthdays until after Freud described the case of "Anna O" in 1895. All the same, you encounter those who suggest the folly of claiming the birth of any real discipline at all, on the point of view that essential frameworks have long been around, just buried by neglect or misapprehension. "Why begin with Freud—or even Wundt or James?" these critics ask. "Why not start with Hippocrates and the four humors, or Augustine of Hippo and the restless interior life given expression in the *Confessions*?" And last of all there rises the party that persists in questioning the legitimacy of the discipline's enterprise wholesale, no matter the incursions of the field's language and concepts into mainstream consciousness: "What right," they charge, "has psychology to be considered an academic discipline at all? Behaviorism mistakes humanity for lower forms of life; psychoanalysis stands as mere pseudoscience, unable to verify its claims; and the contemporary psychology practiced in American universities and clinics relies on subjective self-reports that cannot be feasibly compared the one to the other."

The birth of a discipline is a sign with a meaning worthy to unfold, but just the same, the unfolding counts as a slippery and treacherous exploration. This is so especially in the early stages, before history has fully vindicated the discipline's existence, and before a community of truth-seeking inquirers has settled and stabilized the field's identity. Yet wheresoever the discipline possesses an authentic life, wheresoever the discipline opens the way to insights that previously lacked the means of expression, where the public (however unconsciously) seeks a fresh way of seeing, not only will the discipline find its legs, but moreover the sign of its birth will reward the effort of interpretation. Through interpretation of the events of its genesis, we can begin to discover the discipline's significance, perhaps even its indispensability, as a guide for our future inquiries. The uncovering of foundations, tracing back to the legacy of ancestors and the initial flowering of hopes, can help focus the sights of future students and researchers. Economics, psychology, and sociology, among other more recent disciplines, have benefited from such inquiries. As we will make clear, exploration of the foundations of the study of Christian spirituality—a new discipline drawing from an old storehouse—promises certain treasures not only for researchers but for all spiritual seekers.

SPIRITUALITY AND THEOLOGY: UNITY LOST AND UNITY SOUGHT

The spiritual life of Christians is nothing new: the tradition of Christian spirituality stretches over two thousand years, developing from Hebrew and Greek traditions going back centuries more. The term *spirituality*, when first invoked, emerged from the adjective *spiritual* in the writings of St. Paul, indicating the gift of the Holy Spirit. For Paul, the gift of the Spirit leads to life in the Spirit, drawing individuals into healing relationship with Christ and the church. From the days of Paul, commentators have reflected critically on life in the Spirit, offering tools for the rational grasp of and emotional development within the Christian mystery. The earthy reflections of Egyptian desert fathers and mothers marked out a path of liberation from emotional attachment so as to make space for God's transforming grace, while the influential bishops of the early church coordinated intense Christian devotion with biblical investigation.

In fact, as Hans Urs von Balthasar remarks, for much of Christian history, one would be hard-pressed to understand Christian spirituality and Christian theology as anything but a unitary endeavor. In the High Middle Ages, monastic theologians connected head and heart in rich texts exploring the spiritual sense of scripture, as in St. Bernard of Clairvaux's *Commentary on the Song of Songs*; in such an environment, the expounding of the meaning of the scriptures and mystical contemplation constituted a continuous enterprise. The theologian, in the patristic age and up to the peak of the medieval period, was taken to be one who not only knew *about* God but who knew and experienced God. In the words of Christian ascetic Evagrius of Ponticus, "One who prays is a theologian; a theologian is one who prays."[1]

As von Balthasar judges, the affective and intellectual synthesis of Christian life began to pull apart around the twelfth century, the final period during which the sapiential approach of monastic theology combined a biblical-doctrinal rigor with a rich and dedicated personal piety.[2] As theological inquiry migrated from the monastery to the schools, the speculative bent of "systematic theology" separated from the spiritual-pastoral orientation of Christian practice and ministry, and theology at the desk became remote from prayer on one's knees. The original unity broken, dogmatic theology grew in the modern period to be formally distinguished from spiritual theology, which itself became divided into ascetical theology (focused on the individual's active conformity to God, up until mystical experience) and mystical theology (centering on the "passive" work of God in the soul by way of mystical union). The issue was not academic specialization as such, nor the use of refined scholarly methods, but the loss of the direct encounter with the divine mystery in guiding and shaping theological investigation.[3] In his essay "Theology and Sanctity," von Balthasar laments that after the period of Albert the Great, Thomas Aquinas, and Bonaventure at the end of the thirteenth century, we witness "the disappearance of the 'complete' theologian…the theologian who is also a saint."[4] In subsequent centuries in the Catholic Church, too often the arid scholastic speculation of official theologians stood across a great divide from the prayer and commitment of Christians in the lay and religious state alike. Works of genuine spiritual depth and insight continued to be composed, yet these treatments came to be roped off as exercises pertaining to the "interior life" and thus divorced from the standardized theological curriculum of schools and seminaries. Spiritual autobiographies, reports transcribed by third parties, poems, hymns, and even more speculative treatises seldom crossed over to find their way into the often-formulaic textbooks of spiritual theology.

The outstanding theologians of the middle part of the twentieth century—the forerunners and fathers of the Second Vatican Council such as von Balthasar, Henri de Lubac, Louis Bouyer, Yves Congar, Marie-Dominque Chenu, and Karl Rahner—helped to heal this rift through the recovery of the wider and more integrated tradition. In their retrieval of patristic and medieval thought, Balthasar, de Lubac, and Bouyer shed light upon the mystical center of scripture and the mystical journey into the knowledge of Christ and his passion. Congar, Chenu, and Rahner, who began their careers dedicated to reimagining Aquinas in contemporary terms, reminded their readers that Aquinas's theology is best understood in light of the pursuit of holiness. Even as these two camps clashed and came to view the theological task and direction of the church in opposition to one another, they shared a vision of the reunification of spirituality and theology. The movement of spiritual reinvigoration has extended well beyond the Roman Catholic Church. Theologians across confessions have begun to consistently engage spiritual and mystical texts like the *Showings* of Julian of Norwich, Teresa of Avila's *Interior Castle*, the poetry of John of the Cross, and the journals of Jonathan Edwards.

In the Catholic Church, where the conversation began, the former rationalistic and deductive methods that did little to evoke mystery or encounter with God have given way to nuanced contextual and historical inquiry. Whether achieved through Balthasar's soaring aesthetics, Karl Rahner's reflections on grace mediated in the ordinary round of life, or the communal theology of liberation of Gustavo Gutierrez, the theological re-engagement of the spiritual life has been the abiding concern. For Balthasar's successors, monastic theologians like Bernard of Clairvaux remain inspirations for this ongoing task of the rebinding of intellectual inquiry and spiritual health. Doubtless, their work radiates an authentic ardor seldom palpable from the pens of deskbound theologians. The patient labor of mining these genuine sources of encounter remains essential and alive. We could call this the labor of spiritual reconstitution, approached from the theological side.

THE FRESH IMPETUS

Nevertheless, even as theology grew to reintegrate the spiritual life in the course of the twentieth century, the study and practice of spirituality jumped the fences of its theological farm. Expressions of spirituality and conversations about spirituality flowered in new places: not only within churches; but also, among Christian churches, and among Christians and participants in the world religions. Spirituality also gained traction outside of the churches entirely, including through ecological, feminist, and peace movements. In the academy, not only did non-Catholic Christians begin to engage with an area that had once attracted skepticism, but *spirituality*, the term once inextricable from the action of the Holy Spirit, began to be adopted in accounts of other religions and cultural traditions. In the Christian and Western philosophical traditions, the term *spirituality* had already shifted to signify a difference between the "spirit" and "spiritual" on one hand and "matter" and the "material" on the other.[5] This philosophical sense made possible the more contemporary understanding of the spirit as the "deepest center of the person."[6]

Despite the dualistic inheritance, the study of spirituality took on a holistic hue, seeking to overcome the inner side of the inner-outer dialectic that had characterized the theological rupture and the dualistic split between matter and spirit regnant from the time of Descartes. Late twentieth-century spirituality research considered broad dimensions of human integration and self-transcendence, including politics, gender, and professional activity; this early discourse reflected the view that an understanding of embodiment and its messy complexities is fundamental to an understanding of the human being's transcendent orientation.[7] In the academy, the fruits of this growth include the publication of the French *Dictionnaire de la vie spirituelle*, the twenty-five-volume *World Spirituality* series, and the Classics of Western Spirituality series, now at well over one hundred volumes. To these high-quality texts, a slew of excellent journal articles, monographs, and research tools have been added, while graduate programs and research institutes dedicated to the study of spirituality have taken root.[8]

Although it is appropriate to ask questions about the legitimacy of some shoots on the contemporary spirituality tree, it is equally necessary to accommodate and nurture the expansion. For those who have come of age in a globalized landscape exposed to a wide variety of religious expressions, used to being surrounded by sisters and brothers raised according to different beliefs; those who have been raised in an atmosphere of secularity, whether hostile or indifferent to Christianity; those who have become conscious of how Christian churches and believers have transgressed the Christian principle of universal dignity and equality; those who recognize, then, in the world religions a ray of light, and in the historical expression of Christianity a certain kind of problem; for those, in short, who know in their bones that we must also take as a starting point the often-ambivalent histories and the often-excluded experiences not caught even in the wide net of theological recovery, the endeavor of reconstitution must begin not only from the theological arena, but from elsewhere. The early cry of the advocates for the discipline of spirituality is that, in order to address the new impetus, not only must the canon of spiritual authors be expanded, not only must the underside of the Christian legacy be addressed, not only must the "others" of world religious traditions be admitted as partners, but a different form of inquiry must be established. Herein lies the creative drive behind the birth of the discipline of Christian spirituality.

From its formal foundation as a discipline in the United States in the early 1990s, Christian spirituality—conceived afresh, apart from spiritual theology, that is—has taken as its keynote the study of "lived human experience." The discipline of Christian spirituality aims in this way to reach the transcendent by starting from the ground up. The theological interest in overcoming stultifying and degrading dualisms remains; the effort at a kind of reconstitution aiming at a greater wholeness remains; while a new imperative, an imperative tied also to a broader sociopolitical awakening, has sprung up: "Let us not overleap the experience of the Christian life, which also means the experience of those who have previously been habitually stepped over." Christian spirituality humbly knocks first on this door to gain entry, which has not always been the front door for scholars; once the door swings open, the perspective on Christianity shifts. The multifaceted and frequently surprising social contexts of Christian life become inhabited rather than overridden, spectated, or even ignored. Dialogue partners are also afforded thick descriptions of their spiritual lives and traditions, following a method that begins with critical description rather than normative criteria.

The discipline of spirituality has been remarkably self-conscious from the beginning; such an outlook comes with the territory of having begun through intense conversations about its place in an academic world shorn of previous certainties. Spirituality emerged amid the maelstrom of postmodern deconstructivism in academia and the attendant destabilization of totalizing narratives, suspicion over the power relations inherent to presumptively truth-seeking discourses, and doubts regarding the possibility of founding inquiry on self-transparent bedrock principles. Naturally, for a discipline addressing Christian experience, the relationship with full-throated postmodernism can only be tense: while the thoroughly postmodern impulse pushes toward a skeptical and subjectivistic account of reality, the Christian imagination retains confidence in the trustworthiness of a God who reveals oneself and calls all to the same destiny of communion. However, even this confidence contains a measure of paradox, for the transcendent God is understood to be a hidden God, a God who lies beyond all rational categories, remaining a mystery beyond knowing even in our loving approach.

On the whole, while not forsaking truth or meaning, spirituality gladly takes the postmodern shattering of Enlightenment myths in hand, including the illusion of the separation between a clearly bounded, "pure" object of study on one hand and the disinterested researcher on the other. Spirituality may be a genuine discipline, but its borders are blurred, as it draws liberally from several partners. As for the position of the researcher, the discipline's pioneers insist that the study of spirituality is, in a turn of phrase that has stuck, "self-implicating." In a sense, this claim is true for any field of research, no matter how dismal the science in question. No scholarly pursuit stands so aloof from life that engagement does not possess ethical or practical implications. What we study shapes us such that we change our way of being in the world; all boundaries are porous, the strands of existence ineluctably intertwined.

A child of its time, spirituality brings this increasingly accepted insight out into the open. But all the same, the "self-implicating" badge says more, gesturing toward the profoundly participative dimension of spiritual research, connecting the study of Christian spirituality with personal transformation. Here again, as with the synthesis represented by Bernard of Clairvaux, head and heart unite. Indeed, in its self-implicating character, spirituality resembles good theology; spirituality's stance represents a version of what von Balthasar maintains in his call for a "kneeling theology" that seeks the face of the Lord. But we might also say that the discipline of spirituality, in its fidelity to the concreteness of human experience, kneels before the other kneeling before God.

SPIRITUALITY'S PRAGMATIST INHERITANCE AND POTENTIAL

Hidden Connections: American Pragmatism and the Leading Ideas of Spirituality[9]

The Society for the Study of Contemporary Spirituality first met in November 1992 in San Francisco, California.[10] The setting is fitting—across the bay from the Graduate Theological Union in Berkeley, where biblical scholar Sandra Schneiders had toiled to establish the parameters for the discipline in several founding papers, including "Spirituality and Theology: Strangers, Rivals, or Partners?" (1986) and "Spirituality in the Academy" (1989).[11]

Not only is the San Francisco Bay area an appropriate location for the establishment of this research society, but panning out, the United States proves an appropriate country for its emergence. The discipline's emphasis on lived experience picks up the late career concern of influential Harvard psychologist and philosopher William James, who carved a path upon which many in the United States have followed. James's famous *The Varieties of Religious Experience*, adapted from his 1901 Gifford Lectures, prescinds from analysis according to strict theological categories in order to examine the immediate and direct religious experience of individuals, along with the enduring fruits of their conversions.

James analyzes the accounts of extraordinary mystics preserved within various religious traditions, as well as the chronicles of ordinary Christians from his own time. By deliberately eschewing theological discourse, James aims to concentrate more exactly on the definitive features of the experience of his subjects. Not without a certain level of hopeful naivete, he adopts the personal faith that experience has the potential to unite where dogma previously divided.

From his collected accounts, James delineates four signatures of mystical experience: transiency of duration; ineffability of the experience; the sense of passivity of the subject; and the experience's "noetic" quality (i.e., providing a sense of "enlightenment"). Mystical experience, he conjectures, can be explained through a kind of subconscious permeability. James theorizes that the subconscious is connected to the dimension of mystery James calls "the Unseen." Through openness to the contents of the subconscious, the mystic comes into contact with this region. Whatever its shortcomings, *Varieties* was a watershed text, inspiring the development of the descriptive-psychological mold of appraisal of mystical experience in the academy. So too, in popular practice, James's focus on solitary, absorptive religious experience has influenced the increasingly numerous "spiritual but not religious" partisans on the hunt for the presence of the divine.

Sharing a fence with William James for decades in Cambridge was longtime friend, colleague, and neighbor Josiah Royce, whom James had recruited to Harvard from, incidentally, UC Berkeley. Royce was sympathetic to James's project and equally motivated to find a source of understanding to overcome sectarian and religious divisions. However, he disagreed with James's restriction of religious experience to the experience of individuals, as well as his dependence upon what he sarcastically labels James's theory of the "mysterious upwelling from the subconscious."[12] So as to include additional pathways of encounter with God, Royce speaks of religious insight rather than simply experience. He adds social experience, reason, and the loyalty of persons to a community, among others, to his list of sources of religious insight.

The backyard fence was not only physical: by the time of Royce's publication of *Sources of Religious Insight* in 1912, the two had sparred for decades as proponents of opposing philosophical positions. James ultimately advocated for a version of philosophical pluralism emphasizing the open-ended, unstable "flux and flow" of existence, while Royce defended a version of absolute idealism in which he teased out the nature of the relationship between free individuals and the all-encompassing consciousness of the Supreme Knower unifying them. Though James passed away in 1910, Royce carried on their conversation, developing his approach to metaphysics and religious experience until his own death in 1916.

As these stories go, it was the intervention from beyond the halls of Harvard, the line of thought late to be fully recognized in Cambridge, that initiated the vital breakthrough. Royce's close study of the philosophical logic of the maverick polymath Charles Sanders Peirce (also a friend of both Royce and James) brought Royce's ideas to their most complete and satisfying expression, emboldening Royce to press toward the most substantial articulation of his communal metaphysics in 1913 in the lectures that became *The Problem of Christianity*.[13]

James, Royce, and Peirce may be responsible for initiating a single new kind of conversation about religion, but just as much they represent two distinct trajectories for the conversation's continuation. They also reflect a forking in American spiritual culture. In his focus on extraordinary and spontaneous private religious experience while disregarding collective religious expression, James stands as a father figure for the experimental spiritual individualism that strives to plumb inner depths, break through subconscious resistances, and thereby achieve openness to the transcendent. If not necessarily ignorant of religious traditions, James's descendants are comfortable refraining from expressing allegiance to any specific tradition, seeking the transcendent according to an admixture of practices and beliefs guided by a personal compass. Royce and Peirce, on the other hand, stand as "prophets of community," emphasizing how personal fulfillment is achieved within a social matrix.[14] For Royce and Peirce, the self-transcending inclinations of the individual find their aim through participation within communities of interpretation. Royce's thought is dominated by the decisive contrast between the detached individual—"a lost being"—and the saved person united with a community of charity. The early Pauline churches, drawn together into a unity by the spirit of Christ, constitute the primordial expression of this reality. Rather than the legacy of spiritual individualism, Royce and Peirce point to a path of development through social participation; relationship to the transcendent arrives especially through fidelity to particular communities that nevertheless tend toward an all-embracing solidarity.

These three figures provide a foundational set of leading ideas for the contemporary study of spirituality. Through his turn to experience and attention to religious conversion, James guides the discipline's study of the holistic transformation of the human being. Royce helpfully overcomes the limitations of James's perspective, offering a sketch of the multiple modes of religious experience, and, in particular, the social fulfillment of the individual. Royce also inspires with his expression of the horizon of the spiritual journey through the significance of fidelity to what he terms "the Beloved Community." Peirce's pivotal insight into the triadic form of knowing overcomes the malignant dualisms of thought (inner-outer, matter-spirit, body-soul) that the discipline of spirituality must take as its mission to overcome. Finally, as seminal figures of the philosophical school of American pragmatism, the three together reinforce spirituality's ramifications for the field of theology, inasmuch as pragmatists hold that the meaning and validity of any theory is understood according to its practical, operational consequences. Ideas are known by their effects; theory can only be understood through praxis. For the pragmatists, lived spiritual experience possesses a creative and constitutive relationship—not merely a derivative relationship—to Christian doctrine.

The Triadic Paradigm

In terms of the dynamics of pragmatism, again, however, Royce and Peirce fall on one side and James on the other. The source of the disagreement (a disagreement both epistemological and ontological) leads to another crucial idea for an understanding of self-transcending human experience: the role and structure of interpretation. Peirce, the founder of pragmatism, and Royce, in agreement with Peirce's way of thinking, present a markedly distinct version of pragmatism from James, especially in their exposition of the triadic character of human experience. James proposes an essentially dyadic paradigm of perceptions and conceptions, in which perceptions are "cashed out" in conceptions while valid conceptions give rise to further perceptions. As the interplay between perceptions and conceptions advances, truth is defined as what "works"—the notions that prove useful and beneficial. On Royce's critique, inspired by his close reading of Peirce, James's dyadic scheme fails to explain how conceptions and perceptions translate into one another.[15]

James's approach also ignores a basic dimension of our knowing: our intercourse with other minds. The contents of another mind cannot simply be gained by a direct perception; lacking such a perception, then, no true conception is possible either. A third kind of cognitive process of an essentially social character is required.[16] Royce names *interpretation* as the cognitive process capable of achieving this kind of communication. Consider an ordinary social encounter. In order to know what a friend is thinking, you cannot proceed from sense impressions of their presence in front of you to a conception of their thoughts; you must at the very least interpret their bodily movements and gestures. You may interpret a restlessness or harshness of expression as a sign your friend is upset with you. Your friend's verbal communication, itself an interpretation of their being, might expand your initial understanding. Their speech may also provide a modification or correction of your interpretation, as when a friend says, "It may have appeared as if I was angry with you, but I was actually still processing bad news about my mother I had received just before we met." All the same, their verbal communication continues the process of interpretation, supplying the means for further understanding, as might be the case if you later interpret your friend's hasty departure as occasioned by their rush to tend to their mother.

In this view, it is not the familiar dualism of conception and perception (and the consequent explanatory restriction to a single subject) but the triadic process of interpretation that guides our knowledge of reality. Interpretation is "triadic" because it necessarily includes three terms. Royce uses the example of the translation of an Egyptian text. To understand the intention of the translation, one must invoke the following: first, there is the Egyptian papyrus; second the translator of the text; and third, the person who reads the translation. In the case of the Egyptian papyrus, the interpreter's efficacy depends both on the translator's fidelity to the historical meaning of the original text and their power to make the text comprehensible to future readers.

Interpretation can also be formulated archetypally as the relationship between three persons A, B, and C in which a loyal interpreter B interprets A to C. The mediating agent, that is, the interpreter, forms the glue of this primitive community; the three become a community according to the mediation of the third. Royce's paradigm stresses the ethical basis of interpretation and of community. For interpretation to be successful, the loyal interpreter B must be dedicated to both A and C. Communities of shared loyalty form a generative society, founded upon shared memories and oriented toward a shared hope. For Royce, even when we reflect on our personal experience, we form a triadic community, for our present self interprets our past self to our future self. Accordingly, the experiences of individuals in their solitude studied by James are also inescapably triadic in character.

As Royce and Peirce have it, an understanding of lived experience—both for the one who experiences and the one who investigates—requires the third of *interpretation*. In their view, the process of ongoing interpretation manifests the irreducibly relational character of reality. The philosophy of interpretation becomes the hinge for a communal metaphysics. Peirce called this discipline *semeiosis* (the science of the interpretation of signs), and he dedicated the latter part of his life to its clarification.[17] Peirce's semeiosis recognizes human beings as sign-sending and sign-receiving organisms, bound to community by the real continuity of mind shared by individuals. The individual and community are both fallible for Peirce, but the individual to a far greater degree; the individual's proclivity for error smooths out only through the alert relationship to shared interpretations.

In this vein, Peirce's philosophy facilitates a deeper understanding of Royce's career project interrelating the "sacred pair" of the individual and the community. As with Royce's philosophy, Peircean semeiosis highlights the ethical and communal dimensions of the pursuit of the truth. Peirce suggests that truth can be understood as the conclusion fated to be agreed on by the community of humble, rightly motivated investigators.[18] In appealing to the final opinion of the community, Peirce understands the truth as the goal that we progressively approach yet do not definitively attain in the course of our inquiries. Thus, the total truth belongs to the future.

Addressing Spirituality's Central Questions

This communal philosophy of inquiry applies a kind of metaphysical lens to a profoundly biblical way of seeing. The metaphysics of community coheres with the scriptural narrative of the journey of the pilgrim people toward God, which leads to spirituality's central notion of holistic personal and collective conversion. Peirce's understanding of the constant revision attendant to the humble, shared pursuit of the truth finds agreement with the stance of one ever on the road to God. And Royce, after all, considers interpretation as the search for an essentially spiritual object that is never fully closed down upon.[19] As he suggests in *The Problem of Christianity*, our immediate experience leads us to the quest of interpretation, which points ahead to a transcendent goal:

> The heaven of glittering immediacies answers the quest by saying: It is not in me. Interpretation says: Neither is it in you—not even in your heart; but shows us, through manifesting the very nature of the object to be sought, what conditions must be met if anyone is to interpret a genuine Sign to an understanding mind. And, in the end, interpretation seeks a city out of sight, the homeland where, perhaps, we learn to understand one another.[20]

If spirituality is to be true to the wholeness of lived experience, a triadic, communal metaphysics must stand at its foundation. The core ideas of a communal metaphysics—triadic knowing, the individual's humble participation in the whole, and ongoing personal and collective transformation—resonate with the fundamental tenor of Christian spirituality. As this book proceeds, we seek to unpack the meaning of these principles, as well as to suggest possibilities for further development. At the heart of the proposal is the claim that spirituality, occupied with the study of the human relationship with the triune God, must proceed according to the rule of three.

Thus, a relational-communal metaphysics offers a way beyond the subject-object dualism that has hampered the understanding of spiritual experience and left the mediation of other people and of traditions insufficiently recognized or tacked onto a subject-centered framework. Several fundamental questions, which we will address as we go, cannot be answered adequately according to a philosophy that remains tied to the binary of subject-object, and which labors under formulations that frame spirituality as the subjective experience of the objective reality of God. The following elementary questions, we argue, are best addressed through a semeiotic communal metaphysics:

1. How can spiritual experience be understood beyond the realm of private, ultimately incommunicable experience? How is it that we can ever make spiritual claims that reach beyond our personal experience?
2. How does spirituality make sense of the notion that lived faith has historically been rooted in communal experience and communal forms of expression? How do we account for the fact that the Catholic tradition, among others, holds that spiritual events can be mediated ritually and cultically?
3. How can we understand what it means to relate to a triune God, who according to tradition, reveals himself to us? How does this God communicate with us? What modes of interpretation do we have in order to understand this communication?
4. How is it that a person is changed or transformed in relationship to God? If, as Aristotle maintains, knowing comes through imitation, how does this God manifest to me in a way in which my consciousness and habits are changed? How do people and external events mediate this transformation?

Introduction

RETURNING TO THE FOUNDERS: A TRIADIC PROPOSAL

How can the ideas floated by the three pragmatists in the late nineteenth and early twentieth century contribute to the conversations among the scholars who developed Christian spirituality's approach in the latter part of the twentieth century? What might it mean for the discipline of spirituality to integrate a communal metaphysics along with a triadic understanding of reality? How might spirituality's elementary questions be addressed?

We can start by exploring one of the pivotal founding dialogues between Sandra Schneiders and Bernard McGinn that took place in 1993 and 1994 in the pages of the *Christian Spirituality Bulletin*. In his incisive article, "The Letter and the Spirit: Spirituality as an Academic Discipline," McGinn sketches three primary approaches to spirituality: theological, anthropological, and historical-contextual. The theological approach squares with older definitions of *spirituality*, in which the norm of divine revelation grounds and directs the discipline. Spirituality can neatly be considered, to adopt von Balthasar's phrase, "the subjective aspect of dogmatic theology."[21] In the theological construal of the discipline, anthropology, history, and the human sciences stand less as constitutive players and more as ad hoc interlocutors. The anthropological approach, which McGinn rightly connects with Sandra Schneiders, views spirituality as the "depth-dimension" of human existence, treating human authenticity and transcendence.[22] McGinn notes the advantages of the anthropological approach as compared to the theological: the anthropological approach is accessible for researchers and ecumenical and interreligious audiences and open to the work emerging from outside fields concerned with human experience. However, he finds fault with the vagueness of anthropological definitions, charging that they fail to carve out an adequately delineated or cohesive field.

McGinn's third approach, the historical-contextual, builds on the growing insight into the historically conditioned character of our experience, knowledge, and beliefs.[23] It is historical-contextual in that it "emphasizes spirituality as an experience rooted in a particular community's history rather than as a dimension of human existence as such."[24] McGinn recommends the historical-contextual for its capacity to attend to particular expressions of Christianity across time. The historical-contextual approach brings a specificity that the theological approach often neglects in its return to dogmatic touchstones and that the anthropological approach blurs in its expansive leanings. McGinn ultimately views the three approaches as mutually implicating, and he holds each to be necessary. He gives the historical-contextual a nod as leading to the other two—the historical experience of the community leading to the theological in its relation to the beliefs of a community and their truth claims, and to the anthropological in the ramifications of these historical communities for an understanding of human nature.

In an article in the subsequent issue of the *Bulletin*, Schneiders endorses McGinn's call for the use of all three approaches; however, she expresses pointed reservations about the theological and historical-contextual methods. For her, neither can be definitive. The normative criteria of the theological approach present an obstacle through the premature closure to many of the diverse expressions of Christian spirituality. This limitation is especially evident with respect to the inclusion of non-Christian sources such as native spiritualities, the world religions, and feminism.[25] Schneiders saves her most sustained critique for the historical-contextual methodology. She holds that although history supplies essential data, it does not on its own terms attend to the transhistorical nature of spirituality. She writes:

> One can study the conditions leading up to a conversion experience, the observable conditions of the experience itself, and its publicly available results including first or third person accounts of the experience. But can one study, historically, the conversion experience itself? Or mystical experience as such? Or transformation as religious or spiritual experience?...It seems to me that historical study, while indispensable as a participant in the study of the spiritual life, is not the defining method.[26]

We might suggest that Schneiders detects in the limitations of the exclusive use of the historical-contextual method what C. S.

Peirce would label a tendency toward nominalism. Nominalism is the philosophical position that rejects the existence of universals, holding that only concrete, sensible realities exist. For instance, thoroughgoing nominalism maintains that there is no such general shared nature of "humanity," but rather only unique individual human beings exist. In Peirce's estimation, the nominalistic temper of the philosophy of his time undermined the appropriate belief in the genuine continuity, relatedness, and explicability of reality essential to fruitful inquiry. Peirce considered the scientist who subscribed to nominalism to assent to an ultimate contradiction—denying philosophically the existence of the very general laws and classes he or she studied. (So, too, contemporary skeptical postmodern thought, in its endless deferral of meaning and repudiation of metaphysical realities, can be classed as a form of nominalism.) Though not deliberately espousing nominalist tenets, a strictly historical approach as read by Schneiders remains tied to particulars and does not possess the means to reach or identify general truths. If one remains confined to the historical approach, the multiplicity of phenomena may be described but the vital common realities at the heart of the discipline's inquiry are not penetrated. The conversion experience and mystical experience remain unplumbed at their center. Lacking further support, no accumulation of historical data regarding diverse Christian communities can probe into the ultimate objects of the study of spirituality.

Schneiders argues at last for a deeply interdisciplinary *hermeneutical approach*. By hermeneutical, she intends to signal interpretation true to the historical reality of the experience and comprehensible and meaningful in the present.[27] Schneiders's proposed "approach" (for spirituality depends upon no single method) includes three stages: first, the description of phenomena under investigation; second, the critical analysis of said phenomena; and third, constructive interpretation.[28] Schneiders resists considering spirituality finally according to the terms of any other discipline, denying that it is "reducible to a subdivision, or a moment within, any of these [constitutive] fields."[29] In this way, she takes an important stand for the autonomy of the fledgling discipline. Such claims provide the inspiration for the organic development of spirituality, a vision wherein spirituality develops in interaction with other disciplines, not circling back to a field by which it will ultimately be reabsorbed, but growing, as living things do, into its own rhythms and activities. This is not to say that contact with other disciplines becomes haphazard: in another article, Schneiders names scripture, the history of Christianity, and theology as constitutive disciplines (disciplines that supply fundamental data) for spirituality's hermeneutical task.[30]

Schneiders names the object of the discipline "spiritual life as experience," which, intentionally or not, harkens back to the preoccupation of William James. Her clarifications, however, tighten the Jamesian horizon in one respect and expand it in another. She tightens the horizon inasmuch as she clarifies the focus on Christianity in particular: Schneiders states that Christian spirituality addresses the spiritual life of Christians or the experience of the Christian life, depending on the point of view at hand. At the same time, she expands beyond James's tendency to prioritize special states of consciousness as definitive of religious experience. Schneiders identifies Christian spirituality as concerned not only with ecstatic experience but with the whole project of self-integration through self-transcendence—that is to say, concerned with the experience of the Christian life in its wholeness and its intrinsic aims.[31] In a much-repeated definition, she identifies the *spiritual* aspect of this life as "*the vital, ongoing interaction between the human spirit and the Spirit of God* with both poles receiving equal attention and the focus being on the fact, the modality, the process, the effects, the finality of the human interaction itself."[32] In this definition, an anthropological orientation remains evident (though not exclusive), as she places the stress upon the human pole. This special study of the human side of the interaction—both carrying forward and sophisticating James's first foray into religious experience—ultimately separates spirituality as an academic discipline from spiritual theology.

Returning to the notion of the birth of an academic discipline as a sign worth unfolding, the dialogue between these two pioneers of the study of Christian spirituality lends insight into crucial developmental questions in the discipline. For one, what kind of data, precisely, does spirituality examine? McGinn's attention to the historical communal matrix of spirituality provides a concrete and irreplaceable basis for subsequent inquiry, as Schneiders corroborates. Without neglecting scripture and theology, spirituality is powered by its encounter with history. Much of the significant advancement in spirituality in the twentieth century, namely, the various translations and historical investigations produced in the impressive volumes earlier named, has come through this kind of work. McGinn and his students at the University of Chicago have done a great deal to build up the repository of central, accessible texts within the field through translations and studies of mystical authors. Nevertheless, Schneiders rightly argues that amid this important labor, researchers must not lose sight of the transhistorical heart of the discipline; spirituality must necessarily engage the common reality of spiritual experience rather than merely a multiplicity of expressions.

How, then, can we understand the foundational framework of spiritual experience? Schneiders turns the conversation in a fruitful direction when she defines *spirituality* according to the interaction between the Spirit of God and the human spirit, placing an accent on the human spirit. However, her dipolar framing of the interaction between the Spirit of God on one hand and the human spirit on the other needs assistance, especially in light of the metaphysical clarifications of Peirce and Royce. If spirituality is conceived exclusively according to these two poles, we are left with an impotent dyad. As Peirce and Royce demonstrate, dyads can only be brought into fruitful relationship through the introduction of a third that unites them; every pair implies and requires a mediating third in order to be authentically related. Schneiders's formulation names no intrinsic means of mediation between the Spirit of God and the human spirit.[33] In this respect, such a definition still falls short of marking out a paradigm in which it is possible to effectively answer the foundational questions we earlier outlined:

1. How can spiritual experience be understood beyond the realm of private, ultimately incommunicable experience?
2. How does spirituality make sense of the various inherently social forms of faith expression?
3. What modes of interpretation are available to understand God's self-revelation?
4. How do people and external events mediate personal transformation?

Schneiders's dipolar definition requires a third, mediating agent.

The resolution lies in the community of interpretation. For good reason, Peirce and Royce understand the community of interpretation as an indispensable element of any account of reality. For Peirce, the truth belongs to the community rather than to any given individual; for Royce, the individual remains lost and ineffectual without being tethered to a community. As Royce powerfully attests in *The Problem of Christianity*, not only does the community stand as a second level of reality along with the individual, but the divine Spirit guides the whole, the Beloved Community, into all truth. In any complete account of Christian spirituality, the community formed by Christ must be given due weight, mirroring the way in which St. Paul understands the destiny of each individual as indissolubly joined to the destiny of the Body of Christ.

To speak again in the technical terms of triadic metaphysis, the community of interpretation must be placed in the mediating or reconciling position in order to provide an adequate framework for Christian spirituality. The traditions and experience of the community render possible and explicable the interaction between the divine spirit and the human spirit. As we will explore, the answer to each of our four foundational questions of Christian spirituality must be understood with reference to this community: one, the community deprivatizes and generates individual experience; two, it publicly mediates spiritual realities; three, it facilitates ongoing interpretation of God's action and human development; and four, it models and directs personal transformation. In keeping with Schneiders's critique of the historical-contextual method, the community cannot be understood as *merely* a historical community; it must possess a transcendent basis in order to relate the transcendent God to the human being capable of receiving God. With both a divine foundation and concrete instantiation, the mediating third holds firm as the Spirit-governed interpreter of God to the human person.

Here at the outset, then, we propose the Spirit of God, the human spirit, and the community of interpretation as the fundamental triad that grounds the study and practice of Christian spirituality. This generative triad, we maintain, addresses the major insights of the discipline's founders as they first explored the future of Christian spirituality. Through engagement with the philosophy of Royce and Peirce, this starting point also presents an avenue to substantively address the discipline's core questions. Finally, the interactive process of the unfolding of life in the Spirit connects the intentions of founders and present researchers with the experiential keynote introduced by William James, whose opening salvo effectively established the orientation for the discipline to come. "The life project of self-integration," which for Sandra Schneiders endows the spiritual life with momentum and intention, is but a revised title for what James identifies in *The Varieties of Religious Experience* as the process of conversion.

If we are to name the triad of the Spirit of God, the human spirit, and the reconciling community of interpretation, then we can also name the goal of this matrix of relationships: the transformation of the human person. Along this journey of conversion, not only the individual, but the community too, steps toward transformation—the Spirit of God leading the human spirit and the community alike. In the last analysis, the discipline of Christian spirituality, a sign worthy to unfold, must be unpacked not only through, but also by and for, the sacred community of interpretation.

Chapter One

RELIGIOUS EXPERIENCE MEETS RELIGIOUS INSIGHT

RELIGIOUS EXPERIENCE: THE STATUS OF THE QUESTION

Two Impulses Regarding the Approach to God

FOR CHRISTIAN SPIRITUALITY, the notion of the experience of God is as fundamental as it is elusive. At once, we meet with questions: What does "experience" mean in the first place, let alone "God"? What distinguishes an experience of God from ordinary experience? Do we best speak of gradations of intensity or rather of a sharp divide between the sacred and the profane? Can the religious experience of non-Christians be considered an experience of God? Is present-day experience different in kind from, say, the medieval period? Seeking a clear point of departure, contemporary inquirers often turn first to the writings of the Christian mystics, looking to establish solid footing with the helping hand of those who testify to special intimacy with God.

The Christian mystical tradition tends to speak of the near approach to God in terms of paradox: of an ascent that is also a descent, of loss as gain, of an experience of abyssal fear along with an impregnable sense of security. In the words of Pseudo-Dionysius, the approach constitutes a plunge into the "brilliant darkness."[1] Beginning with Cappadocian theologian Gregory of Nyssa, the image of Moses's encounter with God in the dark cloud at the top of Mount Sinai (Exod 19—20; 32) has been a touchstone for creative exposition of the climax of the mystical journey.[2] Taking place at the veritable meeting point of heaven and earth, of the infinite and the finite, the holy mystery is disclosed but for a brief moment—and on God's terms—just as the greater part of the mystery remains concealed. The ultimate consummation of desire, the journey into the divine presence is also a trial, a leave-taking, a leap into obscurity. When the vision departs and the sojourner turns back down the mountain, the shine of the divine may be upon them, but the content of the encounter remains unspeakable. The intense experience of the presence of God, we are bid to learn, rests shrouded within two clouds: one, the cloud of unknowing that remains amid all experiential knowledge revealed in the moment; two, the cloud that settles upon recall, as the one who has encountered God insists that images and words cannot fully capture what has transpired. Some mists are not to be dispelled—neither empyrean mists nor inner mists. And so it is that many of the guardians of Christian spirituality have displayed a particular contempt, boiling at times into rage, directed at those who seek, as the saying goes, to have their experience of God pinned up like a fly upon a wall; those, they allege, who murder to dissect.

Nevertheless, it is the task of the researcher into the experience of God to probe into this ultimately incommunicable realm of experience and seek to clarify it. The discipline of Christian spirituality understands itself to be dancing on this knife's edge. The question of the nature of the experience of God cannot be skirted, but neither can it ever be adequately formulated. The task requires the appropriate awareness, a sufficiently chastened attitude. The counsel the mystic gives to the novice applies as well to the student, for the study of spirituality constitutes a species of the approach to God: "Remove your shoes before you draw close." This understanding gives a different ring to the discipline's self-implicating character. Not only do the results of research carry implications for one's life as it unfolds, but moreover the approach to the subject lays a demand upon the researcher. The investigator participates in a discourse that requires a particular kind of integrity: you must be audacious in order to approach at all, but you must be careful not to be an audacious fool by forgetting the mystery at the center.

The concern for reverence and proper humility, borne of the otherness and incomprehensibility of God, reflects, as we suggest, simply one side of the question regarding how to address the experience of God. The reverse side of this guardian impulse is the hand beckoning the seeker forward—the appeal to spiritual experience as the thirst-quenching water of life, the deepest human experience of meaning. If the guardian impulse rises against the hubristic attitude that potentially sullies, cheapens, or rationalizes away the divine mystery, then the beckoning impulse—complementary with rather than destructive of the first—recognizes that we must find ways to speak of the transformative experience of God. Through sincere and compelling witness, our religion must express the renewing divine life that animates it. In many of the mystics, the tension between these two impulses is apparent: at once protectors of the mystery and champions of its dissemination, they speak out of both sides of their mouth.

The Late Modern Vision of Direct Experience

In his 1799 *Speech on Religion to Its Cultured Despisers*, the young German Romantic Pietist Friedrich Schleiermacher writes as a champion of access. He seeks to persuade his literary and artistic friends in Berlin that religion stands much closer to what the poets are after than what the moralizing preachers and speculating academicians suggest. Above all, for Schleiermacher, religion is the "feeling of absolute dependence" or the "sense and taste for the infinite."[3] This interior glow illuminates Schleiermacher's vision of the possibility of boundary-transcending spiritual communion. He insists that the "immediate consciousness of the Deity," encountered through prereflective intuition, can be the property of no religious sect, while he marks out a distinct line between what he frames as the tired, dead-eyed dogmatism of most religious folks and the lively awareness of the divine presence common to mystics and authentically religious souls. For the many seeking a way beyond entrenched religious divisions and the theological systems perceived as bulwarking them, Schleiermacher's appeal to immediate, unifying consciousness of the divine generated a liberating hope.

Schleiermacher's shift inspired investigation into "religious experience" for a group of researchers working in the northeastern United States in the late nineteenth century, including G. Stanley Hall, James Leuba, Edwin Starbuck, and most significantly, William James.[4] Through their notion of religious experience, they carried over Schleiermacher's inspiration, but not necessarily the terms of his understanding.[5] The American investigators approached what they called religious experience from the perspective of the budding field of psychology, promoting empirical research methods to collect data from varied individuals and religions. They sought the common center of experience they presumed to exist at the heart of diverse outward expressions of religiosity.[6] The group carried over presuppositions from Anglo-American philosophical circles, wherein raw feeling, sensation, and perception were typically considered on one hand as *experience*, as apart from reflective *thought* on the other.

For the most part today, the "raw" and "direct" estimation of experience, ordinary or transcendent, has been eclipsed by a more nuanced hermeneutical perspective stressing the interpreted and culturally conditioned character of all experience. Recent commentators have addressed how the late modern account of religious experience depends upon and suggests misleading ideas about the human relationship with God, while also distorting the testimonies of saints, mystics, and prophets. The a priori assumption of a shared core of religious experience neglects the significant discrepancies between religious traditions and the attendant divergent forms of experience.[7] Moreover, even as applied to Christianity, these moderns discovered at once less and more than their evidence warrants. In contemporary scholarship, theologians Grace Jantzen, Nicholas Lash, and Denys Turner, among others, show how modernity's marshaling of ideas about religious experience gives plentiful proof of the epoch's overreaching assumptions.[8] For Jantzen, the modern conception of mysticism as "ineffable experience" (James's terminology) misses the fundamental concerns of the mystics themselves, especially the broader social and political significance of their encounters with God. Lash joins the critical consensus that charges the experience-based tradition with neglecting the reality that all human experience is culturally, socially, and linguistically mediated; more precisely, he finds fault with this tradition's tendency—especially prominent for him in James—to reduce the transcendent God to the dimensions of the satisfaction of human need. Turner, meanwhile, makes the most extreme criticism of the bunch: not only do moderns misread mystical writers, he alleges but they have their account exactly backward. Their "experientialism" imposes a false perspective on the anti-experiential theologians and mystics whose apophatic language above all seeks to communicate the impossibility of direct experience of God.[9]

Even when critiques go too far, as we would argue with Turner's for instance, the corrections are essential: the Enlightenment mixture of heady exuberance, anthropocentric pretension, flippant dismissal of traditions, and uncritical universalizing spawned both the forgetfulness of the valuable religious insights of the past and the projection of culturally specific ideas onto the wider world of the time. We are left today with the conclusion that there is no such reality as these previous formulations suggest—no such access to pure or raw perception or feeling, and no religious experience that simply constitutes the unmediated consciousness of the divine. All mature consciousness, even religious consciousness in which observable external sensations are absent, depends upon prior contingencies of formation, habits of interpretation, and received beliefs. Additionally, following any given experience, these processes carry on and actively shape the understanding of the event. When talking about the inner experience of God, the appeal to direct intuition has ceased to predominate. Though it may not be that the best lack *all* conviction, few scholars today discourse upon religious experience without issuing a string of caveats. In a certain respect, the mystic cloud has returned, casting now a hermeneutical shadow.

JAMES ON RELIGIOUS EXPERIENCE

James and the Continuation of the Late Modern Project

Reviewed from the vantage point of criticisms of the late modern understanding of religious experience, William James's account in *The Varieties of Religious Experience* leaves much to be desired. In the first place, he defines *religion*—arbitrarily he notes, taking full personal license—as "the feelings, acts, and experiences of individual men in their solitude, so far as they apprehend themselves to stand in relation to whatever they may consider the divine."[10] James's qualifying remarks notwithstanding, this statement represents the full arrival of quite a profound shake-up in the understanding of religion, only possible within the late modern turn to religious experience. Building on the perspective inaugurated through Schleiermacher's *Speeches*, James does not define *religious experience* according to the private, subjective states of individuals, but rather defines *religion* in these exclusively individualistic and experiential terms.[11] James also adopts Schleiermacher's notion of the specially attuned religious genius who alone grasps true religion. The mystical states of consciousness of the extraordinary religious subject become for James the ideal route to grasp religion at its presumed mystical center. In this respect, James's notion of religious experience begins from the basic form of the privileged mountaintop encounter of mystical union, which is not to say that he consciously invokes this background or that he commits himself to any kind of traditional parameters of understanding. Under the same rubric, James treats the experiences of Catholic saints, Protestant American townspeople, Quakers, Mormons, Transcendentalist philosophers, Buddhists, and Muslims, among others.

Above all, James wants to burst the skins of separate traditions in order to pour religion into a fresh container. At the outset of the twentieth century, his phenomenological evaluation of religious experience carries on Schleiermacher's dream from the dawn of the nineteenth, aiming to achieve an expansive, reconciling, and ultimately universally shared understanding of religion. By evaluating religious experience pragmatically, according to its fruits for life, he seeks to find a path out of the woods of religious rancor and theological sterility. He optimistically imagines that his project kicks off a scientific study of religions. His first major hypothesis is that religious experience emerges from the subconscious mind, which itself is connected to a greater unseen realm. By appealing to the ministrations of the subconscious, James hopes to reach beyond theological explanations that depend exclusively on divine causality without appeal to empirical sources.[12] As James sees the matter, explanation by way of the subconscious bears the promise to open the field to scientific researchers. His theory proposes that the personal transformation of the converted person comes about through the inbreaking of stored subconscious contents into the conscious mind after a period of incubation. James attributes sudden conversions to a developed subconscious self and a permeable boundary between the conscious and subconscious mind. For a person with a harder shell, progress can only be gradual. James argues that this kind of explanation does not preclude the influence of a deity but suggests a secondary means by which higher powers act on the individual.

Despite James's lack of hermeneutical sophistication—relying as he does on the paradigm of spontaneous experience, an unreconstructed notion of a "common mystical core" across religions, and a sketchy theory of subconscious mediation—*Varieties* possesses enduring appeal. Part of the reason for the work's staying power is that many people today still share his presuppositions, despite their flaws; *Varieties*' understanding of religion implicitly encourages the free-floating, experimental personal spiritual quest. His pragmatic, empirical method also strikes a nerve in a practically and scientifically minded culture.

The Conversion of the "Sick Soul"

In addition to the above sources of attraction, James's gifted portrayal of the spiritual journey of the angst-filled "sick soul," born twice through conversion, continues to resonate. James's "sick soul" is an archetypal figure introduced in Lecture VI of *Varieties*, whose journey from melancholy to peace characterizes the path of religious conversion. The sick soul is plagued by the awareness of tragedy, injustice, irresolution, disharmony, failure, and the inevitability of death impacting every existence. The soul's consciousness of these realities produces an unshakeable feeling of gloom.[13] James describes the sick soul not merely to identify a psychological specimen, but to persuade his audience of this psychological type's abundant insight.[14] He argues that in comparison to the constitutionally upbeat person's reflexive optimism, blithely steering around sorrow's gravitational field, this darker vantage point provides a profound and accurate reading of life.[15]

In James's telling, as the conviction of hopelessness on the natural plane of life grows, the "sick soul," who cannot contentedly abide, gives way to the "divided self," who cries out for transformation. The divided self glimpses the possibility of escape from their tortured condition but cannot shake their angst. James suggests that the sole lasting solution for this world-weary condition is rebirth into a new life; the situation cannot be remedied except through a radical reorientation of consciousness.[16] St. Augustine of Hippo's crisis on the precipice of baptism supplies the consummate example of the moment in which the inner division mounts to a breaking point, as Augustine seeks divine regeneration while still caught in a life ordered toward natural gratification, wavering between former habits of desiring and the embrace of a new way of being.[17]

For Augustine as for the many subjects whose stories James catalogs, conversion lies on the other side of the successfully navigated conflict. The vital breakthrough occasions the transformation of "the habitual center of personal energy."[18] James understands this process as the replacement of one center of conscious dynamism for another. In Augustine's case, the desire for God stably gains the upper hand over the attachment to lust, just as for several of the subjects of James's first-person accounts, inclinations to prayer and worship take the place of the attraction to spending nights at the bar and other profligacies. Conversion grants a stable state of assurance, characterized by three predominant features: *affective peace*, *the perception of truths not known before*, and *the appearance of newness and beauty*.[19] The transformation may be well signaled by these three components; taken holistically, the change constitutes a renewal of the existential horizon. As James writes, "The process [of overcoming melancholy] is one of redemption, not of mere reversion to natural health, and the sufferer, when saved, is saved by what seems to him a second birth, a deeper kind of conscious being than he could enjoy before."[20] Amid his questionable religious leveling and psychological hypothesizing, James's attention to the process of conversion stands out as a valuable—and sometimes even poignant—evaluation of personal reorientation in relation to the divine.

KINSHIP AND DEPARTURE: ROYCE'S RELIGIOUS INSIGHT AND SOCIAL EXPERIENCE

Having related an account of James and his influences, the next part of the story treats how, in *Sources of Religious Insight*, Josiah Royce overcomes the deficiencies of James's appraisal of religious experience. His category of religious insight offers a sounder, deeper, and more integrated picture of religious experience. His understanding of social forms of experience provides a more reasonable understanding of mutual influence and interdependence. But to simply describe Royce's attainment of this advance and then to dismiss James would be to fail to say the most important thing, because Royce overcomes James by building on his work—by learning from him, dialoguing with him, and adopting what is best from his enterprising mind. Royce does not just overcome James: in some way, he redeems his project—not entirely until after James's death. The tightest focus on Royce and James reveals them to be as inseparable as they are opposed—carrying on like brothers at the family table who betray an ineluctable loving regard even as their relentlessly sharp exchanges wrack the nerves of the guests. They may battle, but they do so in part because of the depth of their shared ground. They are best treated as kin, which is how they treated each other.

Background and Respective Evaluations of Individual Experience

The Sources of Religious Experience represents Josiah Royce's continuation of his long-standing philosophical debate with William

James.[21] James had turned their conversation in a religious direction with his Gifford lectures, pitting his pluralistic metaphysics against Roycean idealism in the arena of religious experience. James acknowledged that he had Royce in mind from the beginning of the composition, intending to strike a lasting blow to Royce's monistic metaphysics, though he confessed he could not pull off the full confrontation he initially imagined.[22] The division between Royce's idealism and James's pluralism had at this point long been clear, although Royce's significant philosophical developments through his study of the logic of Charles Sanders Peirce would render him something of a moving target.

Sources, originally delivered as the Boss Lectures in Illinois in November 1911 (a decade after *Varieties* and less than a year after James's death in August 1910), picks up the thread during an especially intense period of Royce's ongoing philosophical evolution.[23] Royce gave an indication of his aspirations in a speech delivered months before the Boss Lectures, entitled "William James and the Philosophy of Life."[24] After praising *Varieties* for its intrepid spirit, he diverges from James:

> I do not believe James' resulting philosophy of religion to be adequate. For as it stands it is indeed chaotic. But I am sure that it can only be amended by taking it up into a larger view, and not by rejecting it. The spirit triumphs, not by destroying the chaos that James describes, but by brooding upon the face of the deep until the light comes, and with light, order.[25]

In *Sources*, Royce pursues this effort to build on *Varieties* rather than to dismantle the work. Not only does he ground his sources of insight upon individual experience, but he adopts several features of James's method. Like James in *Varieties*, when Royce sets out to define *religion*, he offers a broad, deliberately nonpolemical, and subject-centered definition, focusing his evaluation of religion on "the postulate that man needs to be saved."[26] And like James, he addresses the question from the standpoint of experiential bases rather than from creeds, dogmas, or theological systems.[27]

The Category of Religious Insight

The process of religious insight Royce outlines in *Sources* is essentially an insight into salvation—both the need for it and the path to attain it.[28] Similar to James in his assessment of the melancholy "sick soul," Royce considers the human being's awareness of interior poverty to direct the grasp of religious truth. As Royce writes, "Unless you have inwardly felt the need for salvation, and have learned to hunger and thirst after spiritual unity and self-possession, all the rest of religious insight is to you a sealed book."[29] Even as the questing person gains assurance, he or she encounters new forms of need, whether lacking in personal meaning, a sense of connection with others, knowledge of God, or commitment to a cause worth living for. Only by passing through want and exposure does the person advance on the way to religious insight; each source of insight lies, as it were, on the other side of need. Royce names seven (nonexhaustive) sources of insight that emerge: individual experience, social experience, human reason, the will, dedicated loyalty, atoning sorrow, and the unity wrought by the Spirit.

By beginning with the individual's felt need and its subsequent fulfillment, Royce self-consciously initiates his stages of religious insight with James's predominant category of individual religious experience. If Royce starts from James's foundation of individual religious experience, the question arises: Is Royce's understanding vulnerable to the same shortcomings as James's view? Is Royce merely another insufficiently critical late modern, another heir to the school of thought that has since been eclipsed? The answer to both questions is no, and the crucial difference lies in two areas: first, Royce's choice to speak of religious insight rather than religious experience; second, Royce's emphasis on the process of development of religious insight.

First, Royce's "religious insight" avoids the implications of direct, spontaneous intuition, providing a greater place for the interpretive aspects of even the most ecstatic encounters with God. Royce rejects James's theory that religious experience emerges from the spontaneous upwelling of the subconscious mind, holding that no such special hypothesis is necessary.[30] Royce takes his approach as the more satisfactory in its appeal to commonsense—proving relevant, he says sarcastically, not just for the specially favored but for "men who have had no such sudden uprushes from their own subconscious natures as James's 'religious geniuses' have reported."[31] When he speaks of individual and social experience, he understands these as modes of knowledge continuous with other ways of knowing; they need not be delimited to forms of pure and exalted intuition or feeling.

Royce's definition of insight further reinforces the holistic notion he has in mind. He identifies three marks of insight, whether religious or of another kind: breadth of range, coherence and unity of view, and closeness of personal touch. Insight affords a power of synthesis, a connected view of the whole that cannot be had without intimacy.[32] In this way, insight blends the view from above and the view from up close, taking in the forest while in contact with the trees. Royce writes, "True insight, if fulfilled, would be empirical for it would face facts; intuitive, for it would survey them and grasp them, and be intimate with them; rational, for it would view them in their unity."[33] Returning to the original discussion about the customary philosophical disjunction between raw experience and reflective thought, insight falls prey to no such binary. Insight transverses rational and prerational ways of knowing, including also the rational knowledge that on the standard view had been left across the gulf from experience. As the hermeneutical turn makes evident, this synthetic grasp is necessary in order to understand experience: to leave reflective thought to one side is also to fail to be able to offer any coherent account of experience, considering the inescapable relationship of any given experience with the structures of thought and meaning that condition its course.

Second, the category of religious insight tracks the dynamic, mobile orientation of the human spirit more comprehensively than James's category. On the Jamesian picture, the appeal to the acts, deeds, and events of solitary "religious experience" freezes a moment in time, rendering the experience essentially an event. The model of insight, on the other hand, captures the truth that religious experience is not a singular phenomenon, but bound up with the telos of the human spirit in its propulsion toward communion—a communion that takes not one but many forms. Royce cites the Letter to the Hebrews in reference to this drive ever forward: "Here we have no continuing city, we seek a city out of sight."[34] If through James's category of religious experience, we have an image of a mountaintop experience, an intense human-divine encounter analogous to a great aesthetic experience, then with Royce's category of religious insight, we have food for the long haul, whatever the elevation—the sustenance shifting as the human relationship with God develops.

The Second Phase of Religious Insight: Social Experience

In the opening chapter of *Sources*, Royce is equally clear on two points: one, that he considers individual experience a valid starting point for inquiry; and two, that he disputes James's restriction to individual experience. He states,

> Now James' whole view of religious experience differs in many ways from mine. But just at the present point in our inquiry, where it is a question of what I should call the most elementary and intimate, but also the crudest and most capricious source of religious insight, namely, the "experience of the individual alone with the divine," I feel my own account to be most dependent upon that of James and my own position to be most nearly in agreement with his.[35]

Royce takes as he gives. Compressed beside Royce's assurance of this close agreement is his expression that the agreement extends no further than "the crudest and most capricious" source of insight. Though James's sole efficacious source of religious experience marks for Royce the indispensable first station of religious truth, it cannot for him be the only stop. He is responsive here to James's severe judgment upon socially mediated religious experience, which James took to be a poor substitute for private encounter with the divine. For James, the general life of churches depends secondhand on the original and authentic gifts of mystically inclined individuals.[36] Ranged beside the mystics' vivid and powerful personal encounters, the social field can only be rendered in monochrome. Royce argues, on the contrary, that it is not social but individual experience that lacks adequacy and finality:

because of the significance of each person's connection with their fellow human beings, the personal encounter with the divine does not fulfill the need for salvation The final goal of salvation depends upon the common realization of a unity of spirit and purpose. Salvation is either social or it is not salvation at all.[37]

Royce ultimately holds that a communal reality undergirds all advances within individual understanding, even if understanding is arrived at prior to communal participation or social mediation. But to arrive at this insight, one has to continue to Royce's seventh lecture, "The Unity of the Spirit and the Invisible Church." As he explains there, a foundational unity of spirit, which is recognized through the loyalty of the individual, weaves the path forward through the seven sources of religious experience. This unity of spirit constitutes what Royce calls "the spirit of the invisible church."[38] Fittingly, at the close of *Sources*, Royce states, "The sources of insights are themselves the working of its [the invisible church's] spirit in our spirits."[39] The higher spirit guides the individual spirit's several passages in the movement toward salvation.[40] Thus, individual experience may suitably initiate the course, but only inasmuch as it leads forward, through its own insufficiency, to the need for social communion. The insight into the spiritual community crowns the process, just as the spirit of the community saves.

Social Conversion: Royce's Debt to James

As Royce transitions from the explication of the individual to the social source of religious experience, he emphasizes a predicament of his own, albeit with a Jamesian ring: the social alienation of the individual wracked by guilt.[41] He points out that remorse is not always felt in relation to God but can manifest as the sense of being an outcast standing out beyond human sympathy and community. As he demonstrates through the literary expression of the overcoming of loneliness in Samuel Taylor Coleridge's poem "The Rime of the Ancient Mariner" and Fyodor Dostoevsky's novel *Crime and Punishment*, the reconciliation of the self-isolating person requires not only a divine but also a social operation. To heal the experience of the loss of fellowship, only the return to fellowship suffices as a cure. And even when guilt and alienation do not lead, positive social experience points to the transcendent, whether through the glimmers of the divine in the face of one's beloved, the intimacy of friendship, or the love awakened through patriotic fervor. Despite the ongoing struggles, tensions, dissatisfactions, and injustices of the social world, a "way upward" becomes apparent.[42]

As with Royce's characterization of the individual's predicament, the social process of conversion Royce sketches through his literary examples accords well with the Jamesian description of conversion: the previously sick and disunified self overcomes an unhappy consciousness to operate henceforth from a new center of dynamic energy. Spurred by the warmth of the communion of a wedding celebration he stumbles upon, Coleridge's Mariner is healed of his former anguished sense of being "alone on a wide, wide sea." Taught about love and sacrifice by the prostitute Sonia, Dostoevsky's Raskolnikov overcomes the guilt that made him an outcast in his own eyes. They both find once more the joy of the social communion of which they had despaired, just as James's sick soul finds peace beyond existential dread. The social transformation, then, includes the essential criteria of James's phenomenological definition of *conversion*: through contemplation of a fresh sense of belonging, the experience of an affective state of peace; through the goodness glimpsed via social mediation, the perception of truths previously unrecognized; and through the protagonists' expression of aesthetic elevation, the appearance of newness and beauty.

Accordingly, they stand on the new, stable platform that conversion delivers.[43] The journeys of Raskolnikov and the Mariner should not be reduced merely to social sagas of reintegration, for each is gifted with a sense of well-being transcendent of their condition prior to alienation. They are each like the prodigal whose horizon expands from an initial hope for reacceptance to the gift of a greater inheritance when his father tells him, "All that is mine is yours" (Luke 15:31 NRSV). As with the prodigal—and James's sick soul, no less—no simple return to the former conditions of existence is possible in the crisis in which they find themselves. They not only move about in a state of existential exile. More to the point, they are wracked by the awareness that their previous way of being would bear no promise of relief. When the Mariner finds God amid the wedding company at the church and Raskolnikov learns love through Sonia's devotion, it is not the emergence of a contingent opportunity to experience fellowship and love that most enlivens and fortifies them but the reality that this opportunity discloses.

James's comment that conversion "does not mean reversion but redemption" applies to both the Mariner and Raskolnikov. Neither the Mariner's potential future separation from the community nor Raskolnikov's loss of Sonia would necessitate the regression to the initial situation of despair. They experience the goodness of human love in its particularity, just as they understand this human love to be a sign of love transcendent of the people and the communities to which they are joined. Royce understands their form of experience in a sacramental sense when he points out that the social world functions as a "hint, or revelation, or incarnation of a divine process."[44] It is this hint that electrifies Raskolnikov and the Mariner. In their newfound joy, we see another form of resolution of the archetypal conversion story first told by James in *Varieties*.

REIMAGINING *VARIETIES*: THE OVERLOOKED SOCIAL ELEMENT

In paging through the conversion experiences James arranges in *Varieties*, it is quite striking to follow the role of actors *besides* the subject of conversion. They are largely marginalized. The assorted characters may be catalysts, but only inasmuch as they lead the central subject away from the outer world and into their own inner recesses. These unobtrusive others bookend the intense interior dialogues, illuminations, and visitations where the action happens. A preacher communicates his experience of spiritual healing to a crowd that contains an alcoholic, only to disappear from view as the alcoholic's inner spiritual drama featuring the devil and Jesus takes center stage.[45] A "young lady friend" sends along a book to a young man, *Natural Law in the Spiritual World*, that contains the words that trigger a lasting conversion; pains are taken to describe her as a mere occasion for what follows.[46] A proselytizing friend runs an errand at a church office and leaves the central subject in the nave to wait for him; in a matter of minutes, the subject has a profound experience of the divine.[47] A crowd at a revival gathers around a man terrified by locutions and the mysterious sensation of being choked, but the man only notices the group after he comes to his senses.[48] In each of these cases, the social element is framed as no more than incidental: even the proselytizing friend is credited as serving as something of a taxi driver rather than as an evangelizer.[49]

We need not follow James's reconstructions to the letter. Looking again at James's accounts, we can entertain a way of seeing attentive to the inescapable ubiquity of social mediation in the unfolding process of conversion. Although in the examples James provides, social experience may be conspicuously absent at the moment of conversion, social mediation goes on in all of the stages leading up to the interior experience. Social mediation informs the personal appropriation of religious experience: for conversion, the effective guidance and directed assimilation of experience is necessary, not only a certain kind of exalted experience. Postconversion as well, the fruits of religious experience show up in the social world through deeds of charity. These interactions, too, are religious sources. With a little imagination, the deliberately flattened marginal characters might be animated into life. For instance, the young female friend, who sends a *spiritual* book after all, might just have been another kind of Sonia—opening the man's mind to love and acceptance—except doing her work in ways not initially accepted by the person in question. The proselytizer may have served, to borrow Royce's words, as a "hint of a divine process," evincing the transcendent despite all his friend's willful resistances to letting his love and friendship break in.

Recollect that the process of conversion is characterized by a push-pull dynamic: the divided self longs for but also resists acceptance and integration of the saving truth. Each story of conversion also stands as the story of a person's resistance to transformation eventually *giving out*—or to put the point in a more personalistic way, the story of the person being won over. In each conversion, there always remains another story to be told from another perspective: the tale of the community's guidance toward transformation. Take Augustine, an exemplar of conversion for James, whose solitary experience in the garden may be the summit of his conversion, but whose path to the garden was paved by his mother Monica, by friends, and by bishops. As Augustine makes clear in *Confessions*, we must not simply understand these assorted characters as notable for the explicit message they convey, as mere instruments of transmission of beliefs. Rather, as Augustine portrays them, they communicate God's love in their very actions, in a kind of sacramental form: Monica in her remarkable fidelity to her son despite his hubris; Augustine's dying friend in his inexplicable resolve to reject Augustine's mockery of Christians; Ambrose, who impresses Augustine as possessing a unique magnetic quality unfamiliar from his experience of secular orators.[50] If retrospective vision paints their influence most glowingly, then this is to be expected: only the integrated self, possessed of a higher viewpoint, can see clearly what the divided self could not entirely acknowledge prior to conversion.

We present these examples not only to point out that social mediation proves central to the process of conversion but also that Royce's particular model of social alienation and social restoration threads through stories about conversion, whether for Augustine or for the subjects from James's collected reports. As Royce indicates in his description of Raskolnikov's guilt and the Mariner's estrangement, an individual's sense of separation from community need not be established through the community's formal exclusion. The sense of alienation can also come from within. There is something particularly modern—even contemporary—in Royce's analysis, wherein the subject constitutes the center of gravity of judgment.

Compare to an ancient or classical situation. In premodern times, exclusion or punishment from the Catholic Church marks a kind of primordial type of separation; the penitent or the exile who endures the painful expulsion from the ecclesial community is understood not only to stand outside the bounds of the community but also to have compromised their salvation, at least in principle. The paradigmatic premodern perspective emphasizes objective, formal, and institutionally mediated judgments, which come to land upon the individual. However, the paradigmatic modern situation (postmodern too) is connected to what Charles Taylor calls an "expressivist" culture and sense of self. In an expressivist understanding, writes Taylor, "the moral or spiritual order of things must come to us indexed to a personal vision."[51] Formal structures of belonging do not become irrelevant, but, even in cases of formal exclusion or marginalization, the individual's *perceptions* of group belonging and fulfillment take center stage. When the stress falls on the feelings and judgments of the individual, the sense of rupture, distance, and estrangement may indeed be entirely subjective; one may formally belong to a given community and still feel oneself to be alien to its life, and this feeling is what counts.

In an expressivist age, the individual's assessment of the religious community takes on greater weight. As long as the community's promises of mediating salvation or of bringing the individual into intimacy with the divine seem to go unfulfilled in the individual's eyes, then the community's efficaciousness and value come into question. The individual is in a way interiorly empowered vis-à-vis the community. However, this power of judgment does not resolve the individual's problems: as we see with the Mariner, the felt disconnection from the community remains a burden. The individual is thrown back on oneself; not only doubt but also guilt and angst trouble the person. James's sick soul is no less prototypical than the Mariner. When the sick soul cries out for help, the soul calls for relief from the disease no community has been able to cure; lost *as an individual*, he or she is also lost *from the community*. No community has delivered the foundational support the soul longs for; no community has stably mediated the saving power that later floods in at the moment of conversion. Now, the sting of the condition is double, redounding upon the community. Not only is the individual estranged: the sense of alienation includes the particularly modern perception of the meaninglessness of the community's forms of existence. The individual may ask whether his or her perception is accurate, but even reserve in judgment does not take away the sense that the community fails to bear life. In this modern-expressivist situation, the renewal of the individual's relationship with the community must be seen as distinct from the classical picture. From the perspective of the individual, the community too comes back to life. Transformation is not just about the redemption of the individual but about the redemption of the community in the individual's eyes.

Keeping with such an outlook, the archetypal Jamesian story of sickness-division-integration can be grasped on the level of the renewal of the individual's orientation to common life. Contrary to James's presentation, the various conversion tales show through as stories of social reintegration. The young man not only has a new basis for a strengthened relationship with the young woman who sent him the book, but also a basis for a relationship with his father, in whose rectory he sits on the night of the conversion. Since his father represents the church, he also represents the potential for reintegration into the larger body. The friend of the proselytizer has for himself a ready-made companion, and likely a spiritual community to walk into besides. The healed alcoholic possesses the bond of rebirth in Christ with the others who have been transformed by the same means, and he meets his company straightaway in the room where his heart changes; likewise, the revival attendee opens his eyes surrounded by new friends of a sort.

Thus, by incorporating Royce's social dimension of conversion, James's account becomes more adequate. From the social standpoint, review again James's criteria of conversion: the affective state of peace or assurance settles not as an absolute individual novelty but as an assurance all the more powerful for the intimations of its reach. It is an assurance that others too have felt. To recognize this power is to be brought into union with those who also testify to it. Such a claim does not need to be metaphysically furnished; revival meetings provide sufficient evidence. So, too, the insight into truth (even a truth gained in solitude) fashions social bonds. The young man takes up his father's Christian faith and the friend of the proselytizer understands for himself what the man has been driving after. And as for the third criterion, the appearance of newness and beauty: in the sight of the convert, not only the natural world but people too are washed clean.[52] Authentic relationship once again becomes possible. As the process of conversion is socially mediated, so are the fruits of conversion social. According to the expressivist perspective, the most notable realities of social disconnection are the individual's feeling of being adrift and the community's impotence in the individual's eyes. Correspondingly, conversion brings about the individual's sense of having a place to stand in a communal life that mediates meaning. The Jamesian notion of interior, spiritual "homecoming" is concretized in the return to the community. The social renewal of the individual culminates with the renewal of the social horizon.

CONCLUSION

The debate between William James and Josiah Royce provides an instructive point of entry into the late modern status of the question regarding religious experience, which has set the terms for contemporary evaluations. In the approach to spiritual experience, James represents what is freshest and most courageous about modern aspirations, at the same time as he epitomizes what is most naïve and perhaps arrogant. In *Varieties*, James brings the journey of conversion into sharp focus, probing into firsthand experience, and opening an important line of dialogue with the field of psychology. These fresh paths are worth following. However, he sorely needs the help of his neighbor, and Josiah Royce obliges. In response to *Varieties*, Royce does not deny the reality of individual religious experience, but by introducing the category of religious insight, he overcomes James's interpretive one-dimensionality. He understands individual experience as part of an unfolding process, guided by the divine spirit, and leading toward a radical commitment to community. With Royce's contribution, the real center of James's attention—rarefied experience on the order of the exalted mountaintop encounter of the mystical tradition—does not lose its relevance but must be understood as connected with this larger process. Even the highest flights of "private" ecstasy are experiences borne of communal origins and bearing communal ramifications, for Moses no less than for the recovering alcoholic.

The experiences frequently taken to be individual—James's "experiences of men in their solitude"—only appear to be so under a certain aspect. Thus, we have offered a second, revisionist way of reading James's phenomenology of conversion by drawing out the presence of social experience as religiously revelatory. We surmise that Royce would underwrite the rereading. Not only did Royce long consider James's limitation to individual experience to be mistaken, but he also consistently took religious experience to be most adequately understood socially. His follow-up work to *Sources*, *The Problem of Christianity*, offers an exploration of social experience in the Christian religion, concentrating specifically on the experience of the Pauline Church.[53] In *Problem*, he explicitly develops a social metaphysics based on triadic relationships. As he fleshes out the relationship between the individual and the social realm, he proposes that reality includes two levels: the level of the individual and the level of the community. This two-plane paradigm may well offer the best Roycean interpretation of William James's account of the conversion of the sick soul. Read strictly on the plane of the individual's experience of transformation, James's archetypal story from *Varieties* remains instructive. However, the most comprehensive account requires the introduction of the communal plane of reality. From this standpoint, James's account gains a wholeness lacking in his presentation in *Varieties*. Such an account would be enhanced descriptively in some of the ways we have suggested, as well as philosophically, through a metaphysical appraisal of social experience.[54]

The relationship between Royce and James finally falters at precisely this social-communal site. We can point out how James's existential-empirical approach to religious experience bears a strong resemblance to Royce's course in *Sources*. We can demonstrate the affinities between the "sick soul" narrative and Royce's vision of social restoration. We can also understand the identity of hope between the two men—how the two were inspired by intentions to overcome Christian sectarianism and to find common religious ground. But Josiah Royce's social metaphysics and his closely connected ethics of loyalty finally separate the two thinkers. One gets the sense that, even after James's death, Royce's greatest intellectual effort was expended in persuading his friend to come over to his point of view. Understanding the two as kin rather than combatants, we must not deem his intentions belated: it is precisely through the great community's hope of social salvation, precisely through our inextricable belonging to one another, that we can understand James's project as redeemed by Royce. To us, too, Royce makes an appeal—especially if, like James, we have accustomed ourselves to concentrating on individual experience. Royce would say that whenever we inquire, a second level—more profound than the first—awaits our attention. Our inquiry into religious experience stands to benefit from his insight.

Chapter Two

COMMUNITY AT THE HEART OF CHRISTIAN SPIRITUALITY

THE REALITY OF COMMUNITY: A PERSONAL DISCOVERY

WHAT DOES IT MEAN to hold, as Josiah Royce does, that not only the individual but also the community is real—that the two constitute two levels of reality? For our purposes, it means, in the first place, to view individual mystical experience as a gateway to an even broader network of human communion in God. The two-plane reality also suggests that we adjust our way of looking such that our understandable infatuation with striking spiritual figures also translates into a healthy respect for the communal commitments and communal contexts that shape them. The shift represents something difficult, not at all automatic; not only, as it were, do we behold the flowering of the individual tree—where our gaze is apt to remain—but we must let our eyes pass down along the trunk, deeper down to the roots, beyond which lies the ever-ramifying network, the immense root system of the forest, that we are bid to recognize as a unified reality in its own right. Because the network is not immediately plain to sight, because we must infer its existence or trust in the work of scientists who discover this dynamic biological interdependence, we can be slow to acknowledge its existence. But just as the tree is a real discrete entity, so too is the forest that sustains it. The saint is a genuine beacon of holiness; so too does holiness belong to the whole.

To fully encounter the reality of community, not just as a philosophical principle but also as an existentially appropriated discovery, requires a conversion—the Spirit-guided reorientation that we identified in the last chapter as the social renewal of the sick soul. The conversion can be especially hard-won: the irony is that we recognize community through a journey in which we come to grips with our solitude. If community is something like the network beneath our feet that sustains, and if we are used to focusing intently on the parade of individual actors above, then is it any surprise that most of us recognize community only once the earth under us trembles and we lose our footing; that we usually begin the conscious journey into community, into recognition and into responsible participation, when the form of common life we partook in prior to mature reflection breaks down?

Speaking of the self-implicating nature of spirituality, as coauthors we each had an experience of recognition of and commitment to community belying our generational differences. John Markey's experience took the form of a journey through the Catholic Church. John came of age after the Second Vatican Council, carrying the expectation formed in childhood that the Catholic Church would gradually adapt its organizations and practices to more contemporary methods and that it would become more unified with the other Christian Churches. He discovered in his first years in college that not everyone in the Catholic Church thought that this was the desired and necessary outgrowth of Vatican II and, moreover, that powerful elements in the institutional structure of the Church resisted just such a movement. It was then that he realized that he had to take responsibility for the change that he wanted to see in the life of the Church, requiring deeper reflection on his community and its tradition in order to more fully understand Vatican II and its consequences.

At about this same time, he was trying to discern his life's vocation, considering a life as either a lay theologian or as an ordained cleric. During this period (about 1985–86), he read the book by Robert Bellah and others, *Habits of the Heart*, describing the crisis of community in American society caused by the unchecked, and even glamorized, rise of what the authors termed *radical individualism.*[1] He realized that this book described him and his generation insightfully and offered a valid assessment of the fundamental problem facing American society. The book also helped him to understand that the most important and countercultural act one could perform within this context was to join a community, especially a community that required a lasting and sacrificial commitment to some good greater than oneself. He consciously began to seek a community where he could put his gifts and talents to good use and that could also challenge him to move beyond inherent culturally conditioned individualism to interpret the world in terms of a wider meaning and purpose.

John ultimately found the Order of Preachers, commonly called the Dominicans, a Roman Catholic religious community founded in the thirteenth century for preaching the gospel through thoughtful and learned evangelization and then by authenticating their preaching through their shared life together. One of the first great theologians to arise out of this new religious movement and to synthesize its practical and theological insights was Thomas Aquinas. Aquinas realized that the Dominicans were successful because they took their new cultural milieu seriously and responded to the emerging situation of the thirteenth century with new theological and philosophical insights. The more that John studied Aquinas, the more he began to ask, "If Aquinas were alive today and living in the late twentieth-century United States, what would he be studying?" It became increasingly clear that Aquinas would not be studying Aquinas any more (or any less) than the medieval Aquinas studied Augustine: the tradition is always the foundation, but not sufficient in itself to meet the needs of the contemporary culture. It was with this question in mind, his own cultural experience of the great need to further understand the relationship between the individual and community, that eventually led him to the philosophy of Josiah Royce.

Michael Ceragioli, a member of the so-called millennial generation, was also raised as a Catholic, in an era in which the ecclesial narrative revolved not around the Second Vatican Council but rather the sexual abuse crisis of the early 2000s. Michael largely disregarded the Church in the latter part of high school and through college, feeling little compunction about stepping away from an organization whose authority did not carry sway among the vast majority of his peers or within the wider cultural landscape. His work out of college as a mental health counselor for traumatized youth was inspired by sincere Christian faith, yet not driven by a strong sense of communal belonging: attending Mass struck him as something like a gratuitous good deed, akin to helping at a food bank for an hour on a Sunday morning. It was only once the enormity of the suffering he faced began to feel like too much for his own strength that he began to reconsider; only once, through the struggles of the families with whom he worked, the consequences of the social rifts and failures in society became impressed upon him as a devastating and perhaps insoluble problem that he sought community in earnest. For Michael, the social situation named in Bellah's *Habits of the Heart* appeared not in the mode of academic sociological analysis but splashed out into the streets in living color, demanding a response, as much from a dawning recognition of personal weakness in the face of collective and personal suffering as from idealistic initiative. The movement into community felt more like an utter necessity than a choice between competing life options.

Whereas John traveled all the while through the Catholic Church, experiencing positive expectation, disappointment, and hope in turn, Michael made his way *into* the Catholic Church, surprising himself perhaps most of all. He entered as one wounded. Being welcomed into the community of St. Michael the Archangel Church in Portland, Oregon, a church that remains active not only on Sunday but every day of the week, Michael experienced healing and a reinvigorated sense of purpose. This mending of spirit came along with a new appreciation for the sustaining power of tradition and, most of all, the joy of participation in a spiritual community. The medical-therapeutic language of healing and recovery gives only part of the idea—accurate insofar as it communicates the sense of being made well, and inadequate to the degree that it signals a passive process like that of a patient receiving treatment. Michael's most unanticipated discovery in his local Catholic community was not that he was cared for and supported, not that God's presence made a meaningful difference, but that in such a space, his own gifts became unearthed in service to others.

We bring up the stories of the authors to emphasize the experiential path into community, which, though as varied as human beings are, invariably retains a sense of discovery of a newfound source of life and carries with it a transformed attitude. Communal commitment feels at once a departure from the status quo of isolated personal striving and the means of personal fulfillment that could not have been achieved otherwise: the discovery of community is also a form of self-discovery.

This theme of the reconciliation of the individual and the community, approached above as an experiential breakthrough, dominates Josiah Royce's thought. Indeed, it is Royce's central concern to demonstrate a philosophical synthesis that need not conclude in either detached individualism or self-erasing collectivism. Royce's contribution is essential to the development of Christian spirituality, the understanding of which tends to be skewed today by the notion of a solitary journey of self-realization, or, from another quarter of the modern mind, distorted as something like the "opiate of the masses." Through Royce's synthesis, we can better grasp the significance of the central triad of the Spirit of God, the human spirit, and the community as the dynamic locus of Christian spirituality. In this chapter, we continue to probe Royce's dialectic of the individual (the human spirit) and the community, revealing their mutual entailment. Adding to the analysis of the social renewal of the sick soul, we examine the features of community that shape the spiritual development of the human spirit. Such reflection on the individual-communal relationship leads to consideration of the Spirit of God, for the three necessarily function together. The role of the Spirit of God provides the concluding note for this chapter and the opening for the next.

JOSIAH ROYCE ON THE DIALECTIC OF THE COMMUNITY AND THE INDIVIDUAL

Overview of the Communal-Individual Relationship

The most complete expression of Royce's thought comes in *The Problem of Christianity* (1913), at the heart of which lies the idea of universal community. In *Problem of Christianity*, Royce expands on the social process of renewal that he addresses in *The Sources of Religious Insight*. He speaks of the later work as a kind of companion volume to *Sources*. Whereas in *Sources* he takes a non-exclusive view of religious experience, in *Problem of Christianity* he treats the principles of Christianity in particular.[2] As with *Sources*, Royce originally composed *Problem of Christianity* as a series of lectures. After suffering a serious stroke in January of 1912, he completed the work at an astonishing pace: Royce delivered the lectures in part in Boston in November and December of 1912 and in full at Oxford from January through March of 1913.[3] Following the loss of his son Christopher and of William James, the lectures communicate the seriousness and maturity of one who chooses hopefulness in full sight of sorrow. The lectures possess a level of clarity, intensity, and spiritual depth that suggests his recognition of the project as an opportunity to offer a kind of parting elaboration of his most dearly held insights on the relationship between the community, the individual, and the Spirit.

In *Problem of Christianity*, Royce's integral philosophical vision of community builds upon Christian sources, namely, the image of the Body of Christ in the Pauline letters. For Royce, both the profound interdependence of human beings and the full realization of individuated personhood are evident in the Pauline elaboration of the Body of Christ. As St. Paul writes in Romans, "We, though many, are one body in Christ, and individually members of one another" (Rom 12:5 NABRE). Paul compares each human being to a part of the body: the absence of an individual part—an eye, a hand, a mouth—spells deficiency or disease, and yet each part of the body has no independent identity or existence apart from the whole body (1 Cor 12:12–26). The one Holy Spirit that animates each member of the community ensures the genuine shared reality of the body (1 Cor 1:13). From the inspiration of this dynamic relational model, Royce constructs his interpretation of reality that unites the individual and the community, the particular and the universal, and the human and the divine while maintaining the authentic integrity of each of the paired terms. He concentrates on three central ideas with roots in the Pauline corpus: the Spirit (the Holy Spirit as source of unity), community (represented primordially through the Body of Christ), and the interpretation of signs (the discernment of charisms in the Pauline churches).[4] Royce's metaphysical and practical insights, although remaining philosophical proposals of wide applicability, emerge then from the experience of these actual Christian communities.

Royce understands the lives of communities as constituted by and actively involved in acts of interpretation that shape the minds of their members and aim toward the realization of shared future plans. A virtually innumerable set of "communities of interpretation" overlap and intermingle in the composition of the whole world of human experience. Unlike the Cartesian style of philosophy that begins with the isolated individual mind, Royce starts with the presupposition that human minds are inherently connected to one another. Human beings strive for the accurate interpretation of existence, and accurate interpretation necessarily requires more than one mind. The dialogue among minds leads to knowledge and to action.[5] In this way, communities of interpretation connect each of us to the rest of reality; the interpretation of signs (ideas, events, images) is the fundamental human conscious process out of which the distinctiveness of individual minds and the distinctiveness of human communities emerge. The individual can only achieve full integrity—can only come, as it were, to serve in freedom as a good eye or ear—through cultivating social ties. Meaningful autonomy emerges only once we acknowledge our interconnectedness and respond to this reality. This picture represents a stark contrast to the American tendency to encourage autonomy through breaking restrictive social bonds or by remaining free from enduring commitments. For Royce, we are "persons-in-community," persons *among* rather than persons *apart*. Our most basic and abiding responsibility is to discover and positively participate within authentic and life-giving communities of interpretation.

These two key responsibilities—discovery of community and positive participation within it—maintain the communal-individual relationship as a dialectic, rather than the domination of the individual by the community or vice versa. Individuals shape communities through their presence and through their interpretive contributions. The first priority of the individual is to distinguish the bent of any group. For Royce, groups may be destructive as well as salvific: not all groups have a right to the name "community." The differences between a genuine and inauthentic community lie in the goals of the community and in its capacity to foster a genuine sharing of life among its members over an extended period. Groups with limited, narrowly self-serving, or mean-spirited goals fail to fulfill the potential of the individuals who comprise them and tend to degenerate into self-destructive violence and disorder over time. Even communities that initially seek good ends can become destructive when monopolization of power, manipulation and oppression of members, and self-serving, short-term thinking eclipses the pursuit of just long-term goals. Through prudent discernment, individuals can strengthen genuine communities and weaken destructive groups by choosing to belong to the former and not to the latter. Once a person begins to participate within a community, their interpretive contributions either fortify the community or contribute to its decline.[6] Herein lies the heart of the dialectic: we may justifiably speak of genuine communities and inauthentic communities, but we speak at the same time of the conditions of individuals, whose ideas and deeds influence and transform the communal reality. To cease to refer to one or the other is to lose an element of reality.[7]

From this standpoint, we can see how Royce develops the doctrine of the two levels of reality: individuals and communities form the "sacred pair" upon which the whole order of the universe is based.[8] Royce insists that a genuinely and loyally united community is a person in "a perfectly literal sense."[9] A community does not merely refer to an aggregate of otherwise detached individuals (in which case only the individual would be real) but is itself a person—a "live unit" with a mind of its own.[10] As Royce remarks, the Christian church was, for Paul, a person—possessed of a coherent plan of life including a common past, present, and future.[11] This primordial community, as well as those genuine communities that have followed throughout history, are thus coherent persons, just as an individual person is, in a sense, a community, constituted by a unified memory of history and future intentions worked out in present experience based on this memory.

Royce asserts the two levels of reality by appealing to human experience. We experience ourselves as individuals, argues Royce, in at least three ways: (1) Our bodies and their direct sensory perceptions are unique. (2) Our minds and their strains of conscious thought are not directly accessible through intuition to any other mind. (3) Our voluntary decisions and the deeds that follow from them are our own.[12] Nevertheless, Royce points out, we do not experience ourselves as individualistic "monads," that is, as wholly separate beings who only incidentally or accidentally relate to one another. We commonly experience a profound unity and interconnectedness with many other people. As proof of the reality of an underlying unity, Royce appeals to the many types of social cooperation that bring into existence the very language, customs, and religions that make our own individual consciousness possible.

Applying Royce's Framework

Royce's paradigm provides an instructive (if today somewhat atypical) way of understanding the human person. To begin to understand yourself or another, you might well start to understand the communities of interpretation in which a given person participates. From a grasp of a person's situatedness within this communal background, attending to the tensions that exist among different communities of interpretation, the ongoing momentum and persistent conflicts of individual minds become more intelligible. Conflicts within the self might be illuminated as conflicts among communities that shape the self. The self can even be understood in terms of the internalization of communities. The creative person might be imagined as one with the capacity to reconcile ideas from disparate loci of interpretation and to communicate across boundaries—a kind of cross-pollinator of different communities. The postmodern condition of the individual, frequently described according to the multifaceted, polymorphous, plural, or even fractured self, should be traced to the individual's incredible exposure to diverse communities of interpretation. Today, our phones and computers can, in an instant, deposit us into the flow of any number of communities of interpretation. This kind of rapid-fire, serial exposure is even more prominent in the younger generations that have habituated themselves to electronic rhythms. The sheer abundance of communities of interpretation in contemporary life exerts a pressure on the individual that leads to a sense of multiplicity within the self—and sometimes even a sense of chaos.[13]

The notion of a communal self is equally relevant for Christian spirituality. An understanding of the self in its communal constitution has ramifications for various disciplines—whether in psychology, indicating a shift of the focus beyond family systems and childhood conditioning to broaden the therapeutic view to better encompass communities of influence; or in history, indicating the dialectical relationship between communities and powerful actors, rather than the mere attribution of the determination of world events to outstanding individuals. Spirituality, in its interaction with disciplines like psychology and history, can seek to integrate communal interpretations. Rather than understanding the psycho-spiritual development of the individual as merely concerned with stages of interior union with God, development must also be treated in relationship to the individual's participation within their social and ecclesial world. The history of spirituality cannot remain focused on the accounts of mystical experience as an isolated body of "mystical literature" without recourse to the way that mystics both reflect and challenge their communities of origin. And in its explicit dedication to lived experience, spirituality must emphasize the communal ground of the individual, thus demanding cultural research to shed light on the nature of contemporary experience. This conscious turn to communities of interpretation begins with the veritable forest root system in order to attain genuine insight regarding the individual tree.

In each of these fields, we can also follow Royce's lead in assessing communities in the way of persons. Rooted in an underlying unity rather than in the consciousness of any single individual, shared groups have minds of their own and tend to develop a shared form of life—a form of life that transcends each of the individuals who belong to them.[14] These interdependent communities are not to be mistaken for the modern ideologies of collectivism. Royce describes "collectives" as soulless organizations that treat their members as things and not as persons. Communities, on the other hand, respect and appreciate the autonomy of their members, while uniting them in common beliefs and activities. A community, a social reality, can and often does work in and through the individual. For Royce, therefore, each person is *both* an individual and a communal being, functioning autonomously as a discrete entity while simultaneously experiencing the social reality of the community. When fully mature, the person bears two interrelated forms of consciousness wherein both forms remain fundamentally interdependent. As with the members of the Pauline body, the individual person can only become fully oneself and reach authentic autonomy by being genuinely loyal to some community; a "mere" individual has not achieved full humanity.

This perspective implies a vision of reality that challenges the default radical individualism of the United States, a vision wherein coexisting and mutually interrelated communities shape unique and mature individuals. Each of these coexisting communities ultimately participates in the life of the one great and universal Community of Interpretation, while this universal community likewise participates in the divine community that we call God. Through Royce, we do more than simply make an appeal to the interconnectedness of all human beings. Rather, we understand this interconnectedness by way of a philosophically coherent vision. Today, we must extend Royce's proposal to include the community of all creation, which also participates in its own way in the community of interpretation. By broadening our perspective beyond that of Royce, and understanding the community as constituted as well by the more-than-human world, we touch upon the shared ground of all living beings. We will clarify this relationship when we turn to the thought of Charles Sanders Peirce in chapter 5.

SIX CONDITIONS FOR GENUINE HUMAN COMMUNITY

Royce provides six conditions for genuine human community. These conditions further clarify the perennial questions surrounding the reconciliation of the universal and the particular, "the one and the many." How can one participate fully at the social level without subsuming one's own individuality? How can communities discover a genuine unity of purpose when composed of individuals with distinct minds and life plans? What is the difference between a genuine community and merely natural associations of people directed toward specific ends and purposes, some of which might harm the common good? Through observation of historical communities and philosophical reflection upon them, Royce's extensive analysis addresses each of these challenges.

First Condition: Complex Social Process Over Time

Royce insists upon the differentiation between communities and crowds, mobs, or mere associations of people. A community is distinguished from these entities by its unfolding over time. As Royce writes, "A community has a past and will have a future. Its more or less conscious history, real or ideal, is a part of its very essence. A community requires for its existence a history and is greatly aided in its consciousness by a memory."[15] A community shares not only a common mind but also the institutions, organizations, traditions, and historical unity that enable it to think and act as a unit over time. The common mind implies the need for a complex and lengthy social process that fashions a psychological unity of many disparate selves.[16]

To build on Royce's understanding of the community as a person, we can observe that this complex process entails stages and patterns of development—and even some of the emotional complexity that we recognize in human beings. When communities confront their past with clear eyes, or, on the contrary, when they fail to face the consequences of their collective actions, they establish their character in the way of human beings. The moral dramas of human beings concerning what we choose to remember, how we understand our role in events, and how we take responsibility for our past deeds are shared by communities. We can see communities according to the decisions they make in the processing of their histories and, relatedly, how they imagine possible futures.

Likewise, when we are sensitive to the relative stage of life a community passes through at any given time, we become more discerning about its needs, strengths, and limitations. A group or a nation—even a religion or civilization—can be young or old and relates to its past and future accordingly. With the community that supports and directs the study of Christian spirituality, the SSCS, we might conjecture about the moment in which we are living. The discipline has survived its birth years and found its first foothold. In the old world of theology, spirituality remains a youth—full of promise, possessed of an unmistakable allure, and yet still unable to shake a certain self-consciousness. We are, in a sense, passing through a period of late adolescence, psychologically speaking the crucial period of the establishment of identity that necessarily involves a degree of narcissism. During this phase, questions of fundamental orientation and differentiation are asked in a concentrated turn to the self in order to prepare for a purposeful future with others—in order to be ready to take one's place in the world. Through the successful solidification of identity in emerging from the relatively narcissistic phase of youth, the capacity develops both to give out of one's own experience and receive from others with openness. From this standpoint, we can ascertain some of the tasks of the near future for the Society for the Study of Christian Spirituality—for the incipient phase of mature adulthood—which must naturally include the transition to a dialogical role within the academy. As we write a text sharing a vision for the discipline, we recognize that the time comes for intensive contact with other communities of inquiry, a chief concern of a discipline established on the inclusive basis of an anthropological hermeneutic.

Second Condition: Expanded Self-Interpretation (Acquiring New Memory and Hope)

The social process functions fundamentally as a process of individual selves taking on the shared past and expected future of a community in such a way that these selves can act concurrently and singularly within the community in the present. This social process creates over time what Royce calls "communities of memory and hope." To join a community of memory and hope, the individual extends his or her personal consciousness to assimilate the vaster and richer consciousness of the community. As Royce writes:

> When many contemporary and distinct selves so interpret, each his own personal life, that each says of an individual past or of a determinate future event or deed: "That belongs to my life," "that occurred or will occur, to me"—then these many selves may be defined as hereby constituting, in a perfectly definite and objective, but also a highly significant sense, a community. They may be said to constitute a community with reference to that particular past or future event, or group of events, which each of them accepts or interprets as belonging to his own personal past or to his own individual future. A community constituted by the fact that each of its members accepts as part of his own individual life and self the same past events that each of his fellow-members accepts, may be called a community of memory…[and] a community of expectation or a community of hope.[17]

For the individual, the process requires the interpretation—in truth, the reinterpretation—of one's life in terms of a communal life and communal narrative.[18] This does not mean, however, the diminishment of the individual but rather an enlargement—an extension into a common past that they may not remember and into an ideal future that transcends the span of their earthly existence. The enlargement reaches back to the founding of the community and ahead to its hoped-for culmination. Take the example of one's life as an American citizen: although my name does not appear on the Declaration of Independence, I may consider the event to be a part of my personal past, saying, "*We* declared independence from England." Similarly, I may take personal responsibility for the future of the United States even though I may not live to see this future: "I am willing to give my life for the country so that *we* can be free," or: "I am willing to stand for the dispossessed though the progress may be slow or indiscernible."

The individual track and field events at the Olympics, among other events, demonstrate the difference made by the extension of the self in otherwise individual activities. The Olympian's representation of their country impacts the spirit in which they participate. The athlete's understanding of the effort they put into their solo event, that is, of their private preparation, becomes inextricably connected with their representation of their country. After a track and field athlete wins an event, they waste little time before jogging to the stands to drape their nation's flag around their shoulders, indicating that they do not compete for themselves alone. As much as they celebrate their achievement, they celebrate their place among a particular company, most notably the past outstanding representatives of their country. Participation welds them to their national story in a special way; numbered among Olympians past, present, and future, they come to see their own life as caught up in this greater design of representing their nation on the world stage. Whether a gold medalist or non-placing competitor, the athlete effectively participates amid several different communities, each of which becomes central to their personal narrative: their national track and field community, their nation, and the community of Olympians, to name a few.

Royce understands this kind of appropriative activity to be essential for the well-being of the individual. The power of extension of oneself is grounded in a basic need of the human being:

> This power itself rests upon the principle that, however a man may come by his idea of himself, the self is no mere datum, but is in its essence a life which is inter-

> preted, and which interprets itself, and which, apart from some sort of ideal interpretation, is a mere flight of ideas, or a meaningless flow of feelings, or a vision that sees nothing, or else a barren abstract conception.[19]

Royce's analysis echoes the idea of the spiritual journey outlined in *Sources*, with the soul passing from a condition of ineffectual and sometimes even desperate isolation to integration through relationship with a community. The ability to view one's life in terms of a greater communal (and, finally, cosmological) whole gives individuals the ability to widen their own lives by consciously and freely participating in a community of memory and hope greater than the physical and biological limits that life naturally imposes.

Third Condition: Real Communication

In order for the community to function as a unit, distinct individuals must be engaged in ongoing and fruitful communication about past events and future aspirations, the deeds and persons who make up the community, and the common ideal that binds them together. This communication should be characterized by intentional and rational dialogue that includes as many members of the community as possible in critical reflection on their common life and shared goals.[20] To facilitate progress, the whole community must share a common language or discourse linking them to their traditions while nevertheless remaining open-ended.

Royce insists that communities require common forums where both "views of life" and "ways of life" can be discerned and shared. Communication does not stop at discursive exchange but must also include the sharing of lives. This sharing happens through the sharing of gifts and talents of each person with the whole community. Rather than the melting or blending of various persons into a monolithic mold, this process entails the coordination and orchestration of many lives into a single, unified, yet internally diversified life. Here Royce invokes the Pauline metaphor of the body and even compares the community to an orchestra.[21] The group's interdependence enables the whole to act as one body—or, on the other metaphor, to achieve a symphonic rhythm and flow.

Certain members of the community facilitate the group's communication through a role Royce designates that of the "interpreter" (or "interpreters"). Much like a conductor coordinating an orchestra to harmonize the sections of instruments, the interpreter helps the community interpret itself *to itself*. The interpreter is responsible for guiding the community to ever-greater unity while simultaneously drawing out the unique contributions of each of its members. The interpreter serves the community most effectively by building up the individual members and encouraging the dialogue of the whole community over time—thus, according to the foundational dialectic, enriching each and enriching all. Interpreters are important at all levels of society, global and local alike. In the Catholic Church for instance, the pope functions as an interpreter in conducting and harmonizing the world church, just as pastors, catechists, and social services coordinators act as interpreters for the parish. Equally, those who function as voices of conscience for a nation or a group are interpreters. A head of state designing public policy, a journalist evaluating these same policies in light of the common good, and a comedian offering incisive commentary on the policies' concrete effects each in their own way fulfill the role of interpreter.

Fourth Condition: Shared Past Events

For individuals to make the community's life their own and achieve the mutual dynamism of which Royce speaks, they must understand themselves in relation to some readily identifiable events. Commemorative acts and ritual events recalled, nurtured, and sustained by the whole community serve this purpose.[22] Returning to American communal identity, the signing of the Declaration of Independence functions as a pivotal past event. Americans born in the United States and American immigrants alike annually recall this event through Fourth of July celebrations, a way of identifying the founding event with the personal histories of those whose births followed long after the actual founding. For the Jewish people, the exodus event and the Passover celebration function in the same way. For Christians, the paschal mystery of Jesus's death and resurrection and the sacraments of Christian initiation that commemorate this event (baptism, confirmation, and Eucharist) assume this foundational role.

The rituals from Judaism and Christianity profoundly unite the individual with the community, for they bring the individual into an active relationship with the very foundational events they celebrate. The Greek term ***anamnesis***, which translates *zecher* in Hebrew, often defined inadequately as "recollection" or "remembrance," describes the character of these commemorative events. In its fullest sense, ***anamnesis*** means to make a past event present, an act that sweeps the person who commemorates it into participation with the past deed.[23] In baptism, for instance, the participant ritualizes the movement from the death of an old way of life to the birth of a new life in Christ, recalling but also being conformed to Jesus's being raised from the dead (Rom 6:3–6).[24] *Anamnesis* communicates the full depth of the member's relationship to central shared past events, which are not only observed but meaningfully appropriated.

Fifth Condition: Voluntary Cooperation

For Royce, participation in shared past events stimulates the power of self-interpretation vital to individual autonomy within community. It is self-interpretation that provides the key to Royce's ongoing effort to solve the problem of the relationship between "the one and the many." In his developed theory of community, a genuine unity of consciousness depends upon the distinct minds of a variety of individuals, for conscious cooperation only comes about through the free choice of self-interpretation of the individual. Genuine community cannot be coerced or imposed. Cooperation must be chosen, developed, and sustained over time; cooperation must become, indeed, a kind of "conscious art."[25] It is not enough for a person to be born into a particular community—neither for the individual nor for the community. Communities are genuine to the degree that mature members consciously, critically, and freely make a commitment to the life of the group.

The issue of the free commitment of the individual dominates the discussion of the community today, informed especially by the social crises of the past century. Dystopian novels, including *1984*, *Brave New World*, and more recently, *The Handmaid's*

Tale, focus attention on possible social futures that subjugate the individual and thus positively militate against the formation of genuine communities. Not only do these works send out warnings through their portrayal of the tendencies of real and present social trends, but they also pose questions about the potential for deception at the personal and social levels. When we walk away shaken, it is usually because we recognize our own present-day social patterns of infectious delusion and mesmeric ideology that prevent awareness as to the deficit of free and critical participation in our communities. As the heroes of these works show, the struggle for liberation into authentic communal forms of life is always also a struggle for individual consciousness regarding the repressive measures that threaten freedom.

Sixth Condition: Loyalty to Loyalty

As we witness in the American context, the structures and practices of society do not necessarily foster a spirit of cooperation. How do commitment and cooperation emerge in the public world? And in the individual prone to self-interest and conflict, how are salutary habits developed? Royce's answer is that love empowers conscious cooperation that would otherwise be impossible:

> Love furnishes that basis for the consciousness of the community which intelligence, without love, in a highly complex social realm can no longer furnish. Such love—such loyalty—depends not upon losing sight of the variety of the callings of individuals, but upon seeing in the successful cooperation of all members precisely that event which the individual member most eagerly loves as his own fulfillment.[26]

When Royce equates loyalty and love, he does so with purpose. Royce's "notion of 'loyalty' was essentially a universalized and ecumenical interpretation of Christian *agapic* love."[27] Love functions for Royce as an interpreter of sorts, empowering the kind of self-interpretation required to build up the conscious unity and cooperation that moves us beyond our confined individual scope. Love engenders a type of vision or insight that enables a person to remain loyal to a deep-lying unity that cannot, in fact, be seen at any one time. The insight of love impels the individual to constructive and other-directed action, transforming the self in its light. Love seizes the individual rather than being a kind of power strictly identified with the person's own will. "Love, when it comes, comes as from above," writes Royce.[28] This source of love transcends both the individual and social levels of reality, although it works through both. It must finally be seen as divine.[29] Thus, the ultimate source of community lies in the intervening and creative power of the love that is a gift of the Spirit of God.

THE BELOVED COMMUNITY AS REALIZATION OF THE COMMUNAL PROCESS

In *The Problem of Christianity*, Royce introduces a term to describe the kind of community that emerges from the interaction between the Spirit's love and the sacred pair: "the Beloved Community." The Beloved Community is a great community of communities brought together by the "Interpreter Spirit"—at once invisible, dispersed, and incomplete and yet utterly real as it is actively created through dedicated thoughts and deeds.[30] The Beloved Community stands as an ideal for the individual, who concretizes this ideal as a reality through acts of loyal service and mutual interpretation. In the fulfillment of limited personal purposes, the individual participates in the worldwide community encompassing past, present, and future. This great community also reflects the ultimately triadic nature of the relationship that includes the individual and the community, with the commitment to what Royce calls "the eternal" as crucial to the healthy relationship between self and community.[31]

Loyalty to the Beloved Community proves the highest form of individual loyalty. For Royce, the creation of the Beloved Community is the final religious aim and, thus, the final horizon of personal religious experience. Likewise, local and particular communities reach their full authenticity through their participation within the Beloved Community, which includes but also exceeds their specific aims. For Royce, the realization of this ultimate community of interpretation becomes the practical norm guiding personal and social action. Royce writes at the close of *The Problem of Christianity*: "Judge every social device, every proposed reform, every national and every local enterprise by the one test: Does this help towards the coming of the universal community?"[32] When the answer is yes, says Royce, continue apace.[33]

In her late works, spiritual author and theologian Barbara Holmes (1943–2024) communicates a vision of the Beloved Community for our times. Especially in the final years of her teaching, Holmes referred to the notion of the Beloved Community to inspire shared action in a politically, socially, and racially divided nation. In *Joy Unspeakable: Contemplative Practices of the Black Church* and *Crisis Contemplation: Healing the Wounded Village*, Holmes studies contemplative gatherings in African and African American communities as inherently social events that express the full range of human emotions (running the gamut from anguished moaning to delighted acclamation) before the God who suffers and rejoices along with God's people.[34] Holmes addresses what she identifies as "crises of the one and the many," a designation that should give a sense of compatibility with Royce's way of thinking. For Holmes, these crises are "not the story of the husband who takes you to dinner to ask for a divorce," but the "infliction of trauma upon a group or community."[35] Holmes looks to Hurricane Katrina in New Orleans and Hurricane Maria in Puerto Rico, during and after which the national government and political parties treated the vulnerable as second-class citizens, as characteristic events in which the need for a mobilized "village response" becomes clear.

Even when the village is seemingly abandoned, the village reflects far more than an isolated group. As Holmes remembers, through the perilous times of her upbringing in the American South, when repeated acts of violence against her community were all but assured, she recognized that she was not alone. As she says, "There was a community with me in my present reality; there was an ancestral community in another reality, holding me safe; and there were communities unfamiliar to me whose historical trajectory paralleled mine and could teach me something."[36] Holmes's experience of three-level communion demonstrates the essential ingredients of Royce's idea of the Beloved Community. In Holmes's perceptions of the present community, she recognizes that she suffers as no "mere individual" but belongs to those around her. At another level of depth, the ancestral community reaches through the material conditions of her neighborhood, however bleak, and connects her to sources of memory and hope. The extension across time and space does not stop at ancestral figures: in attesting to her relationship even to unfamiliar communities, Holmes glimpses the village's relationship with the historical and global whole. She goes on to say that her small community depends on and conveys the Spirit of God interwoven throughout creation, which upholds the community of inspirited life across the earth.[37] Holmes's love that irradiates the whole of the earth is but another name for Royce's love from above—a love that comes to a point in and through the life of her threatened community. According to such an appraisal, the undeniable experience of mistreatment and isolation does not unequivocally describe the battered village, which remains sustained by the universal community as part, while also sustaining the greater community as facet.

CONCLUSION: ROYCE'S IDEA OF COMMUNITY IN THE AMERICAN CONTEXT

We identify Royce's thought on the relationship between the community and the individual as a *dialectic*. Too often, American sentiment—both in opinion and in practice—has favored a dichotomy rather than a dialectic, and to ill effect. In his later career, psychologist James Hillman (1926–2011) used to draw out, by way of needling provocation of the crowds he addressed, what he considered the destructive abandonment of communal and political engagement. Walking onto the stage, he would immediately ask the audience, "How many of you in this room are here with your therapist?" After giving a moment for hesitant hands to rise, he would continue, "Well, do you know that *you* are the issue with this country? You—intelligent, conscientious, economically comfortable people—you are spending your best energies working through your woes in private rooms, and meanwhile, the outer world is falling apart."[38] Although Hillman's reproach is perhaps overstated, it is difficult to deny its force—and not only because he criticizes therapeutic culture as a therapist. Hillman hits upon a one-sided ethos that has become deeply ingrained in American culture.

Patterns in therapy present just one facet of this phenomenon; it may just as well be glimpsed through patterns of settlement and consumption. Wary of the collectivism that coursed through Europe, Asia, and the former Soviet Union in the twentieth century, overwhelmed by social divisions at home, and often equipped with extraordinary financial resources, Americans of means have tended toward public withdrawal, driving a retreat to castles of private enrichment. Exclusive gated communities have become normal for middle-class families, springing up ever further from the heart of the city. Both the pool room and the swimming pool, gathering places of old, have become fixtures of personal property—while for many, reaching any public place without a car becomes something like a chosen impossibility. The more recent turn toward remote work and social communication accelerated by the COVID-19 pandemic has built on these patterns to further isolate and even dissociate human beings from a stable relationship to place. Today, we hear mounting concern regarding the technological captivity and concomitant public disengagement of the younger generations—and for good reason. However, historically sensitive observers point to precursors long before Generation Z, gesturing to the philosophic strains of American individualism in Emerson and Thoreau, and further back to the Enlightenment-era social philosophy in the air at the foundation of the American republic.

Royce's dialectical approach speaks to and constructively critiques this legacy, as well as the centrifugal inclinations of American life today. Over against individualistic constructs of human experience, Royce's formulation of human experience offers a clear account of reality as composed of two irreducible elements: individuals and communities. It also offers an ideal in the form of the Beloved Community that conjoins human beings across time and space. The Roycean paradigm provides both a theoretical and practical alternative to radical individualism. For Royce, modern understandings of community as a mere voluntary aggregate of otherwise separate and "independent" individuals not only misrepresent the nature of community but misapprehend the very nature of reality itself. By mistaking individual subjective experience as the sole foundation of reality, modern thought (and the postmodern thought that has followed) has unwittingly fostered an ideology of individualism that has increasingly diminished the ability of human beings to achieve genuine autonomy and individuality. This false and misleading emphasis on individualistic constructs of experience has been especially devastating when applied to religious experience. Without the essential social and communal dimension of religious experience, a person cannot fully recognize or respond to God's gift that such an experience genuinely represents. A rich and fruitful communal spiritual tradition operates hand-in-hand with the spiritual progress of individuals.

Still, the notion of a generative spiritual communal reality goes against the grain of American life. St. Michael the Archangel Parish in Portland, Oregon, where Michael discovered community, provides something of an icon embodying the complex status of community in the United States. Judged by a first impression, this hub of communal life is easy to dismiss. Since the church's founding in 1903 as a parish for Italian immigrants just south of downtown, the city has developed densely around the site. Sleek apartment towers constructed in the last decades dominate the neighborhood, casting an evolving pattern of shadows on the old red brick church; rays of sunshine break through the windows for only a sliver of time each afternoon before the sun once again falls out of view. During rush hour, car horns penetrate the sanctuary walls—to overcome the horns, the priest must raise his voice a register—and buses shake the seats on the right side of the sanctuary ever so discernibly as they swing around the corner. The building's red brick façade (reddish in fact, as it is never entirely clean) is as fragile as it seems: the church requires seismic upgrades the parish cannot afford. In the case of an earthquake, parishioners are instructed to run for the exits.

Meanwhile, the parish's initial ethnic identity lives on more in the memory of some long-established families than in the overall makeup of the parish. At present, St. Michael's is operated by missionary priests from Argentina and attracts people from all four quadrants of the city and the suburbs. As young families begin to have kids and move further from the city center, they face the necessity of juggling their dedication to the parish and their increasingly busy and geographically remote home lives. Many other young people have moved to new cities entirely, often returning as nostalgic visitors to the community that nurtured them. All parishioners contend with the discomfiting reality of homelessness in the vicinity of the parish. The church has initiated a residential service year centered upon weekly street routes to connect with this growing distressed population. Nevertheless, some former parishioners have been driven away by their fear of the unpredictable and jarring behavior of the surrounding mentally ill homeless.

St. Michael's mirrors the fraught and fluctuating condition of American community in the twenty-first century. Created as a haven for a culturally and linguistically isolated immigrant group, the parish is now racially diverse, and full as it ever was in the early days; all the same, given American geographic mobility, the St. Michael's community has become as much a diasporic as local. Coming across this parish stuck between Portland's latest tall glass structures, you might consider it as an utter misfit—like a small, chipped desk made of fading wood in a home filled with stainless steel appliances and the latest smart technology. But for all that, the church retains its attractive pull, overflowing with a life one might dare to say that the apartment buildings lack, and reaching out to those poor and diseased who are repelled by the solid reflective doors of the sounder structures.

It happens sometimes that a resident who lives alone in the tower across the street (most residents live alone) peers down from above and wonders what goes on inside the church. It has even happened that, moving from curiosity to participation at St. Michael's, a tower resident has said that they have been saved by this humble community. One can perhaps detect, alongside their vociferous gratitude, a subdued note of generalized, undirected resentment, as if an important truth had been kept secret from them. Their experience evinces the nuanced truth about community in America. Like the old church enveloped in shadows in downtown Portland, community often lacks immediate allure. We do not always know whom to hold accountable for community's neglect—the national spirit of radical individualism that conditions consciousness or the individuals who tend to overlook community or cut loose from it. (The fact is that the "sacred pair" declines together as it advances together.) But no matter the turns of public opinion and private behavior, the community expresses a form of life that each person seeks, whether with a vague and mostly unconscious ache or with an obvious, desperate desire. The secret cannot forever be kept, for, as Royce puts it and spiritual experience corroborates, the community *saves*. The healing, integrating power of genuine community in the life of the human person is a secret that Christian spirituality must transmit, in its content and no less in its methods.

In the introduction, we introduced Sandra Schneiders's definition of the spiritual dimension of Christian life as "the vital, ongoing interaction between the human spirit and the spirit of God." We also spoke of the necessity of identifying the community as a mediating agent between the human being and God. Through Royce's elaboration of the dialectic of the "sacred pair" of the individual and the community, we have primarily developed the anthropological side of the formulation to make greater sense of the role of community in the fulfillment of the human spirit. The human person only grows and flourishes—only becomes oneself—through the discovery of and breakthrough into communal participation. By consciously engaging in a complex historical social process through participation in shared past events and present dialogue, the individual takes on an expanded self-interpretation and thus acquires a new kind of memory and a new kind of hope impossible for the detached individual. Thus strengthened, the person develops as an active agent who bears responsibility for the community that they have entered, becoming empowered to engage in interpretation that advances the aims they are now united in seeking. The orientation that arises in the individual dedicated to their community—the attitude of love—ultimately points beyond the individual and the community to a source of power that comes from above. In this respect, the Spirit of God proves to be the sometimes-apparent, sometimes-hidden presence that secures the harmonious and efficacious relationship between the community and the individual. To the Spirit, we turn next.

Chapter Three

THE ROLE OF THE SPIRIT IN SPIRITUALITY

INTRODUCTION

AMONG THEOLOGIANS AND spiritual teachers in the Western churches, the problem of the neglect of the Holy Spirit has become something of a trope.[1] This can only be a good thing, as the trope indicates a change in the direction of the winds, a renewed awareness of the significance of the Spirit in theological reflection and the spiritual life. We can identify a variety of reasons for the historical downplaying of the Holy Spirit, a pattern prevalent especially from the post-Reformation era through the Enlightenment: a restricted, "pyramidal" notion of church authority stifled awareness of the Spirit that acts, as it were, in defiance of the closed figures of our geometries; likewise, a lopsided philosophical rationalism, arm-in-arm with a heightened individualistic ethos, tended to write the mobile, unitive, and often subtle Spirit out of the equation.[2] However, since the middle part of the twentieth century, "the long-forgotten member of the Holy Trinity" has begun to garner theological proponents, spurring a vision in many cases animated by increased awareness of the very impoverishments attendant to ecclesial rigidity, rational hypertrophy, and radical individualism.[3] In the renewal of an appreciation of the limitations of human knowing, as well as in the consciousness of deficits of participation in Christian churches, the Spirit finds its representatives. The defense of mystery and the defense of the marginalized also stand as implicit defenses of the Spirit, which breaks a path out of the petrifications of the present. These are likewise defenses *by* the Spirit, not only for the Spirit. It is the work of the Holy Spirit to encourage just such an awareness of the need for transformation, for it is ultimately the Advocate who, through receptive souls, speaks on her own behalf.

Another way to describe the action of the Holy Spirit is to say that the Spirit empowers both interpersonally and intrapersonally. Interpersonally, the Spirit that blows where it wills stands as the means of empowerment for individuals sidelined by exclusionary practices (see John 3:8). The Spirit brings fresh air into underventilated spaces, opening the way to meaningful and constructive participation for previous outsiders in the lives of our churches. As in Jesus's time, the boldness imparted by the Spirit challenges institutional myopia, leading to the development of a broader community of charity.[4] In one and the same motion, the Spirit provides an intrapersonal or interior strengthening: the Spirit empowers from within to a recognition of the love of God and to action that emanates from and sustains this divine current of love.

We can see the Roycean dialectic manifest in the Holy Spirit's action: the fulfillment of the individual and that of the community are inseparably conjoined. When we emphasize the inclusion of marginalized persons according to the principle of the dignity of each person—that is, inclusion *for the sake of the individual*—we are but half right. Equally, we must include the marginalized *for the sake of the community*, which in due time withers when not animated by the gifts of the full body. And just so, when the human person and their gifts are wrongly shut out—when the community is thus deprived—it is always, on the final account, the Spirit that has been denied.

In this chapter, we build on the foundations already laid to explore the role of the Holy Spirit in Christian spirituality. We are mindful of the problematic philosophical and theological legacy. Amid the divisions and oppositions of spirit-matter, subject-object, and inner-outer, the Western mind has had trouble holding space for the third. These dualistic frameworks, too, are wrapped up in the historical neglect of the Holy Spirit, whose reconciling work is antithetical to antitheses. In short, an appropriately "pneumatological imagination" thus must make two advances in order to overcome the (already rightly disparaged) status quo: *(1) The pneumatological imagination must find a way to include the sources of human experience that have been suppressed as a consequence of the Spirit's neglect. (2) It must replace paradigms that split for those that unite—trading the closed geometries of two for the perpetual creative motion of three.*[5]

The ideas we have introduced thus far prepare for this broadening of perspective. We have shown already that the transformation of the "sick soul" represents, along with a newfound awareness of God, the renewal of one's relationship with community. Likewise, in exploring the "sacred pair" of the community and the individual, we have identified the reciprocal relationship between genuine individuality and genuine community. Having thus started from the roots and traced to the tree, we are now set to look skyward to the Holy Spirit—the Spirit that came upon the primordial Christian community at Pentecost, and that earlier drove Jesus, the fully realized human being, ahead on his mission.

The experience of the community and the experience of the individual person lead toward an understanding of the effects of the Holy Spirit; attending to these communal and individual experiences provides inferences about the Holy Spirit's "nature" or "character." In this way, we are following the pragmatist approach to explore the identity of the Holy Spirit, that is, understanding the idea according to its practical consequences. We perceive the Spirit inferentially outside of ourselves in the lives of those people and communities open to God and God's transforming presence: in, for instance, personal witness to joy and peace; in a colleague's evident shift from closed-heartedness to generosity; in bearing witness to a stranger's magnanimous care for the poor; in a friend's reawakened hope during a time of distress; and in the reception of inspired teaching. Through these experiences, we become aware of the Spirit. So, too, in our interior lives, the consoling, intangible perception of presence, as well as clearer visions, insights, and directives, bring us to the knowledge of the Spirit that lies at last beyond our comprehension. The transformation of our own habits, ways of thinking, and bodily actions—the Jamesian "shift in the center of consciousness" that results from conversion—points to the Spirit in action.[6] In the first part of this chapter, by placing these communal and personal effects against the backdrop of scripture and the paradigms we have explored so far, we home in on the role of the Spirit in spirituality. In the second part, through evaluation of the effects of the Spirit shown forth in the charisms, we reflect upon how the Holy Spirit works contextually and diversely in concrete communities.

THE HOLY SPIRIT AS TRANSFORMER: THE SCRIPTURAL WITNESS

A central contention of this book is that conversion, which names the process of spiritual growth, entails the transformation of the lost individual into a situation of belonging within a united community. Considered within this paradigm, the Holy Spirit is, simply put, the transforming agent that lies behind this human transformation, as well as the transformation of community and cosmos. The Spirit guides the individual person free of the "divided consciousness" William James describes and into healing and wholeness—a work, as we have seen, inseparable from the formation of a united, saving community.

The individual and the community constitute an interdependent dyad, but we can only talk about these two in isolation as long as we temporarily prescind from the work of the Spirit. When we treat the relationship between the "sacred pair" in depth, we recognize that we must eventually appeal to the agent, named or unnamed, that *guides* the individual to conversion, *leads* into communion, *empowers* participation, *strengthens* group resolve, and *unites* to the shared body. To understand the actual dynamics of this third agent's action, we need not conjecture, for scripture supplies the account that fills in the philosophical insight. Indeed, the language associated with the Spirit in scripture invariably comes to mind whenever we speak about the individual's fulfillment within community. The scriptural witness to the Holy Spirit identifies the agent of stimulation and reconciliation without which the dialectic of community and individual would be left unanchored.

Philosophically speaking, the Holy Spirit represents the necessary third—or, in Royce's terms, mediating third—that facilitates the creative union between individual and community. As scripture testifies, the Spirit catalyzes and directs the individual's relationship with Christian community. We need not restrict the Spirit's role to Christian community, privileged locus though it may be. The portrait of the Holy Spirit that emerges in the Hebrew Scriptures and in the New Testament provides an indispensable starting point the evaluation of the work of the Spirit in our lives.

THE HOLY SPIRIT IN THE HEBREW SCRIPTURES: CATALYST AND GUIDE

From the start of the book of Genesis, we see the part of the divine life we name the Holy Spirit acting in a special relationship with all of creation and with the human being. The Hebrew word translated into English as *spirit* is *ruah*. *Ruah* literally means "breath" or "breathing into," with original reference to a strong, rushing desert wind. This "breath" connotes a life source that can be transmitted to someone or something. In Genesis 1:2, the *ruah* of God "moves over the waters" of chaos and darkness out of which God creates the heavens and earth. In Genesis 2:7, God creates humanity from the soil of the earth, breathing life into the human body until the breath becomes the human being's own. The Hebrew mind knows nothing of later dualistic antitheses between spirit and body: the *ruah* animates the body, possessing a subtle corporeal nature rather than being understood as an incorporeal substance.[7] The divine *ruah* is a source of force, action, and life. The *ruah* serves as catalyst of the whole of creation and a profoundly intimate link between the human being and God.

Throughout the Hebrew Scriptures, the divine "breath" acts in this dual manner: as a transformative force at work in the world and as a personal link to the divine life empowering new religious consciousness, inspired prophecy, and creative interpretation of the will of God. The general understanding of *ruah* that pervades the primary texts of the Hebrew Scriptures reaches a unique fulfillment in Jewish Wisdom literature. The Hellenistic notion of Wisdom comes into such close approximation with the *ruah*, or more precisely, its Greek equivalent ***pneuma***, that the two are virtually identified in their actions and effects.[8] Wisdom, personified as a woman, helps human beings penetrate into the heart of existence, opening up the complexity and mystery of life to those who trust and follow her.[9] By way of relationship with Lady Wisdom, the human being gains a new vision and a new critical frame of reference from which to judge reality. The texts also give us our first real personal biblical imagery and metaphor for the third person of the Trinity: a beautiful and wise woman mentor who attracts and leads into ever-deeper realms of knowledge and love. These texts suggest that the relationship with the ***pneuma***, like that of Lady Wisdom, provides an intimate and transformative experience that lifts the human being to a new level of conscious awareness about the world and about his or her relationship with God. If in Genesis the Spirit figures most prominently as the creative source of life, in the Book of Wisdom, the Spirit appears also as the enlightening guide that beckons the human being ahead into the life of God.

THE HOLY SPIRIT IN THE NEW TESTAMENT: THE COMMUNAL AGENT

The pneumatology of the New Testament develops particularly in the Pauline Epistles, the Acts of the Apostles, and the Gospel of John. The Synoptic Gospels, written after the Pauline letters, depict well the inseparable relationship between Jesus and the Spirit: Jesus possesses the fullness of the Spirit and shares his own spirit with his disciples after his death and resurrection. In the narrative accounts of Jesus, his life signifies what the human life completely open to the Spirit looks like. This valuable insight notwithstanding, the Pauline texts and the Acts of the Apostles offer arguably the most direct understanding of New Testament pneumatology. The Pauline texts, written explicitly as the outworking of an understanding of the paschal mystery, offer sustained theological reflection on the Spirit in the context of the Pauline missionary communities. The Acts of the Apostles provide a kind of spiritual-historical record of the Spirit's activity in building up the Body of Christ, giving witness to the Spirit's unique "working relationship" with early Christian communities. The Gospel of John, which we review briefly at the close of this section, also offers valuable insights into the unique guidance and fortification provided by the Spirit in the postresurrection church. In our summary tour of New Testament pneumatology, we wish to draw out how this pneumatology stands, in fact, as a communal pneumatology, evincing the Spirit's action as transformer of the "sacred pair."

The Spirit in Paul

Paul holds a privileged place among New Testament writers for two reasons: one, he is unique in that he personally saw Jesus; and two, he ponders in considerable detail the theological significance of Jesus's resurrection, taking into view his own experience and that of others with whom he communicated. Paul considers a wide range of experiences: his letters address the gifts and challenges that develop from the manifestations of the Spirit in the communities he founded. As the letters respond to various doctrinal and pastoral problems that require an understanding of the intentions of the Holy Spirit, they give an essential account of the Spirit in relationship to communal Christian life.

In Paul's reflections on the Spirit, the relationship between the Spirit and Christ proves a persistent theological question. Among other texts, 2 Corinthians 3:17–18 reveals the significant bond between the risen Christ and the Spirit. Paul writes:

> Now the Lord is the Spirit, and where the Spirit of the Lord is, there is freedom. And all of us, with unveiled faces, seeing the glory of the Lord as though reflected in a mirror, are being transformed into the same image from one degree of glory to another; for this comes from the Lord, the Spirit. (2 Cor 3:17–18)

Notice that Paul seems to suggest the identity between Jesus and the Spirit. The identity is, for one, *functional*: wherever the Spirit of God is present and acting, the risen Christ is also present and acting. But Paul indicates more than a functional identity: he points to a *vital identity* as well. Whoever possesses the Spirit of

God possesses the risen life of Christ as well.[10] A personal encounter with the Spirit connects one directly with the paschal mystery and allows one to share in its fruits. By asserting a functional and vital identity between the risen Christ and the divine Spirit, Paul likewise asserts that, in the encounter with the Lord, one receives the Spirit in an utterly powerful and transforming way, and vice versa. The Spirit of God transforms believers into the image of Christ, reflecting back his glory as they look upon the divine reality with "unveiled faces." The growth of the believers "from one degree of glory to another" indicates that the resurrection offers progressive and intensive growth and transformation in the Spirit.

Thus, the new life offered through the paschal mystery represents a historical process continued through the power of the Spirit, a power grounded in the vital identity of life shared by the Spirit and the risen Christ. In this portrait, Paul carries forward the consistent role of the *ruah/Pneuma* throughout scripture: the Spirit functions as the divine principle of empowering and saving enlightenment. Such an experience gives believers the authority and the hope to testify to the saving power of the resurrection. Paul offers us a view of the work of the Spirit that is liberating rather than controlling, encouraging cooperation with God's purposes rather than unthinking submission. Not only does the Spirit help us to finally see God, but just as much to *desire* to see God.

In Paul's Letter to the Romans, this understanding of the renewing current of life—flowing by way of the paschal mystery and into the community of believers—reaches something of a systematic presentation. In chapter 8, Paul's reflections on the implications of Christ's death and resurrection reach a crescendo:

> You are no longer ruled by your desires, but by God's Spirit, who lives in you. People who do not have the Spirit of Christ in them do not belong to him. But Christ lives in you. So you are alive because God has accepted you, even though your bodies must die because of sins. Yet God raised Jesus to life! God's Spirit now lives in you, and he will raise you to life by his Spirit....Only those people who are led by God's Spirit are his children. God's Spirit does not make us slaves who are afraid of him. Instead, we become his children and call him

> "Abba." God's Spirit makes us sure that we are his children. His Spirit lets us know that together with Christ we will be given what God has promised. We will also share in the glory of Christ, because we have suffered with him. (Rom 8:9–17 CEV)

Paul presents an understanding of human existence as transformed through the paschal mystery in the power of the Spirit. A vision of "mutual indwelling" emerges: Christians dwelling in Christ, Christ in Christians, Christians in the Spirit, the Spirit in Christians. Through the Spirit, we are incorporated into Christ—given a share in his risen life and conformed morally to the pattern of his life. This pneumatic transformation enables righteous living that manifests God's presence to others. The power of the Spirit also gives a new personal history: we take on the story of Jesus Christ himself in such a way that Christ's story becomes our story, and his relationships become our relationships. This means that we enter into the family of God in a radically new way: we gain access to the Father and are united with the rest of God's children who have been adopted in Christ. In the unity of God's children, the Spirit achieves not only an individual but a social and communal transformation.

Paul explores the social and communal dimensions of pneumatic transformation most thoroughly in Romans 12—14 and 1 Corinthians 12. In both instances, he examines the Christian community in terms of the interrelationships among the parts of the body, a metaphor we touched on in the last chapter. He also insists in both cases that the fullness of the Spirit can only be experienced within community, not in some kind of mystical isolation. The Spirit builds up community through *charismata*: gracious gifts that reflect particular instances of *charis*, or God's saving activity (grace). As Paul writes, "To each is given the manifestation of the Spirit for the common good" (1 Cor 12:7). The interrelating and mutual sharing of these charisms makes community possible and renders the Spirit more fully manifest. This manifestation of the Spirit is ultimately the manifestation of the presence of Christ, for it is the sharing of the *charismata* that ties together the Body of Christ. The union transcends particular spatiotemporal communities, as well as purely human communities. As Paul explains in

Romans 8, the Spirit connects each community to the universal community and ultimately ties the whole universe into the life of God.

Pentecost in Luke–Acts

Like the Pauline letters, the Gospel of Luke and the Acts of the Apostles treat the relationship between the power of the Spirit, the paschal mystery, and the life of the Christian community. However, the narrative form of these texts accentuates different dimensions of the action of the Spirit than does Paul. The Gospel and the Book of Acts, which make up a two-volume unity, were composed after the Pauline epistles, likely in the early 80s CE. They were written for a community of predominantly Gentile Christians. In the formal prologues to both the Gospel and Acts (Luke 1:1–4; Acts 1:1–5), the author makes clear the intentions of the respective volumes of the study: the first volume recounts Jesus' proclamation of the kingdom; the second, the Christian community's proclamation of the risen Christ. Thus, the Gospel of Luke details the life, mystery, and paschal mystery of Jesus Christ, while the Acts of the Apostles concentrates on the coming of the Spirit and its life and activity through the Christian community.

In the Pentecost story of the Acts of the Apostles, we find the paradigmatic "Spirit event" of the New Testament. Mary and the disciples receive the Spirit and become capable of speaking boldly about Jesus to foreigners in languages unknown to them (Acts 2:1–13). This initial event leads to a series of "pentecosts," the likes of which still go on today. For the author of Luke–Acts, the transformative power of the Spirit in these events leads to the formation of a new community, as described in Acts 2:42–47 and 4:32–36. This community is characterized by a radical sharing of life, including a literal sharing of goods, while finding its deepest center in the sharing of one heart and mind.[11] The Spirit is mediated through the witness of others, which often leads to or coincides with a personal experience of the Spirit. The Spirit endows the community with the strength to overcome their fears, doubts, and inertia, thereby sparking transformation not only by bringing people together but by imparting a unique, direction-shifting mission to the communities it touches. In summary, in the Acts of the

Apostles, the Spirit moves Christian communities out beyond the boundaries within which they had imagined themselves confined.

PNEUMA AND *PARAKLETOS* IN THE GOSPEL OF JOHN

In John's Gospel, the Spirit inspires authentic worship of God and serves as the source of divine enlightenment that guides the disciples of Jesus in faithful witness to his resurrection. John also introduces the term *Parakletos* to refer to the Spirit in Jesus's Last Discourse. This is the only place in the fourth Gospel and in the whole of the New Testament where this term appears. The Spirit's role as Paraclete, or "Advocate," evocatively brings out the Spirit's transforming power within the Christian community.

In two central texts early in the Gospel, Jesus refers to the essentially pneumatic or spiritual character of all authentic worship of God. When the Pharisee Nicodemus inquires about the meaning of Jesus's declaration that one must be born a second time (or from above; John 3:3), Jesus answers in part: "no one can enter the kingdom of God without being born of water and Spirit [*pneuma*]. What is born of the flesh is flesh, and what is born of the Spirit is spirit" (3:5–6). Later, Jesus proclaims to a Samaritan woman:

> But the hour is coming, and is now here, when the true worshipers will worship the Father in spirit and truth, for the Father seeks such as these to worship him. God is *pneuma*, and those who worship him must worship in spirit and truth. (4:23–24)

These texts dramatically indicate that the Spirit designates a central reality in which both Jesus and the Father participate. To be reborn in or worship in the Spirit is to enter fully into the very mystery of God's own life revealed in the incarnate Christ. Jesus is "the way, the truth, and the life" (14:6–7), and the Spirit makes his saving way, truth, and life accessible to all those who are open to its transforming power. In light of this saving transformation, temple worship and all other forms of institutional religion are rendered secondary to and at the service of authentic Christian worship. Jesus comes to offer new life, and those who want it will be given it through his own flesh and blood and his spirit, the source of all life. John alludes to this basic formula throughout the Gospel: to share in Christ's life is to share directly in the divine life (John 15:4–5; 17:21).

In the course of Jesus's Last Discourse, he promises that he will send a Paraclete (***Parakletos***) after he is gone to confirm the faith of the disciples and guide them in their postresurrection mission (John 14:16; 14:26). Among the rich variety of meanings and connotations of the term *Paraclete*—including "defender," "advocate," and "counselor"—the legal and forensic interpretation stands out. The Paraclete whom Jesus sends is both an attorney, who will convict the world of its guilt in rejecting Jesus, and a witness, who will come to testify on behalf of the disciples of Jesus who remain true to him. The Paraclete stands by, encourages, and strengthens those who proclaim Jesus as the risen Christ.

The Paraclete also teaches and guides the disciples by instructing them in the light of the resurrection as to what they must now say and do in the name of Jesus. Jesus implies in the Last Discourse that he is, in fact, the first Paraclete, as he promises to send "another Paraclete" (John 14:16). The second Paraclete will come to continue and prolong the work of Jesus and to teach the disciples as he had done, conforming them to Jesus's likeness. John's Jesus realizes that the disciples are not ready to understand all that he has to teach them. The second Paraclete that they will receive, Jesus's very own Spirit, will teach them all truth and lead them in the ways of divine wisdom—that is, the truth and wisdom that the Spirit receives from and shares with Jesus (John 14:26). Jesus, in turn, shares only what he has learned from the Father. Thus, for John, human beings who experience the transforming power of the Spirit enter into a triadic relationship with the Spirit (***pneuma***), the Son, and the Father. This relationship is the new life that Jesus came to bring and the salvation that he promised to all believers. For John then, the Holy Spirit, as Advocate, not only protects and defends the community of faith, but also guides the community into the fullness of the divine life, much like the figure of Lady Wisdom who leads forward in the Hebrew Scriptures.

SUMMARIZING THE COMMUNAL ACTION OF THE HOLY SPIRIT WITH REFERENCE TO ROYCE

In reflecting on the presentation of the Holy Spirit in scripture, we see how the Spirit acts as an agent of communal transformation, adding a dimension to our understanding of the sacred pair. To summarize how the Spirit operates in relationship to community, and indeed, in relationship to the dialectic between the individual and the community, we can correlate the actions of the Spirit in scripture with Royce's principles of genuine community.

- Holy Spirit guides believers toward an *expanded self-interpretation that secures them within a community of memory and hope*. This process begins through conversion in the Spirit that transforms one's sense of self in conformity with the kingdom reality Jesus preaches. The Spirit transforms the orientation of the whole person, which enables participation within the Christian community of memory and hope. The Paraclete continues to mediate the risen Christ to the community. It is the ongoing work of the Spirit to configure the expectations and hopes of individuals to the universal promise of salvation. The Spirit constantly renews faith in Jesus and the hope of a communal eternal life that flows from this faith.
- The Spirit facilitates *real and efficacious communication, helping the community to interpret itself to itself*. The interdependent sharing of the ***charismata*** through the Spirit's gifts, such as teaching, preaching, and healing, unites the community not only in a common set of aims but also in a sharing of life. By way of the concrete sharing of life as well as the insights and discernment occasioned by the Spirit, the community comes to a deepened level of self-understanding. Through the Pentecost event, the Spirit is poured out upon all believers, renewing

each according to their unique character and role in the community. The radical personal sharing of resources and of life, the fruit of the "pentecosts" described in Acts, marks a higher order of communication of self.

- Spirit places the community in a *living relationship to shared past events*. Through granting the believer participation in the "mutual indwelling" of the Father, the Son, and the Spirit, the Spirit links the believer to the paschal mystery. The Spirit does not merely forge an "ideal" relationship but rather connects one to Jesus's historical passion, death, and resurrection. The Spirit animates the communal celebration of these events, rendering their celebration a participative affair (genuine ***anamnesis***) rather than a mere spectated memorial service.
- The Spirit, *the agent of "love that comes from above," inspires a higher loyalty in the human being*. The fullness of revelation about the Spirit is that it not only acts as the source of unity and the sharing of gifts within each community but also as the bond uniting each particular community into the wider communion that forms the Body of Christ. This community of communities also depends on a mutual sharing of gifts and of life to function as a coordinated body. The divine ***pneuma*** orchestrates and sustains this interaction, as it unites the universal community of communities with the Body of Christ. From this picture, we can understand how the Holy Spirit effectively fashions what Royce calls the Beloved Community.

The Holy Spirit functions as the mediating third, or just as well, *animating third*, that brings about the generative life of Christian communities who follow the Spirit's lead. As both the Hebrew Scriptures and the New Testament relate, the Holy Spirit, working at the heart of the progress of human societies and of creation, asks for keen attentiveness and the willingness to respond to a new source of insight. If, like the disciples, we toss out our all-too-human closed geometries, it is not so much because we have learned to reflect with more exactness but because—pentecost by pentecost—we have been led clear of the lines that once contained our imaginations.

THE CHARISMS: EXPERIENCE OF THE SPIRIT

The *charismata*, or charisms, the gifts that the Holy Spirit diffuses throughout the community, are indispensable to our understanding of the Spirit. As the veritable sparks of life that create community and hold it together, the charisms represent the chief effects by which we come to know the Holy Spirit, the great signs of the Spirit's action. Paul lists various charisms, including, among others, prophecy, teaching, exhortation, evangelization, healing, administration, speaking in tongues, and interpretation of the Spirit (Rom 12, 1 Cor 12, and Eph 4). The gifts given differ according to the Spirit's choice, with each in its own way contributing to the vitality of the Body of Christ (Rom 12:3–8). Paul's list, not to be taken as exhaustive, reveals the common purpose of the charisms, leading toward personal repentance and faith in Jesus Christ and coordinating the community in a shared mission.

Judging Charisms Rightly

The inner logic of the charisms is straightforward enough; nevertheless, the evaluation of the Spirit's gifts has posed a perennial problem for Christian communities. Where we find the first explicit identification of the charisms in scripture, we also hear straightaway of their distorted interpretations. Paul chides the Corinthian community for placing too much emphasis on the spectacular charisms of speaking in tongues and prophesying. He reminds the carried-away Corinthians that the greatest of the gifts of the Holy Spirit is love (1 Cor 3:13). His concern is to keep the Corinthians from falling into partisan divisions and self-assertion and, thus, neglecting service to the community and harming unity (1 Cor 1:10).

The Role of the Spirit in Spirituality

Since the time of Paul, the history of communal religious life bears out two different tendencies toward lopsidedness: the *Corinthian tendency* to prize the unusual and impressive at the expense of the ordinary and constructive on one hand, and, on the other, what we might call the *hidebound tendency* to dismiss extraordinary experience as dangerous.[12] The Corinthian tendency errs by a kind of excess, the hidebound by deficiency. The excess condition overvalues superficially impressive forms of the Spirit's action—in the worst of cases, leading to exaggeration and empty displays intended to gain esteem or power. On the side of deficiency, we witness the routinization of spirituality leading to the settling of a stale, unmotivated atmosphere in which the empowering gifts of the Spirit are not even sought. Whether due to complacency or the paralysis of fear, many communities cease to seek the renewal the Spirit offers. The relationship between these two forms of imbalance can be subtle. Corinthian spiritual ostentatiousness often generates its opposite, leading to the total disavowal of personal religious experience among the disaffected, even less flashy forms. Meanwhile, the apathy and decadence of routinized religious culture can give rise to undue emphasis on more inflated spiritual experiences as compensation for the generalized perception of lifelessness. In any case, the tenor of the prevailing cultural and religious atmosphere necessarily colors a group's underlying attitude toward the charisms.

In a sense, the dialogue between James and Royce about religious experience reflects the same species of difficulty we discover in the evaluation of charisms: Royce stands to James essentially as Paul does to the Corinthian community. While James focuses on special and apparently extraordinary manifestations of God's presence, Royce points out that our experience of God is often more humble and more muted than we might be led to think. Royce rightly fears the same distortion in James's thought that Paul detects at Corinth: he echoes Paul's concern that precisely in our focus upon attention-grabbing and impressive gifts we often find ourselves losing the recognition that even the most singular gifts are given for the good of others. Nevertheless, should we see the wisdom in Royce's counter to James, we cannot rest content with the designation of James as simply peculiarly and personally misguided by a kind of Corinthian inflation. In his turn to special religious experience, James must be understood as a seeker responding, however indirectly, to the general climate of the malaise of New England establishment churches. In other words, he may have become a sort of Corinthian in part in reaction to the greyness of a hidebound religious world. Through this slim window into American religious history, we spot some of the complexities and oscillations attendant to the emergence of different attitudes regarding spiritual experience.

All this is to say that our cultural context—and our specific relationship to that context—frequently causes distortions in our understanding and appraisal of the charisms. In the American context, we must be on guard for the impact of radical individualism upon our conception of the Spirit's action. Refer, for example, to the conventional label assigned to a public figure—a politician, athlete, or actor—as a "charismatic" person. Such a term picks out a person as especially captivating, as someone with the power to exert influence or draw others to them through the force of their personality. As it generally stands with linguistic evolution, such a term identifies an aspect of the spiritual meaning of "charismatic" while losing its deepest center. Indeed, two vital realities fail to translate to this contemporary secularized variant: first, and most obviously, the reference to a divine source, with the charisms standing as the diverse gifts of the one divine Spirit (1 Cor 12:4); and second, the notion of divine "charisma" as given for the purpose of the common good (1 Cor 12:7). As we evaluate the charisms, then, we must bear in mind these two essential reference points in order to see without prejudice. Contrary to the cultural ethos, we must keep in view a perspective on the charisms that understands them as manifestations of God working in a particular way through a person, and no less as directed toward the good of the community.

This double reference reminds me of an encounter I, John, had while preaching a retreat about God's care for the poor to members of the Mobile Loaves and Fishes ministry in Austin, Texas. The ministry sends pick-up trucks around the streets of the city to take food and supplies to the homeless population. At the end of the retreat, a man came up to me and said dejectedly, "This retreat was inspiring, but it made me realize that I have never really been around the poor. I have been working with this ministry for fifteen years, and I have never gone out with the trucks to distribute food. I am ashamed to say that I don't have a relationship with the poor." I asked him how he was a part of the ministry. He said, "I am a mechanic. When a truck breaks down, I get a call, and I take the truck into my shop to fix it, sometimes working through the night so that they can send it out in the morning." Trusting a flash of inspiration, I told him, "Well, it seems to me that it isn't true what you said about not having a relationship with the poor. Your work on those trucks is your relationship with the poor. Without you, they might have the Loaves and Fishes ministry, but it wouldn't be able to stay as the *Mobile* Loaves and Fishes ministry for long. You may not be handing out meals, but God is feeding the poor through you." Trust me when I say these moments of uncannily tuned insight are not a daily occurrence for me. Regardless of my role, what the mechanic required was an understanding of the charisms, even if he and I did not use the term. By expanding his notion of his relationship with the poor to include his role within a community that serves the poor, and in turn, by identifying this role as a conduit of God's action, he could begin to appreciate his gift.

How Charisms Develop and Where They Lead

The mechanic's role in the community exemplifies the "grassroots development" of the charisms. The Spirit coordinates and animates the community by both discerning and calling forth the gifts of its members. The charisms emerge from the *combination of the natural talents and dispositions of the person and the needs of the community*. In the context of the Mobile Loaves and Fishes ministry, the mechanic possessed the talent to meet the need for dependable distribution of food and supplies to the homeless. Not all gifts, talents, and abilities are Spirit-given charisms. Needs develop as the community emerges, and the charisms emerge depending on the dispositions of the members of the community. When a gift constitutes a stable and essential part of the community's functioning toward an end consonant with the gospel—as is the case with our mechanic's work—we have reason to consider that gift a charism.

The regular free sharing of gifts indicates a healthy community. The conversion of the community remains foundational in the ongoing work to identify and make use of charisms, so that the work of the community may be led by the Spirit and not fall into narrow, predetermined, or selfish ends. A converted community will show forth the very elasticity and openness, but also the firmness of intention, of the Holy Spirit.

In short, the purpose of the charisms is service. As we read in the First Letter of Peter, "Serve [***diakonia***] one another with whatever gift [***charisma***] each of you has received" (1 Pet 4:10). The word for service, ***diakonia***, can also be translated as "ministry." The mechanic may render the Mobile Loaves and Fishes Ministry mobile, but it is his service, as well as the service of the whole, that makes the Mobile Loaves and Fishes Ministry a *ministry* according to the full dignity of the designation. In any given ministry, the Spirit operates with a certain precision to build up the kingdom of God, empowering people according to circumstances to take on particular roles of service. To quote Ephesians: "He [Christ, working through the Spirit] gave some as apostles, others as prophets, others as evangelists, others as pastors and teachers, to equip the holy ones for the work of ministry, for building up the body of Christ" (Eph 4:11–12 NABRE). We need not lay aside a commonsense understanding of the necessary distribution of talents in any given situation, but neither should we forecast precisely how the Spirit who blows where it chooses will work. The Spirit is not fixed to a predesignated means of action—and the Spirit often surprises—while the Spirit still operates to bring about a recognizable good. A board of directors calls for one set of gifts, a classroom another, and a ministry like Mobile Loaves and Fishes a third. Each authentic charism is also a service to the whole, not to be confused with the glorification of a "charismatic" individual.

As we do not know the Spirit except by its fruits, in seeking to identify the Spirit at work, we are always bid to ask whether signs of the Spirit are present: "Is there love here? Joy? Steadfastness? The genuine desire for unity?" (cf. Gal 5:22–23). Likewise, we can apply our discernment to the famous passage of Matthew 25:31–46, with the recognition that the Spirit judges as Jesus does: "Are the naked clothed? Are the sick visited? Are the poor fed?" When we can say yes to the first two sets of questions, as with the Mobile Loaves and Fishes ministry, we can next ask, "And how are these deeds accomplished?" The second answer is the key to identifying the charisms: the Spirit finds the path to serve the poor, to bring love where love has not been, and to accomplish a unity that lies beyond our powers alone. In the highest sense of the word, the Holy Spirit is a pragmatist, seeking the effective way forward to faith and unity through the means available. Whether the roles and tasks involved in bringing about these transformations mesmerize, or whether the humble jobs of love simply get accomplished, we can discern the Spirit at work through these deeds.

Charisms, the Spirit, and the Experience of Meaning

Finally, by reference to the charisms, we recognize another Holy Spirit–directed good that has been particularly elusive in the contemporary era: the discovery of meaning. Royce discerns that the individual devoid of conscious relationship to a community is like "a pot that bubbles dry." However, just as we pointed out that the sacred pair of individual and community requires the anchoring of the Spirit to provide an impetus and an orientation, the sense of purpose of the individual's life is not simply resolved by investing one's energies in a larger group, no matter how enriching this group may be. Royce understands well this need for something more. The community does not present an escape from the questions that would otherwise disturb the lone individual; it does not provide once-and-for-all answers to personal doubts; it does not substitute the personal conscience for a kind of codified collective superego. The kinds of groups that merely shift the burdens of existence in such a manner fail to qualify as genuine communities—on Royce's criteria or any other sound assessment. These groups often reflect dangerous perversions of common life, for they are established at the cost of the individual trading in their autonomy for a false sense of security or peace.

As compared to such destructive groups, the genuine community involves each individual actively and responsibly in its shared mind and shared purposes, receiving its inspiration from the love that emanates from a source that transcends the community. In other words, if personal meaning is secured by and through the community, it only emerges through coordination by the Spirit. The charisms exemplify such a relationship. The meaningfulness of the work of the healer, teacher, or administrator who participates in the community rests in their link to the Spirit, their mutual indwelling with the divine mind that works co-creatively with and through them. What perspective could ever denigrate or dismiss deeds that emerge from this basis? No genuine service can be undermined by comparison to other more putatively accomplished actions elsewhere, through reversals of progress, or through the failure to be appreciated. Meaning, after all, cannot be judged comparatively; if meaning is authentic, it is in some sense absolute and inalienable, beyond reproach in its resplendent particularity that bespeaks a deeper source. Thus, the value of a Spirit-inspired deed is established not by any extrinsic standard but by the very relationship with the Holy Spirit. It is not mere participation in community but participation in a community given life by the divine breath that provides a bedrock source of personal meaning.

CONCLUSION

It is helpful now to return to the two major advances necessary for a resilient "pneumatological imagination": the inclusion of forms of experience previously suppressed or overlooked, and the creative potential of a triadic paradigm by which to understand the Holy Spirit's work. What we noted in the previous chapter about the participatory character of an interpreting community, which finds its own rhythm in the flourishing of its individual members, applies to the creative work of the Spirit. Stated positively, a community open to the Spirit generates activity that is coordinated according to the whole and individuated in its parts. Put negatively, a community that does not actively engage each of its members, or fails to welcome new members, has also failed in some manner to hear and engage the Spirit. Needless to say, the verdict on many of our churches is a harsh one.

Our effort in this first area (inclusion of varied forms of experience) implicates the second (the triadic imaginative framework). To be fixated upon the redistribution of power as an end in itself—to remain, that is, within the closed dialectic of the individual and the community—misses the need to discern according to the guidance of the Spirit. The scriptural portrait of the Spirit identifies the initiating, abiding, and above all *animating* mediator that invigorates and directs the dyadic interpretation of the individual and the community.[13] Royce also makes this move by pointing to the guidance of a divine spirit at play in the formation of a community dedicated to goodness. Remaining in touch with the Spirit generally leads to more rather than less urgency in the rebalancing of the social and ecclesial order. The Spirit empowers the community to overcome the sources of undoing that always threaten to turn human groups in the direction of stinginess, depravity, and bitterness, the very antipodes of the fruits of the Spirit; and the Spirit dissolves resistance to change and the acceptance of new modes of life, liberating from the fear that paralyzes so many human groups. The dreamed-of "big tent" of an inclusive community can only stand upright as long as all three poles of the pneumatological imagination—the divine spirit, the human spirit, and community—are secured and linked together.

The charisms—and especially their appropriate interpretation—provide the experiential center of this pneumatological imagination that flows between the poles of the human spirit, the divine spirit, and community. In light of the flourishing of Pentecostal movements, along with the continuing presence of the global "Charismatic Renewal" initiated in the Catholic Church in 1967, we have to be encouraged by the worldwide fervor for the Holy Spirit, and specifically, by the evidence of the desire for an experience of transformation in the Spirit. However, as St. Paul reminds from the time of the very first charismatic movement, no amount of enthusiasm circumvents the need for discernment. In a different key, Royce's dispute with James all but rehashes the situation of Paul's Corinthian church and Paul's response, as Royce likewise emphasizes the range of forms of spiritual communion over and against impressive spiritual experience. Their conclusions align: to be open to the exceptional without sacrificing the quotidian, and to identify the individual gift without losing sight of the common good—such are the virtues of the Spirit-led community.

Chapter Four

EXPERIENCE THROUGH THE EYES OF CHARLES SANDERS PEIRCE

THE LINGERING SIGNIFICANCE OF EXPERIENCE

IN THE PRECEDING CHAPTERS, we addressed necessary elements for a viable understanding of the nature of religious experience. The account we adopt must center on personal conversion without giving way to "mystical individualism," and it must recognize the primacy of community without neglecting the action of the Holy Spirit. As we suggested, we should not expect to find any utterly decisive clarity in our formulation of "religious experience." The removal of all vagueness is neither necessary nor desirable for a discipline oriented toward mystery. What we strive to attain is not final clarity but an appropriate degree of clarity. And what we cannot do without is coherence; the account we adopt, though permanently open to expansion and revision, must nevertheless hang together.

Herein lies the failure of the late modern understanding we have sketched. The Jamesian voyage, raising the flag of direct, spontaneous encounter with the divine, sailing with the hopes of unifying far-flung realms through appeal to a common core of universal experience, runs aground on the rocks of interpretation. Like the more naïve explorers of the New World, the voyage encounters the greatest difficulty in presuming too much in the way of immediate understanding. Subjected to the reality of the mediation of all experience through traditions, through culture and language, and through the human body, the ship splinters. In short, James and the late moderns, although often hermeneutically ambitious and even sophisticated, pay insufficient attention to the way that interpretation conditions experience at every level.

Suitably, in Josiah Royce, the next effort emerges from a thinker especially close to the Jamesian aspiration and especially concerned with the task of effective translation. Royce's opening of the field of religious experience to the social dimension posits the constitutive influence of others upon the religious experience of the individual. His category of religious insight releases the Jamesian private subject from an otherwise inalienable solitude, introducing an understanding of the spiritual life as an ongoing process lured forward by the Spirit that fashions community. Royce's account overcomes the major errors of James: he rejects the sketchy hypothesis of the subconscious upwelling of religious experience, and he attends to the complex contextual embeddedness of the human being. While James's notion of religious experience focuses on exceptional subjective events and tends toward compartmentalizing dualisms between raw sensation or pure intuition on the one hand and second-order reflection on the other, Royce's "insight" prioritizes processes over events, describing a synthetic, holistic form of cognition bearing an unmistakable telos.

Given the resilience of the term *experience*, however, we cannot simply dispense with the idea altogether. At the present stage, then, we intend to give the notion of experience the level of the clarification required, without, as it were, dissolving the cloud wrapped around the mystery. For Royce, too, this attention to experience is indispensable. Religious insight remains an instructive way to conceive of the full process of the human interaction with God, but even within Royce's master category, the language of experience remains pivotal. He invokes experience in *Sources* and again in *Problem*, when he affirms that all religious experience of any mode must *at least* be individual experience.[1] Turning to Christian spirituality in the present day, the clarification of experience proves equally crucial. Born into the academy under the banner of "lived human experience," the discipline cannot abandon a commitment to the notion of experience without also giving up its claim to autonomous existence.

REALISM AND NOMINALISM: TWO WAYS OF UNDERSTANDING EXPERIENCE

For the task of understanding experience, we must do more than simply renovate the craft that the late moderns built. Royce grasped this need for a new construction in the field of philosophy, stated most clearly when he proposed his most complete "social metaphysics" in his final year of teaching at Harvard. Instructed by Charles Sanders Peirce's logic, his communal metaphysics extends the argument made in *Sources* to arrive at an even sharper articulation of the social nature of reality.[2] Royce explicitly expands his notion of experience as well to include any sort of event or affair that occasions interpretation.[3] The ongoing social process of interpretation of experience leads the community of humankind toward the truth.

Royce's metaphysics takes a different approach from the philosophical "nominalism" predominating since Descartes, appearing in a new guise in Kant, and coloring the approach of subsequent modern philosophers, including James. This tradition renders experience the delimited domain of private subjects processing an ultimately inaccessible reality through sense data and introspection. The Cartesian tradition finally concludes that we only have sure access to individual perceptions, which do not necessarily correspond to reality. In understanding the development of knowledge through socially mediated interpretation, Royce maintains the human link with reality through the community's ongoing process of inquiry.

Like Royce, Peirce took the Cartesian construal of experience as his longtime target. If Royce and James are kin of a certain order, then Peirce is the third brother of the family—the brilliant prodigal whose waywardness elicited their sympathies as his ingenious ideas shaped and challenged their own.[4] Peirce perhaps recognizes and names best the philosophical muddle of the era. As a dedicated reader not only of the modern philosophers but also of the ancients and the medievals, he discerned the inadequacy of the Cartesian starting point. Peirce viewed himself as a kind of Aristotle of his time as well as an inheritor of the Scholastic philosophical tradition of Thomas Aquinas and John Duns Scotus.

Peirce's creative appropriation of these traditions leads him to a more expansive epistemological approach than his contemporaries. Peirce rejects the Cartesian foundationalism arrived at through methodological doubt, instead adopting a "Scholastic" methodology. In an early paper, "Some Consequences of Four Incapacities," he enumerates four principles of the "spirit of Cartesianism" as compared to the Scholastic philosophical bent:[5]

> 1. It [Cartesianism] teaches that philosophy must begin with universal doubt; whereas scholasticism had never questioned fundamentals.
> 2. It teaches that the ultimate test of certainty is to be found in the individual consciousness; whereas scholasticism had rested on the testimony of sages and of the Catholic Church.
> 3. The multiform argumentation of the middle ages is replaced by a single thread of inference depending often upon inconspicuous premises.
> 4. Scholasticism had its mysteries of faith, but undertook to explain all created things. But there are many facts which Cartesianism not only does not explain but renders absolutely inexplicable, unless to say that "God makes them so" is to be regarded as an explanation.

As a proponent of a realism of universals, Peirce identifies his position most closely with the Scholastic realism of Duns Scotus—albeit reframed to gain freedom from the substance metaphysics of Aristotle and the medieval Catholics.[6] Along with Scotus, Peirce holds to the notion that laws and general types are real rather than figments of the mind. In his 1871 book review, "Fraser's *The Works of George Berkeley*" he gives a succinct definition of the "Scotistic" notion of realism: "The real is not whatever you happen to think of it, but is independent of your mind or mine or that of any number of persons."[7] As he reasons, the realist position is distinguished from the nominalist stance on the question of whether natural classes such as horse and man correspond to something that members of the class actually have in common. The realist says yes, while the nominalist posits that the classes emerge from the way the mind is "similarly affected" by objects that do not actually resemble or relate to one another.[8] For Peirce, nearly the whole of modern philosophy, beginning with Descartes, falls prey to this second view he designates as the nominalist prejudice against the realism of universals.[9]

The contrary positions of nominalism and realism represent more than mere differences of opinion: realism reflects the genuine continuity that prevails between items in the world and between the world and the mind. Laws and general types are real because of the continuum that underlies them, which Peirce demonstrates mathematically.[10] He later labels this the doctrine of *synechism*, from the Greek *synechḗs*, composed of the roots *syn*, "together," and *échein*, "to hold." In the introduction, we presented the basic unity and intelligibility of reality as a tenet of the discipline of spirituality, implied by the doctrine of creation. For Peirce, traveling by another road, the discipline's article of faith—that reality hangs together—is logically discoverable.

In the same book review, Peirce also defines the real as the final consensus of a reasonable community of inquirers.[11] This notion should not be understood as a violation of the aforementioned principle that the real is "independent of any number of persons," for it does not imply that the opinion of the community, whatever that may be, *counts* as the truth. Communities do not make something true merely by the force of their belief. Such a view would suggest a relativism antithetical to Peirce's thought. Rather, this formulation emerges from Peirce's confidence in the fundamental harmony between the mind and reality. As the human mind is continuous with reality, human beings are attuned to reality, fit to discover the truth despite their proneness to error. The mistakes of individuals are overcome by the community of truth-seekers, which smooths out the variety of individual errors. In our shared efforts, as Peirce puts it elsewhere, "each of us is in an insurance company."[12] And although communities themselves err, humanity's essential fitness for the truth leads to the approach of the truth over the long run. Such a perspective guides Peirce's "turn to the community" in contrast to the Cartesian-Kantian "turn to the subject." In this way, the Peircean move is born not of a romanticism or communal mysticism but rather develops as an outgrowth of his realism.

Peirce's two related positions—the assent to real generality and the turn to the community of interpretation—stand as the first essential elements in the new construction of experience, breaking cleanly from the regnant Cartesian approach. Post-Cartesian philosophers conventionally follow Descartes's initial turn inward in the search for certainty in a world of untrustworthy impressions. They begin from a problematic initiated by the division of reality into subjects and objects, attempting to describe how a self-conscious subject interacts with the objective world that purportedly stands outside of the subject. Positing the unknowability of things-in-themselves in the objective world, the proponents of this tradition build on the subject's processes of knowing. The general epistemological account, abiding through Locke, Hume, and Kant, understands the subject as receiving concrete sense impressions from the outer world. These sense impressions are devoid of general characteristics; the subject imposes an order on these impressions that does not exist in nature. (In the subject's imposition of order, we can read the nominalist position that general classes emerge from the mind being "similarly affected" by entirely unrelated entities.) From concrete perceptions, the mind derives abstract, universal concepts. This subjective interrelation of concrete percepts and abstract concepts constitutes the fundamental dynamic of cognition.[13] Instead of the real continuity between mind and world as well as among the various entities in the world, the account centers on a subject that remains locked within a closed world of perceptions and conceptions.

American theologian Donald Gelpi (1934–2011) labels this account a dipolar construct of experience.[14] Gelpi was fond of saying that such a paradigm implies that "experience takes place between one's ears," failing to give an adequate account of something as simple as a conversation at the grocery store. The specter of solipsism has long haunted the Cartesian tradition. We should notice that the Cartesian construct's dipolarity extends beyond the dichotomy between perceptions and concepts: initiated by Descartes's first retreat, the whole motion of thought, at every stage, is ruled by the split into twos. Beginning with the whole of reality, we divide into the objective world "out there" and subjective experience, and then divide subjective contents into perceptions and concepts.

By encompassing *relations*—relations that are themselves rendered intelligible according to the principle of generality that connects individuals—Peirce and Royce's social-interpretive approach overcomes the habit of division. Relations are the third that connects two other realities: thus, the logic of relations entails a triadic rather than a dyadic construct. Take the shopper and the checkout attendant at the grocery store, who do not remain two unrelated agents engaged in their own closed loop of sense impressions and concepts. The interpretation of one another's behavior through verbal communication and body language is the third that connects the shopper and the attendant, the relation that unites the two inherently related beings in a common understanding. Whether through recourse to the language of relation, interpretation, reconciliation, or mediation, the triadic construct moves opposite to the dyadic: where the Cartesian tradition severs, the triadic construct conjoins.[15] Better put, the triadic construct describes the already-extant connectedness of reality.

PEIRCE'S PHANEROSCOPY: A TRIADIC ACCOUNT OF EXPERIENCE

Much like Royce, when Peirce addresses experience, he expands the notion's reach. He develops a holistic understanding of experience through what he dubs the science of *phaneroscopy*.[16] *Phaneroscopy* is derived from the Greek ***phaneron*** (what is visible or manifest) and ***skopein*** (to view). Peirce defines *phaneroscopy* as "the collective total of all that is in any way or in any sense present to the mind, quite regardless of whether it corresponds to any real thing or not."[17] Peirce wants to include the full picture, "the total content of consciousness," including outward events, concepts, and fantasies.[18]

When Peirce coins a neologism, he does so in order to offer a clarity of thought otherwise lacking—and usually, in order to transcend the nominalistic connotations into which philosophical language had fallen. We could compare *phaneroscopy* to phenomenology, as *phaneroscopy* is also engaged in the description and categorization of experience. However, Peirce resists the term *phenomenology*, for he wants to avoid reinscribing the Kantian duality between the phenomenon and the inaccessible noumenon that gives rise to it. By the same token, in choosing *phaneroscopy*, he rejects James's construct of *pure experience* as an excessively limited (not to mention incoherent) notion.[19] For Peirce, it is not only the instantaneous states of consciousness that "come into view" but memory and our regular mental habits as well.[20] Peirce refrains from the nominalist move to place an "objective reality" outside of the phaneron: the phaneron includes both the "how" and the "what" of consciousness—both the manner in which we receive reality and the elements of reality themselves.

Beginning with the whole field of consciousness liberates Peirce to create a genuine inventory of the elements that present themselves to the human being. Peirce seeks to identify the fundamental "Categories" of the phaneron, the genuine organic classification of the distinct elements of experience. In Western philosophy, the delineation of fundamental categories of reality goes back to Aristotle's *Organon*, a history with which Peirce is familiar. Aristotle's categories constitute a comprehensive set of attributes that describe, in general terms, everything that can be experienced—formally, a list of all the kinds of things that can be the subject or predicate of a proposition. Aristotle's ten categories are substance, quantity, quality, relation, action, affection (or passion), place, time, position, and state. In his *Critique of Pure Reason*, Kant revises Aristotle's categories, deriving a series of twelve based on pure logic. In Kant's system, the a priori categories serve the purpose of reducing the "sense manifold" of impressions to an organized unity. Peirce's effort at elaboration of the categories began with his close reading of Kant. As a young man, he used to spend hours each day reading *Critique of Pure Reason*, but he became disenchanted, concluding that Kant's categories are riddled with arbitrariness and redundancy, ultimately unserviceable because of their lack of attention to experience.

Thus, Peirce honors the project but refutes the conclusions of his predecessors. He does not mind adopting the definition of Aristotle: categories are those realities "which are so utterly disparate as to have nothing in common."[21] Yet, he explains that his categories cut through the logical and phenomenological confusion that hampered previous systems: "My list differs from those of Aristotle, Kant, and Hegel, in that they never really went back to examining the Phenomenon to see what was to be observed there....They simply took current conceptions and arranged them."[22] For Peirce, again, the "phenomenon" does not imply a dichotomy between what is apparent and what lies behind appearances. Peirce's direct examination of the phenomenon dispenses with the complex jargon and a priori postulates of previous systems of categories. In this respect, Peirce demonstrates an affinity not only with Royce but also with James. They each share the American impulse to disburdenment, aiming for a fresh start on virgin territory. Just as James, impatient with sterile reasoning, dispenses with convoluted, self-justifying theological formulae to understand religion anew in terms of experience, Peirce abandons the inconsistent and unclear foundations of his philosophical predecessors, basing his categories firmly on experience—and the whole of it at that.

Through grounding his categories on experience, Peirce's plain ambition is to propose a philosophical system of perennial relevance. Listen as he explains his approach to the categories in "A Guess at the Riddle."[23] He is full of confidence in the significance of his approach and full of desire to persuade, despite his anticipations of resistance and misunderstanding. We hardly know whether to take his grandiose first line seriously: "To erect a philosophical edifice that shall outlast the vicissitudes of time, my care must be, not so much to set each brick with nicest accuracy, as to lay the foundations deep and massive."[24] Although he expects opposition, he hopes that his system will serve inquiry of all forms:

> The undertaking which this volume inaugurates is to make a philosophy like that of Aristotle, that is to say, to

> outline a theory so comprehensive that, for a long time to come, the entire work of human reason, in philosophy of every school and kind, in mathematics, in psychology, in physical science, in history, in sociology, and in whatever other department there may be, shall appear as the filling up of its details. The first step toward this is to find simple concepts applicable to every subject.[25]

The result, worked out over time with increasing independence, is bracingly bold and marvelously elegant. Peirce proposes a return to a kind of Pythagorean mysticism of number. His proposal is this: there are three categories of experience, three *modes of being*, only three, and they are always before us. He names them *Firstness*, *Secondness*, and *Thirdness*. He is concerned with establishing the master categories of three to replace Cartesianism's preoccupation with (or entrapment by) the number two. He is never short of definitions and expositions; like a teacher trying out different ways around a topic to reach students, he is most concerned that the paradigm gets across. In "A Guess at the Riddle," he unveils the categories according to a kind of intuitive unfolding from simplicity to complexity: "The First is that whose being is simply in itself, not referring to anything nor lying behind anything. The second is that which is what it is by force of something to which it is second. The third is that which is what it is owing to things between which it mediates and which it brings into relation to each other."[26] Speaking in a more empirical-practical register elsewhere, he defines Firstness as *quality*, Secondness as *fact*, and Thirdness as *law*. Qualities are akin to feelings, flavors, or tones (e.g., the experience of redness), representing a form of pure particularity and possibility.[27] Although we can gesture toward qualities, they cannot be experienced in and of themselves but rather always inhere in a world of fact. Facts correspond to what Peirce calls the "outward clash" of the world—the brute action and reaction of the physical world. Facts render the possibility and particularity of qualities concrete and actual. Laws are real generalities, or habits, that make predictions possible. Laws describe the predictable, constant, patterned character of reality that enable representation of the world. Amid all technical distinctions, Peirce remains capable of swinging back to the intuitive foundations of his categories. In a pithy formulation based on the meaning of the first three Pythagorean numbers, he rhapsodizes, "*One* was the origin; *two*, stalwart resistance; *three*, mediation and beauty."[28]

Despite the mystical overtones, Peirce does not merely advance his doctrine of categories as a special revelation beyond all probing and questioning. Rather, he works out the categories by pointing to their presence in ordinary experience, demonstrating their irreducibility through mathematical graphs, and communicating their intricacies across a nearly inexhaustible series of examples applied to a range of disciplines. His playful examples are carefully composed. A man musing, walking down the street in total self-absorption and obliviousness to his surroundings, reflects Firstness in his undifferentiated quality of being. A heavy beam falls from a building and knocks the man on the head, representing Secondness in its raw resistance.[29] Though Peirce does not allude to Thirdness in this example, the man's arrival at the principle that walking absentmindedly through city streets is dangerous would exemplify Thirdness in its generality. Another example: if any beginning is first (in its potentiality), and the end is second (in its finality), then the process that leads from first to last is third (as the relationship between them).[30] For Peirce, Firstness, Secondness, and Thirdness demonstrably carve nature at its joints. Any appeal to a fourth category can be understood comprehensively by explanation in terms of arrangements of threes—while only by abstraction can we separate the fundamental three, for all that appears within the ***phaneron*** appears together in the guise of Firstness, Secondness, and Thirdness.

RELIGIOUS EXPERIENCE ACCORDING TO PEIRCE'S METHOD

Peirce's elaboration of triadic categories provides another way to express the problem with the late modern account of religious experience. Peirce is resolute that only a leap into a triadic system can overcome the woes of nominalism. He detects the nominalism implicit in each dyadic system, even in those that seek to establish a realist methodology as a corrective course. According to

Peirce's reading, any realism worthy of the name must begin with a triadic construct. Thus, the Peircean approach renders the shortcomings of James's account inevitable. James remains beholden to the Cartesian tradition. His restriction to private, mystical experience fails to amount to a realistic account of religious experience: James's mystical experiences stand for him as the exclusive empirical facts of religious experience. Accordingly, if we consider James's religious experience through the logic of the categories, mystical experience functions for James as the only meaningful form of Secondness. Unless warmed by mystic light, the service at the soup kitchen, the shared rituals of worship, the commitment of the piano player, and the gesture of concern for one's neighbor—all these facts of life—stand outside the pale of religious experience. For James, these quotidian experiences may perhaps be the fruits of the more primary mystical experience, but they cannot themselves be basic mediations of the divine. The impoverishment of the category of Secondness prevents continuity among a range of different classes of experience; nominalism shows up most glaringly in James in that his "mystical experience" operates unilaterally. From its foundational and originary position, James lifts mystical experience clear of mutually implicating relation.[31]

Applying Peirce's categories on the other hand, what we call mystical experience indeed possesses the value that it bears a strong sense of Secondness, to be compared to the experience of Secondness in a human relationship.[32] The experience of divine presence is analogous to the presence of an embodied, physical relationship—a kind of Secondness that is relational rather than discrete. However, in religious experience, mystical experience qualifies neither as the exclusive form of viable Secondness, nor as bereft of Firstness or Thirdness. In fact, James's marks of mysticism capture elements of Firstness and Thirdness. "Ineffability," which James identifies as a kind of inchoate feeling, reflects Firstness in its openness and possibility. The "noetic quality" of mysticism indicates the illumination and deeper ground of knowledge that suggests the general ideas of Thirdness. We can see in this way how mysticism displays relative or characteristic (rather than absolute) Secondness.[33]

Operating with a different set of concerns, Bernard McGinn captures the dimension of relative Secondness in his definition of mysticism as the "attempt to express the direct consciousness of the presence of God."[34] McGinn's language of presence and directness suits the real encounter characteristic of mystical experience and reflective of Secondness.[35] In keeping with his favored historical-contextual approach, McGinn draws his definition of mysticism not from philosophical speculation but directly from the self-reports of a historical figure: the definition comes from St. Teresa of Avila's *Autobiography*, where she refers to the "consciousness of the presence of God."[36] By making recourse to a framework devised from within Christian tradition—and delivered for the edification of the local and extended community, no less—McGinn signals the relationship between mystical experience and the broader field of religious practice and thought. McGinn's multivolume historical study carefully places mysticism within the schools, social movements, and geographies that influence its expression, thus ensuring that interpretive grounding does not fall away in favor of a premature abstracted picture of "mystical experience" across times, places, and religions. McGinn too resolutely opposes mystical foundationalism: he writes that the mystical element in Christianity should "be seen primarily as a process or way of life rather than being defined solely in terms of some experience of union with God."[37]

McGinn's historically situated appraisal of mystical experience provides a starting point for further investigation, offering a form of open inquiry compatible with Peirce's markedly different approach. From a philosophical perspective, Peircean realism facilitates what McGinn accomplishes by way of a historical-contextual approach: the nonreductive interpretation of what we refer to as mystical experience. Just as McGinn's method assures interpretive depth, Peirce's observation of the undivided *phaneron*—distinguishing without separating the replete field of consciousness—guards against the dissociative tendency that pulls mysticism away from the soil that nurtures it.

Bearing both approaches in mind, we can appropriately place mysticism within the discipline of spirituality. As McGinn rightly notes in the article "Mystical Consciousness: A Modest Proposal," the mystical element deserves a central place within Chrisitan spirituality, as mysticism constitutes the "inner and hidden realization of spirituality through a transforming consciousness of God's immediate presence" and represents the "goal to which spiritual practices aim."[38] This way of understanding mysticism remains open to all three worlds of experience: Firstness in the implied attraction to the divine presence that begins inchoately and leads to the goal intended by spiritual practices; Secondness in the living encounter within time and space, specified as "direct presence" in McGinn's former definition and "immediate presence" in this definition; and Thirdness in the "consciousness" that interprets and lends meaning to the encounter with the divine presence. Once more, we recognize the value of Peirce's replete realism. In contrast to James's schema, Peirce's philosophy pushes in the same direction as Royce's process of religious insight: his *phaneroscopy* provides the thoroughgoing triadic, logical categorization of experience that retains the wholeness and interdependence of the field of experience. We leave the more extensive elaboration of mystical experience to researchers who specialize in this domain. To get at the depth of Peirce's contribution, however, we need to say more about the interpretation of the three modes of experience Peirce identifies. We turn next to his theory of the interpretation of signs, known as semeiotics.[39]

SEMEIOTICS: A SIGN-SENDING AND SIGN-RECEIVING SYSTEM

Because Peirce understands signs to be the basic and pervasive ingredient of reality, semeiosis, or the theory of signs, becomes the fundamental and abiding preoccupation of his philosophy. Semeiosis emerges from an epistemology that starkly refutes Cartesian foundationalism. As we addressed, Descartes establishes the modern philosophical method when he seeks to establish indubitable knowledge based on direct inner intuition of clear and distinct concepts. By ignoring all potentially deceptive external impressions and looking within for the ideas that stand up to any hypothetical challenge, Descartes grounds his philosophical project upon the ideas that emerge through pure introspection. These direct intuitions stand as the bridge to the unknowable reality-in-itself. Peirce, however, denies that we in fact experience the direct intuitions of the Cartesian type. Where Descartes imagines an intuitive capacity that grasps the indubitable bedrock of experience, Peirce recognizes instead a series of inferences leading to the supposed "pure intuition." Identify any cognition, argues Peirce, and you will find behind it a series of previous cognitions. Knowledge of the internal world is never given via unmediated insight but depends on external observations. The seemingly interior experience of anger, for instance, cannot be understood purely internally, but always relative to an outer object that gives rise to it.[40] In this view, the search for understanding must shift its primary focus from the identification of unmediated intuitions to attention to the chains of signs that in fact constitute intercourse with reality.

In this respect, Peirce aligns with the contemporary critics of the late moderns noted in the previous chapter. We can see how James, as a representative late modern thinker, capitulates to the above mode of thought in his account of religious experience. James hypothesizes that the subconscious mind mediates the divine in the subconscious' connection to the unseen, putatively divine realm. Religious experience is the "bubbling up" from the subconscious once the floodgates have been opened. The more porous the subconscious is to the unseen, and likewise the conscious mind to the unconscious, the greater the intensity of religious experience. This paradigm mirrors the Cartesian turn inward in the search for direct intuitions. What can the mystic gain from others except clutter and confusion? The in-touch person need not look out toward communal influences. Especially if ideas come from less gifted individuals, they can only distract from the primary encounter with the divine. Likewise, the gifted individual need not pay excessive attention to dogmas or creeds, for their own rich form of exalted experience is the very fount of all such notions in the first place. The most trustworthy source for James, as for Descartes, is intuition in its purest form, leading to a kind of unpolluted contact with the divine. Mystical religious experience functions for James the way in which clear and distinct ideas function for Descartes: just as Descartes's indubitable ideas are the foundation stones of philosophy, James's mystical experience operates as the grounding principle for all of religion.

Following Peirce's thinking, as with the understanding of

emotion through a chain of cognitions, a prior chain of cognitions can always be excavated to show something more than pure intuition at play. The encounter with God (as authentic as it may be) cannot depend solely on subconscious mediation. In describing religious experience, we must invariably refer as well to a series of interpretive events The consequences of Peirce's critique are clear: the interpreted character of all experience demands appeal to a semeiotic process. For instance, the mystical visions of St. Teresa of Avila are best grasped—in fact grasped in a manner consonant with Teresa's own understanding—not merely as Jamesian special states of consciousness but as signs: Teresa's visions of Mary and Jesus emerge from a chain of signification including Teresa's particular life experience and her formation within her religious community and tradition. What is true of religious experience is also true of experience on the whole. Since we can only think in signs, signs are the key ingredient of our reality. More precisely, they are the condition of all experience whatsoever. Peirce's expansive phaneron, including the endless and unrestricted dance of all that is present to the mind, is a semeiotic arena.

Although Peirce later refines his terms, one early definition provides a good, if somewhat imprecise, sense of the basic character of a sign. "A sign is something which stands to somebody for something in some respect for something."[41] As with the categories, the sign is triadic: to fully describe a sign, one must refer to the sign, to what the sign stands for, and one to whom the sign is related. To eliminate any one of these components is to compromise the full dynamic of a sign. Take smoke emerging from a burning building as a sign of a fire. For the sign of smoke to function, the smoke must represent something (the fire), while someone (say, a person driving by) must witness and take stock of the smoke. The triadic relation then stands between the sign, the object of the sign, and the effect that the sign produces, or what Peirce calls the *interpretant*. In the above example, the smoke is the sign, the object is the fire, and the concern of the driver is the interpretant. The driver's concern becomes another sign to be interpreted. In this scenario, the driver's concern may lead her to call the fire department, and the signification process continues.

Semeiotics entails this ongoing process of translation, response, and further action. Each sign, by standing as a representation to an actor, indicates a course of action. In the example of the sign of the smoke, this chain of action is evident: the smoke triggers the driver's concern, leading then to the phone call, and the call to the arrival of the truck. Through the mediation of signs, the future influences the present. The call to the fire department, for instance, is directed to a possible future that the driver seeks to facilitate: the arrival of fire trucks on the scene to put out the fire. Through their active relationship to the future, signs make things happen in the world; they cannot be understood as purely subjective exchanges. As the links in the chains of relational processes that generate action, reaction, growth, development, and change, Peirce's signs have a living character.

Precisely in this organic character, Peirce's triadic semeiotics differs from the semiotics of the Swiss linguist Ferdinand de Saussure, whose system, developed later than Peirce's in the early twentieth century, is often associated with the term.[42] Saussure bases his semiotics on human language as the prime exemplar and model of all sign systems.[43] Grounded in the relationship between signified and signifier, Saussure's system is a dyadic construct. Saussure restricts signs to linguistic entities: the signifier, a word, intends the signified object through an arbitrarily established linguistic relationship.[44] Peirce, on the other hand, does not limit signs to language, nor to intentional human expressions: cloud formations, animal markings, paintings, and the gurgling of a stomach represent some of an indefinite number of signs. While for Saussure, signs are specifically human instruments of symbolic representation, Peirce maintains no such cleavage between the human and the nonhuman world. Signs do not come from the mind but emerge from the fabric of the world. Each human mind is the product of the semeiotic process, the "self that is just coming into life in the flow of time."[45] Both interpreter and product of signs, the human being stands within a larger whole. As with Peirce's related synechistic doctrine, human rapport or continuity with the cosmos is fundamental to semeiosis. A philosopher's abstract reflections, a conversation at the grocery store, and a hawk's swoop toward an open field are each rooted in semeiotic exchange at the heart of life processes. The implicit Cartesian division in Saussure's conception between human mental linguistic-symbolic systems and the external material world plays no role in Peirce's organic semeiosis.

Peirce's recognition of the diversity of types of signs led him to establish different kinds of classifications of signs, a developing system he expanded and tinkered with until his death. Understood according to the kind of object that gives rise to a sign, for instance, Peirce distinguishes between three types of signs: icons, indices, and symbols. An icon relates to its object by similarity or analogy: a painting of a person is an icon of that person; the onomatopoeia "whoosh" is an icon of the wind. Icons, in their indistinction from the object, reflect Firstness.[46] Icons stand at the beginning and end of the semeiotic process—at the beginning as the most direct likeness of the object, and at the end, when the sign process comes to rest with an image.[47] If an icon mirrors its object, an index is something distinct from the object that points to it. An index relates to its object by standing in real relationship to it, directing attention to the object without describing it: the red bumps of chickenpox are an index of the disease. Indexes "move" thought away from the object, thus reflecting the difference inherent in the world, or the clash of Secondness. The symbol is determined by convention: "E Street" in Washington, DC, is a symbol for the street that runs to the Capitol.[48] Symbols are unique to human beings; they are the only type of sign that Saussure's system includes. In their generality, symbols reflect Thirdness.

Peirce's semeiotics informs his understanding of inquiry. We live in a world of signs, both natural signs and human-made signs. The whole organic world, from an amoeba to a tree to a human being, participates in a sign-sending and sign-receiving system.[49] Signs reflect the continuity between the mind and the world that Peirce advances in his doctrine of synechism. Our communities operate according to a shared understanding of signs, which they interpret with varying degrees of complexity. Through intercourse within these communities—that is, through the shared process of the interpretation of signs, we come to the truth. The arrival at the truth is the arrival at the conformity of signs to their ultimate objects, a process centered on shared inquiry. The epistemology outlined is both optimistic and skeptical. In a community of inquirers, the individual participates most constructively by adopting an attitude of contrite fallibleness. Not only does the community make knowledge possible through communication, but the community checks the individual's oversights and misinterpretations as knowledge develops. The individual must always be ready to learn—always prepared to revise their former beliefs in consideration of new information that emerges from the community of inquiry. Collective knowledge builds over time according to testing of concrete cases. Attentiveness to facts in relation to theories, the new data of Secondness that challenges the received notions of Thirdness, leads to a dynamic movement toward the truth. Experience, broadly considered, begets interpretation, and interpretation leads toward truth.

Formally, this process begins with what Peirce calls an abduction, a third class of logic he develops alongside the received logical classes of deduction and induction. An abduction is a form of inference that represents a sort of educated guess at a pattern, generalization, or principle that explains some aspect of reality. For Peirce, the movement toward an abduction first arises through surprise at a dimension of experience elusive to one's understanding.[50] An abduction offers a potential means of reasonably explaining the puzzling phenomenon or data. Abduction is an organic form of reasoning, imaginative and rational, that reaches out for a probable explanation.[51] Deduction follows from abduction: from the initial explanation, deduction predicts what other kinds of previously unobserved data will emerge through testing if the abduction is true. As Peirce writes, "Deduction first points to the premises and their relation, and then shakes its fist in your face and tells you 'Now, by God, you've *got* to admit the conclusion.'"[52] Induction draws a general conclusion from the cases that deduction singles out. In summary, abduction provides a hypothesis; deduction identifies implications of the hypothesis; and induction, by verifying the deductive conclusions, verifies the hypothesis.

CONCLUSION: PEIRCE ON THE ROAD TO AN ACCOUNT OF RELIGIOUS EXPERIENCE

In eschewing any effort to retrofit dualistic paradigms, Peirce's triadic semeiosis demands a thorough re-visioning of experience. Peirce refuses to acquiesce to the strict separations between subject and object and appearance and reality that dominate the post-Cartesian mind. He refuses, in short, to set up experience on one hand and the putatively esoteric reality underlying experience on the other. This is not to say that Peircean semeiosis neglects the dialectics of veiling and unveiling, presence and absence, fullness and emptiness, that we find, for instance, in mysticism. Rather, the Peircean semeiotic approach lends credence to what we can call the fundamental *realism of mystery* in religious experience. Mystery is not a mere mirage, not a mere private fantasy located in the head and standing beyond interpretation but a reality to be interpreted while never exhausted.[53]

In fact, as French psychoanalyst and philosopher Michel de Certeau makes clear in *The Mystic Fable*, the approach to God via mysticism entails a semeiotic process, precisely by way of penetration into the previously concealed dimensions of reality and of God's loving presence. De Certeau refers to "the secret" that drives the seeker onward. He writes, "The secret is the precondition for hermeneutics. There can be no interpretation without the supposition of something hidden to decipher in the sign."[54] Even when our knowledge remains partial, even when that which is revealed indicates an ever-deeper abyss, we remain engaged in this "deciphering of the sign." We might go even further and say that *only* when our knowledge remains incomplete, only when we travel on as seekers of the truth that lies out ahead and deeper still, are we authentically engaged in the deciphering of the sign. As we stated, for Peirce, the interpretation of a sign leads to a further sign capable of interpretation, and the subsequent interpretation clarifies the initial sign in turn. Peirce's sophisticated realistic semeiosis, directed invariably to the not-yet-fully-manifest truth, thus proves an aid rather than a hindrance to our understanding, providing language and categories for the encounter with "the secret" at the center of spiritual seeking. Certeau's mystic "who cannot stop walking" in search of the beloved meets a kindred spirit in Peirce's ideal philosopher, who quests after a truth simultaneously real and unfinished.[55]

So, too, to continue with de Certeau's remarks, the relational character of Peircean semeiosis stands out in the pursuit of the hidden. "The secret," says de Certeau, "introduces an erotic element into the field of knowledge. It impassions the discourse of knowledge."[56] The erotic-relational connection is obvious: eros functions as a third that mediates between the desirer and that which is desired. Still, we might question de Certeau's formulation: Does the mystical secret *introduce* an erotic element into the field of knowledge, or is this erotic element rather always in some respect included, perhaps just more or less obviously so? Does our pursuit of philosophical knowledge not also depend upon a fiery, impassioned desire to penetrate the as-of-yet-unknown? Can we not invoke Diotima's speech in Plato's *Symposium* that places eros as the active agent, the in-between *daimon*, that drives one from the sense of lack to the acquisition of a good?[57] And should we not recall that the Greek god Eros possesses particular mythical connections with hermeneutical Hermes, who leads souls into hidden realms as well as to the interpretation of every sort of message? No matter how we understand the parameters of the relationship between eros and knowledge, we can affirm with de Certeau the key role of the mediation of eros in coming to knowledge of the hidden.

For the modern mind, eros stands as a decidedly uncomfortable term: insofar as the modern project pulls back into the domain of a private, thinking self, the erotic character of the pursuit of knowledge remains obscured. The solipsist, that perfect Cartesian, is hardly an erotic being—just the opposite! We must finally be firm that only a thoroughly relational metaphysics like Peirce's can accommodate the erotic element in the knowledge of the mystical sign, wherein eros connotes a creative third. Only a thoroughly relational metaphysics possesses the resources to overcome the legacy of the still-problematic modern disjunction between ***gnosis*** and ***eros***—two terms, which, when seen in their synergy, indicate a relationship that includes but is not limited to mysticism.

Indeed, through the identification of interpenetrating-yet-distinct modes of experience (categorized according to Firstness, Secondness, and Thirdness), Peirce's account of experience preserves us from a kind of mystical tunnel vision while maintaining a place for mystical experience. Mystical experience is an important type of religious experience (characteristically evincing Secondness in the communication of direct presence), yet to elevate mysticism to the status of paragon and model of all religious experience repeats the nominalist error of falsely positing a purportedly unimpeachable subjective foundation from which to build out the rest of one's understanding. Peirce holds on the contrary that our reasoning "should form a chain that is no stronger than its weakest link, but a cable whose fibers may be ever so slender, provided they are sufficiently numerous and intimately connected."[58] To work with Peirce's metaphor, the fibers of the cable of religious experience may include a mystical sense of union with the divine presence, the various forms of social experience Royce enumerates, as well as others, including religious ritual and aesthetic joy. By the same token, Peirce's science of *phaneroscopy* is inclusive of "all that comes into view," whether pure possibility, brute fact, or general ideas. Like Royce in his elaboration of religious insight, Peirce maintains experience within a broad web of mutual relations and emphasizes the social process of interpretation. The discipline of spirituality, committed to a thick, participative account of experience, can likewise adopt a social, realistic, triadic method of interpretation through an understanding of experience as constituted by the mediation of signs.

As we imagine pathways for the development of Christian spirituality, one final advantage of Peirce's philosophy must be brought to the fore: openness to communication with the more-than-human world. Whereas the capsized modern project retreats to the domain of the private subject, Peirce's realism understands human beings as radically embedded within the world and continuous with the world's life processes. We are inextricably configured within a sign-sending and sign-receiving system that transcends merely human construction. Just as philosophy and the sciences have been limited by the Cartesian dualistic framework, our spiritual imaginary has too often fallen short of appraisal of both the human relationship with creation and the way that God works through the "book of nature." Religious experience must also be open to the greater community of creation, not only the community of human inquiry. As Belden C. Lane writes in *The Great Conversation: Nature and the Care of the Soul*: "We're surrounded by a world that talks, but we don't listen. We're part of a community engaged in a vast conversation, but we deny our role in it."[59] To come awake to this conversation has become the spiritual imperative of our day.[60]

With respect to reaching beyond human exclusivity, we can note how Peirce's semeiosis informs, among other disciplines, the emerging field of biosemiotics, which explores "the communication and signification found in and between living systems."[61] Christian spirituality scholar Mary Frohlich recognizes this field as possessing ramifications for spiritual practice, including the implicit invitation to "reconsider the value of some modes of spiritual practice that have been in low esteem in the modern period, such as dreams, visions, and shamanic journeys."[62] Given a Peircean semeiotic approach to spirituality, not only can we find ways to validate previously dismissed spiritual practices, but we can also attend to their specific sign character and thus coordinate them within the expanded framework of experience Peirce charts. An integral account of experience and an integral ecology productively partner in a spirituality that meets the more-than-human world as a part of our spiritual landscape. Historically laden as we are with minds of division, work remains in our conversion to this more holistic way of seeing. In the next chapter, we take up the matter of conversion—the nature of the process, the obstacles to its realization, and the hope by which it is guided.

Chapter Five

CONVERSION

INTRODUCTION

OUR INQUIRY INTO RELIGIOUS experience has led us to a conclusion that may seem paradoxical, but only at first glance: there is no particular genre of experience to be labeled simply and unequivocally as "religious experience." To chase after a pure form of religious experience constitutes a certain kind of rainbow chasing—ultimately, the pursuit of a nominalistic specter. We approach our target more subtly and more appropriately when we attend to the process of spiritual development within a coherent account of human experience. By appealing to the category of "religious insight," we locate our understanding in an interpretive matrix that brings into focus all three worlds of experience: the pure possibility that arises through desire for the transcendent (Firstness), the fact(s) of events both imaginative and external that mediate God's presence (Secondness), and the meaningful interpretations of God's action that endow our spiritual lives with purpose and intention (Thirdness).

As Josiah Royce points out, our first religious insight is not the consciousness of being saved but the awareness of the need to be saved.[1] Genuine religious insight, first and foremost, pushes you out of a state of spiritual inertia, conveying the significance and urgency of finding a community to which you can give yourself sincerely and charismatically. Your dedicated service to a Spirit-led community becomes the lifetime task toward which the nascent insight points. The horizon of religious experience remains forever ahead: not only does your dedication to a community outlast you by way of the community's continued existence, but the vanishing point of religious concern directs you beyond to the hope for salvation within an everlasting communion. In this way, the *experiential impulsion toward the future* is foundational, not only according to application of the pragmatic method, but for the understanding of the essential form of the encounter with the transcendent.

Since the meaningfulness of religious experience relates to the transformation intended in the person and the community, no account of religious insight is complete without an understanding of conversion. Conversion represents not a single decisive event but an unfolding dynamic at the heart of the Christian life. How do we interpret the significance of mystical awakenings, deeds of participatory service, the sense of overwhelming compassion for a stranger, a prophetic message delivered to a community, or any number of instances of a generously understood sampling of the varieties of religious experience? How do we assess the authenticity of our putative encounters with God? How do we make sense of the integration of our experience in different domains, domestic and public—judging whether it leads closer to God or not? To ask these questions means to ask where experience leads, and so to take up the reality of conversion, that is, the normative understanding of human transformation.

PART I: CONVERSION, AN AMERICAN PREOCCUPATION

Let us not be too abstract—too prompt to supply definitions of *conversion*—before identifying the place of conversion in the American context. "Conversion" is in the air and in the soil—uniquely the stuff of the American academy as well as the stuff of the streets. Not only did William James feature conversion in *The Varieties of Religious Experience*, but his empirical research (along with that of Granville Stanley Hall at Clark University) initiated the psychological study of conversion at the outset of the twentieth century. James was only bringing the intellect to bear formally upon the grassroots culture of American religiosity, which developed out of the great revival movements scattered across the regions and the centuries. Wherever we look in American religious life, whether we start in the present with the charged style of evangelical preachers and the repentance-inflected rhetoric of American politics, or whether we track back to the precursors of such a style in the early Puritan settlements; whether we stay back East, or head West to the mission churches in which conversion and colonization were entangled, we find the idea of conversion playing a leading role in the formation of the American character and sensibility.[2] The experience of conversion drives even the expressly secular American-born program of Alcoholics Anonymous—which, incidentally, founder Bill Wilson acknowledged was indebted to James's *Varieties*.[3] Perhaps most strikingly of all, the twentieth-century spiritual heroes of the American landscape accentuate the theme of conversion. American prophets such as Dorothy Day, Thomas Merton, and Martin Luther King Jr.—our larger-than-life spiritual icons—both powerfully called others to transformation and personally enacted what they proclaimed.

Now, considering the breakthrough theological contributions of Canadian Bernard Lonergan (1904–84) as well, the explicit attention granted to conversion must be seen equally as a uniquely *North* American preoccupation. Lonergan posits the "conversion of the subject" as basic to the practice of Christian life and as fundamental for theology, averring that "reflection on the ongoing process of conversion may bring to light the real foundation of a renewed theology."[4] Lonergan offers a clear starting point for defining *conversion*. He frequently describes conversion as a change of the subject's course of direction that involves what he labels "an about-face," or a repudiation of the characteristic features of one's previous way of life.[5] In his definition, Lonergan captures the sense of the New Testament term *metanoia* (often translated abruptly as *conversion*), which indicates a reorientation of mentality and of one's guiding values.

Lonergan extends his understanding beyond the classical religious interpretations of conversion, as he includes intellectual and moral conversion alongside religious conversion.[6] In a late paper, Lonergan also writes of "affective conversion" as the transformation of the feeling life of the subject.[7] Each form of conversion stands in a mutual relationship to the others: conversion in one area supports the full transformation of the personality, while recalcitrance in one area obstructs holistic transformation. The novelty of Lonergan's contribution, then, lies not only in his understanding of conversion as foundational for theological inquiry but also in his insight into the additional modes of conversion and their interrelationship. Donald Gelpi has since expanded and developed these categories to include five different forms of conversion: religious conversion (in particular, Christian conversion), intellectual conversion, affective conversion, personal moral conversion, and sociopolitical conversion.[8] Gelpi holds that each form of conversion focalizes the movement from irresponsibility to responsibility in a certain domain of experience.[9] Gelpi's detailed development of Lonergan, which we will explore in greater depth throughout the rest of this chapter, offers a differentiated understanding of holistic conversion.

The Gelpi-Lonergan perspective represents an important advance upon James's scholarly elevation of the conversion theme in *The Varieties of Religious Experience.* Although James's narrative of the reunification of the "divided self" attends to the transformation of affect, morality, and intellect in religious conversion, James conceives these changes predominantly as consequences or lasting indications of either religious conversion or a more general psychological reorientation. James's analysis is valuable up to a point, capturing the experience of conversion, but he does not examine the question of moral, intellectual, or affective conversion as potentially independent modalities. From the standpoint of spirituality, these realms of experience are worthy of treatment as essential dimensions of human experience. Given the anthropological orientation of spirituality named by Sandra Schneiders, any mode of human transformation falls under the purview of the discipline. Equally, these modes of conversion are significant in their impact on personal and communal religious conversion.

From inside faith communities, we recognize the value of a sharper and more differentiated explanatory framework. Tensions, disagreements, and one-sided attitudes show the need for a holistic account of conversion. We may be sincere in our faith and still wind up sidetracked by patterns of emotional wounding, leading to interpersonal strife as a result. So, too, we encounter community members changed by an experience of the Holy Spirit who remain defiantly closed-minded with respect to evolutionary theory or climate change—or who remain unmoved by the suffering of people in other parts of the globe. And then there are genuine Christians who are the first to meet the poor with soup and blankets during a cold snap yet fail to take accountability for dysfunction in their private lives. In each instance, we gain insight through attention to a particular mode of conversion. In order to accurately identify the legacy of emotional wounding and the potential for healing, we speak of affective conversion; to meet the question of tenacious perseverance in beliefs that do not stand up to scrutiny, we appeal to intellectual conversion; for responsiveness to social realities outside the neighborhood, we talk of sociopolitical conversion; and for persistence in destructive behavior that harms friends and family, personal moral conversion.

Following Gelpi's lead, each form of conversion engages a different realm of experience and so relies upon different norms of judgment to grasp the movement from irresponsibility to responsibility. To be responsible is to be accountable according to the norms appropriate to each domain: for affective conversion, this means accountability for the health of emotional responses; for intellectual conversion, the truth of personal beliefs and the guiding frameworks that inform beliefs; for moral conversion, the values one communicates through one's personal choices; and for sociopolitical conversion, the causes for which one stands.[10]

By beginning at the site of the issue, we hone our understanding of the unique situation of each individual and the community. Whether assessing communally or individually, we soon find that each of these modes of conversion relates to one another and to religious conversion, and that religious conversion promotes conversion in other areas. The human being is an integral whole, and so, as with the evaluation of any organic whole, we can begin at any point and find our way to any other. A fine-tuned holistic account of conversion enables us to view the human being in something of the way a medical doctor diagnoses: the doctor serves the patient best by starting with the organ whose symptoms present most outstandingly, knowing that he or she works to heal not only the liver or the kidney but the whole patient. In offering spiritual guidance, operating as a doctor of the soul, the clarification of the modes of conversion relates to the task of discernment. Proper evaluation identifies and guides the experiential impulsion toward the future in the unfolding relationship among the human spirit, the divine spirit, and the community.

THE FIVE MODES OF CONVERSION IN DETAIL

As we have begun to show, Donald Gelpi's sophisticated work creates an effective platform for spirituality's engagement with conversion. Not only does Gelpi expand on Lonergan's spare comments, but he grounds his thinking in the triadic, relational metaphysics of Royce and Peirce.[11] Gelpi's elaboration of the dynamics and counterdynamics of conversion accounts for the way that the modes of conversion interact. A dynamic of conversion refers to the way in which the presence of conversion in one area supports and fosters conversion in another. A counterdynamic indicates how the absence of conversion in one realm distorts or subverts conversion in another.[12]

Gelpi also attends to the theological rationale for the distinction between the natural modes of conversion and religious conversion. Theologically speaking, intellectual, moral, sociopolitical, and affective conversion constitute "natural" rather than "supernatural" forms of conversion. Whereas the supernatural requires reference to God's call and the human being's response (that is to say, grace), the natural forms of conversion can be understood without explicit recourse to the divine initiative. However, the natural forms of conversion facilitate the human being's relationship with God through the cultivation of truthfulness, goodness, emotional balance, and concern for public welfare—and God may well be at work in each of these shifts. Likewise, the supernatural conversion to faith in Jesus Christ encourages and instigates additional forms of conversion.[13]

For the natural modes of conversion, Charles Sanders Peirce's account of the normative sciences clarifies the distinctive domains that apply to each. The "normative sciences," for Peirce, are those investigations that reflect on shared social experience and advance through shared inquiry. Peirce defines the normative sciences as the inquiries dedicated to "the science of the laws of conformity of things to ends."[14] Reasoning according to the classical or transcendental ends of beauty, truth, and goodness, Peirce posits three normative sciences. The end of esthetics is beauty, the end of ethics goodness, and the end of logic truth. As Peirce applies his doctrine of the categories, esthetics studies its end "as it presents itself," and thus treats Firstness; ethics focuses on its end relative to action, and thus treats Secondness; and logic, in the relation between its end and representation, treats Thirdness.[15] According to their psychological aspects, esthetics reflects Firstness through feeling, ethics reflects Secondness through reaction, and logic Thirdness through thought.[16]

From this basis in the categories of experience, an ordering of the normative science becomes apparent. Logic depends on ethics, as ethics is "the theory of *right* reasoning, of what reasoning ought to be, not what it is."[17] Ethics, as "the theory of self-controlled, or deliberate conduct," is of a wider purview than logic, which studies only self-controlled conduct directed to representation. Ethics requires ideals to guide its conduct: these ideals are supplied by esthetics, the science that inquires into "that which is objectively admirable without any ulterior reason."[18] Peirce also considers esthetics the study that treats the *summum bonum*, the supreme ideal. His ordering of the normative sciences is an order of relative grounding rather than a kind of supremacy: esthetics grounds ethics, and ethics grounds logic.[19]

Building on Peirce, Gelpi coordinates the normative sciences with the forms of natural conversion. Esthetics informs affective conversion: the affectively converted person becomes capable of perceiving the genuinely beautiful. Ethics orients moral conversion: the morally converted stably brings about the good. Finally, logic guides intellectual conversion: the intellectually converted responsibly pursues the truth.[20] Additionally, the ordering of the normative sciences is significant, as, by analogy, affective conversion grounds moral conversion and moral conversion grounds intellectual conversion. This pattern of ordering is not to establish an absolute or rigid relationship among the modes of conversion but to note their relative primacy in light of the normative sciences. *Visio precedes ratio*, according to the medieval dictum.

The stable attraction to the vision of the authentically beautiful impels the commitment to goodness, which establishes the spirit of responsible investigation of the truth. The order of these relationships provides clues to manifestations of disorder as well. As Hans Urs von Balthasar writes, "[Beauty] will not allow herself to be separated and be banned from her two sisters [truth and goodness] without taking them along with herself in an act of mysterious vengeance."[21] When we sometimes believe that trouble clearly stems from the intellectual or moral sphere, we are bid to look deeper to see whether certain *mysterious acts* in fact emanate from the disruptions at the affective level.

Affective Conversion: Features and Relationship to Depth Psychology

Following the Peircean ordering of the normative sciences, we start with affective conversion, which pertains to Firstness. Affective factors are something of the sleeping giant that has the power to invigorate our understanding of holistic conversion and, likewise, Christian spirituality. Affective conversion has received its most significant attention in the field of depth psychology. With the publication of Sigmund Freud's *The Interpretation of Dreams* in 1899–1900 and Carl Jung's *Symbols of Transformation* in 1911–12, the foundations for a kind of revolution of human self-awareness were laid. The insight into the influence of repressed feelings in human behavior, specifically the hypothesis of the unconscious determination of conscious attitudes, represented a profound challenge to the modern notion of the rational, autonomous self on the ascendancy since the time of Descartes. Freud went so far as to gesture to the parallel between the Copernican revolution and the perspective emerging from depth psychology. As Richard Tarnas distills Freud's comparison: "Just as the Copernicans had displaced the Earth from the center of the universe to reveal a much larger unknown cosmos of which the Earth was but a tiny peripheral fragment, the Freudians displaced the conscious self from the center of the inner universe to reveal the much larger unknown realm of the unconscious."[22] For Jung, an awakening to the significance of the unconscious reflected the tall order of the age to come: "We have not understood yet that the discovery of the unconscious means an enormous spiritual task, which must be accomplished if we wish to preserve our civilization."[23]

Jung's designation of the discovery of the unconscious as an inherently *spiritual task* came to set him apart from the Freudian scientific materialist paradigm; while Freud saw spiritual experience as regressive fantasy or rationalization, and thus as essentially pathological, Jung's practice and research led him to conclude that the human being's connection to the transcendent provides the key to psychological wholeness.[24] On this point, the link with William James is salient: James's studies in *Varieties* influenced Jung directly as he worked out his ideas on the unconscious. Additionally, James's thought traveled to Jung indirectly: Jung picked up his central idea of the "numinous" from Rudolf Otto, who was influenced by James's phenomenology of mystical experience. In their appreciation for the spiritual dimensions of human experience, the mysteries of the human being's inner depths, and the relationship between the individual and the "suprapersonal" sphere, James and Jung display a remarkable resonance. Shortly before James died, he met Freud and Jung on a trip the two made to the United States for Freud's 1909 lecture series at Clark University. James's impressions bear out his distance from Freud and his affinity with Jung. James suspected Freud to be "a man obsessed by fixed ideas," while he enjoyed Jung's company.[25] Jung noted that they "got along excellently with regard to the assessment of the religious factor in the psyche."[26]

Recollecting the influence of James on the discipline of spirituality—we have recognized him as a sort of "proto-founder"—the connections with Jung, the resistances to Freud, and the timing of the advent of depth psychology are of decided significance. The discipline of spirituality was born through the Jamesian ancestral line; as we unpack the discipline's potential, "the sign we unfold" includes a particular relationship to depth psychology, which in its fundaments, carries forward James's inclinations. Remember that James opened the door to an empirical study of religious experience as a psychologist preoccupied with the nature of human experience and alive to the mysterious pull toward "something more." We may question James as Royce does on his conception of the relationship between the individual and the "subliminal realms," or the role of the "mother sea" in spiritual experience; we may estimate his hypotheses underdeveloped, or his metaphysics incoherent, but we do not thereby depart from the groundwork James paved for a form of psychological inquiry possessed of reverence for the transcendent dimension of human experience. Thus, spirituality emerges subsequent to, and in some respect, *out of* the intellectual revolution that dethrones the conscious mind from its dominant position in exchange for the rulership of the processes that work beneath the surface of the mind's awareness. Spirituality emerges in continuity with a tradition of exploration of the unconscious that understands this work not as a mere unveiling of biological drives but as a spiritual task. Although the task has been unevenly executed, prone at times to devolve into a tug-of-war between overweening psychological hypotheses and dogmatic religious defensiveness, the fundamental awareness of the unconscious (to put it paradoxically) remains a gift.

However, this understanding of the unconscious is a gift that we seldom receive with open arms, for, in order to claim it, we must step down into shadowy and fearful regions, must enter the veritable basement of the human soul where the giant slumbers. Whether working with others or oneself, the difficulty of affective conversion lies in the confrontation with unacknowledged and unwanted dimensions of the personality. To bring painful memories and habitual behaviors to the surface awakens strong defenses and unlocks frozen negative emotions, leading to an often-arduous journey to healing.

The discernment of affective conversion is more straightforward than the process. The absence of affective conversion contributes to rigidity, insensitivity, pessimism, and insincerity in all dimensions of life—moral, intellectual, and religious. Genuine affective conversion bears fruit in imaginative flexibility, receptiveness, creativity, and enthusiasm across the board. Affective conversion is closely connected with the capacity to appreciate and draw life from the beautiful (or the "admirable"). Principally, affective conversion *animates* the other forms of conversion: when the slumbering giant does not break through the basement door and sow chaos throughout the house, its vitalizing power suffuses the personality with strength and joyfulness.[27] In relation to intellectual conversion, when fear and anger do not hinder a person's thinking, intellectual versatility and creativity emerges.

With respect to moral conversion, not only do moral ideals become suffused with a certain beauty, but moral deliberation becomes sensitized to the range of human experience and engaged with the intricacies and depths of the human heart. And the Christian life, when animated by affective conversion, communicates the best of the missionary spirit, punctuated by an exuberant desire to share the joy one has received through relationship with Jesus Christ.

Affective Conversion and Spiritual Experience

Sadly, in the encounter with psychological truth, our churches have seldom proven more courageous than the average individual: crises have forced a reckoning with wounding and dysfunction, and even then, the reckoning has come with considerable reluctance. In the sexual abuse scandals that have roiled churches, psychologists have too often been summoned like firefighters, called upon only once the building catches flame. But now, in the wake of numerous conflagrations, the insight into the significance of emotional transformation can hardly be ignored—or so we hope.

The basic challenge here is the need to discern the presence or absence of affective conversion in a religious context. Psychological knowledge must be carried both with shrewdness as to the spiritual distortions that emerge from affective roots, on one hand, and, on the other, an imagination alert to transcendence. Good psychological analysis lays bare, patiently pulling off disguises one by one to discover the concealed face of the psyche. Deficient analysis overdoes the unmasking, doing violence to the reality it seeks to expose, crudely reducing the highest to the lowest. Again, openness to transcendent influences and higher motivations, even if held as a bare possibility, shapes the encounter with human affectivity. The "genital eye" of Freudian psychology, for instance, may indeed spy out the psychosexual basis for presumably noble motivations, but bereft of the eye of the heart as well, fails to cultivate the disposition that detects the salutary spiritual ground of relationships. When spiritual guidance and partnership come to be aggressively reinterpreted as sublimated sexual longing and nothing more—when St. Francis and St. Clare of Assisi, St. Francis de Sales and Jean de Chantal,

Teresa of Avila and John of the Cross are no longer seen with the eye of the heart—then we have lost the vital thread of their work. Yet, we must remember cases like the exploitative spiritual direction of Thomas Philippe and Jean Vanier, wherein the unmasking of hidden motivations and techniques of manipulation proved so necessary and yet so difficult.[28]

The dual awareness of both distorting affective factors and constructive spiritual impulses names a challenge not only in discerning authentic spiritual experience but also in discerning the future paths of Christian churches. In a climate where religious skepticism runs high, systemic inattention to affective factors in the shaping of the putative spiritual expressions of individuals and communities threatens the very credibility of Christian faith. Whether it is the unacknowledged anger of a preacher that leaks into sermons prophesying God's coming vengeance on humanity; the unaddressed violence and confusion in the hearts of YouTube carnival barker clerics who condemn members of the LGBTQ population according to a religious justification; or the peremptory exclusionary practices from ecclesial leaders that emanate from a defensive hold on authority, when unconscious affective wounds drive religious positions and policies, not only does the body of Christ suffer, but the name of Christ takes on negative and unwarranted associations. In the leadership of churches, the capacity to discern and appropriately respond to affective distortions ensures an ecclesial integrity that prevents the growth of cynicism.

To navigate between the harm of affective unconsciousness on one side and psychological reductionism on the other, William James's pragmatic principle of spiritual experience remains useful. In his own time, James notes the prevalent ascription of psychological "diagnoses" to historical mystics, along with the charge that their experiences were "nothing but" the result of epilepsy, hysteria, melancholy, or some other neurosis. James responds that affective irregularities and struggles may be a part of the explanatory cause of extraordinary encounters with the divine, but the transcendent dimension of the experience is not thereby discredited.[29] For James, St. Teresa of Avila may indeed be suffering from a neurosis, and her experiences of God indeed related to her illness, but to hypothesize as such does not undermine the possibility that her visions and auditions reflect genuine experience of the divine. As James argues, the efficacy of an experience to bring about a change for the better in oneself and others provides the truest test of authenticity. Affective disturbances and problems can be the conduits of divine action: the charity that emerges from them (or remains absent) will tell whether this is so.[30]

James's reasoning has some merit. However, we need to modify his principle to encompass a spiritual paradigm that better acknowledges discrete mystical experiences in relation to the entire process of conversion. Accordingly, mystical experience is not the foundational "root" of other "fruits" of transformed behavior but itself a fruit of a communally mediated journey into God. When we ask about spiritual authenticity, we need not necessarily pursue particular experiences to their particular results but rather look at the holistic, relationally oriented conversion achieved. From this basis, we gain confidence in our discernment of the role played by the presence or absence of affective conversion. The failure to deal responsibly with one's shame, guilt, anger, and fear proves a problem both relationally and religiously. When we see the spoiled fruits of divisiveness in contemptuous preaching, incendiary opinion-spinning, knee-jerk legislating, and exploitative spiritual counseling, we detect the absence of affective conversion. Following a more capacious version of James's maxim, however, we need not rush to explain away emotionally complex encounters with God as "nothing but" affective pathologies.

Moral Conversion

As affective conversion pertains to Firstness through the responsibility for one's feelings and orientation to the beautiful, moral conversion pertains to Secondness through responsibility for one's actions and orientation to the good. Moral conversion hinges on a fundamental respect for the dignity and personhood of others communicated through consistent action. The morally converted person stably abides by the "golden rule," treating others as they would like to be treated. Through the habitual dedication to a good higher than personal self-interest, moral conversion leads to authentic freedom. This moral freedom is not the freedom from constraint celebrated according to the ethos of radical individualism but the freedom to embody genuine values in one's deeds.

In the American context, the appeal to moral conversion has often been subtly misdirected through tacit connection to a solipsistic, nominalistic philosophical and cultural background. Ralph Waldo Emerson promoted a vision of the freedom of the individual, whose moral strength lies in "self-reliance," as emerging precisely through the break from the constraints of institutions. William James would have heard Emerson's voice as a child: Emerson was one of the many guests of distinction who sat at the dinner table of William's father, Henry Sr., William carried forth an Emersonian aversion to the stunting effect of dependence upon social convention—in Emerson's parlance, the "hobgoblin of little minds." Their shared defiance of unthinking conformity is a stance both moral and intellectual—moral in the commitment to the good despite social norms and even laws, intellectual in the pursuit of the truth through the refusal to capitulate to popular error. The stance is also true to the reality that moral conversion frequently means gaining autonomy from the values of the dominant culture or one's social unit. Emerson's early abolitionist stance displays the historical truism, harkening back to the trial of Socrates, that moral action often requires standing against the consensus view and risking oneself in the process.

However—and here is the point on which Peirce and Royce push back against both Emerson and James—the appropriate separation from or repudiation of inauthentic expressions of community does not mean the total retreat from community as a normative power but the establishment of loyalty to a higher community. For Peirce and Royce, total self-reliance is impossible, for our own thought comes to us from the outside in, developing dialogically rather than through a Cartesian turn inward. We all belong to communities and depend upon these communities, even if these communities do not take shape according to the designs of our geographic and temporal neighbors. Peirce gives his vision something of a scientific stamp in the idea of the "community of inquiry" that pursues the truth over the long term according to empirical testing and mutual correction.[31] Royce's "Beloved Community" more strongly evokes ethical-religious dimensions developing from a Christian transtemporal imagination. These visions converge, as Royce understands that the beloved community functions as a community of interpretation, while Peirce recognizes that the community of inquiry depends finally upon the goodwill of its members and a transcendental hope to reach the truth. According to such a perspective, the morally converted may rightfully stand apart from the crowd—indeed, they usually will—but they remain firmly within communities of memory and hope in service to the good.[32]

Invariably socially mediated and socially directed, moral conversion *orients* the other forms of conversion toward genuine values.[33] Moral conversion entails the repudiation of behavior that harms one's community, the greater community of humankind, and oneself. We see this orientation toward genuine values in the stance of the minority of scientists at Los Alamos Laboratory who withdrew from the project because of the clear devastation of life that they perceived would follow upon the construction of the atomic bomb. They were largely dismissed by their peers, who tended to justify their own continued participation on the grounds of their pursuit of objective scientific truth.[34] The unpopular moral stance of the dissenting scientists demonstrates how moral conversion can guide the use of the intellect away from destructive aims and toward generative goals.

The scientists' moral dissent has only come to be validated more widely in time. In a lecture at MIT in 1947, Manhattan Project Director J. Robert Oppenheimer acknowledged the shared moral responsibility among the scientists, even being moved to speak in a religious key: "In some sort of crude sense which no vulgarity, no humor, no overstatement can quite extinguish, the physicists have known sin; and this is a knowledge which they cannot lose."[35] In the contemporary debates around artificial intelligence, we can identify a similar tension between technical development and appropriate moral restraint. Although AI leaders, developers, and government oversight bodies are not engaged in building a weapon (at least not in the literal sense), their task presents a related set of challenges: where the heady excitement of technical and scientific creative advance meets the ethical concern for human dignity and welfare, moral conversion is required to provide orientation. As the development of the atomic bomb prefigured, we live in an age in which clear moral analysis must be courageously brought to bear on issues of immense scope and interpersonal and technical complexity.

Discriminating between the Need for Moral and Affective Conversion

Whether we recognize it or not, we frequently ponder the relationship (as well as the borderline) between affective and moral conversion. Often, our own holistic conversion brings us to this general insight: what once stood as an unqualified moral judgment of a person or group becomes moderated by our growing awareness of affective factors. Our process of coming to grips with scarring interpersonal relationships helps us to understand the relative primacy of affective conversion. Many of us grew up with a childhood classmate who harmed us or targeted other kids in a way we could hardly believe. The first judgment here, especially when we are going through the rough encounters, tends to be moral: we run home to Mom and Dad decrying our peer as *mean*, *bad*, or even *evil*, and no amount of counsel or explanation from a parent could talk us out of our trenchantly held position. However, when we later meet the maligned student in a chance encounter or when we review our childhood memories with a friend, we realize that our picture was not entirely well-informed. As we belatedly digest the details of our peer's home life—tragedy, neglect, parental alcoholism, abuse, or some combination thereof—we recognize that the child grew up in a psychologically unhealthy environment that left them with emotional wounds; that the emotional problem lies beneath what we had deemed merely a singular moral defect; that our peer was nowhere near morally free enough to be labeled "evil" without hesitation.[36] Informed by such a perspective of the influence of affective factors, our hardened hostility begins to melt into a more liquid sympathy. So many of our adult empathetic epiphanies take this form: the shift of reference from moral judgment to emotional insight, or, put differently, the reading of moral conversion in the light of affective conversion.

Once again, acute insight into holistic conversion illuminates ecclesial as well as interpersonal situations. In churches as in personal relationships, greater affective awareness invariably qualifies our moral judgments and shifts our way of identifying problems. Despite the resistance of churches to painful affective self-evaluation mentioned earlier, the aforementioned "psychological revolution" has made its mark. Religious educators, guides, and confessors now routinely recognize the situations in which they should refer their charges to therapists to give them the appropriate kind of attention. In line with this shift, we can better judge the general transition from hardline, sin-centered preaching to an approach more sensitive to the role that emotional suffering plays in the spiritual life. The transition to suffering as a focal point—and the corresponding emphasis on mercy—leads to a more supple ecclesial style awake and responsive to the depths of human wounding.

In the Catholic Church, Pope Francis's call for a "field hospital" church presents an excellent example of the precedence of the affective over the moral. As Francis set out his thinking in a famous statement,

> The thing the church needs most today is the ability to heal wounds and to warm the hearts of the faithful; it needs nearness, proximity. I see the church as a field hospital after battle. It is useless to ask a seriously injured person if he has high cholesterol and about the level of his blood sugars! You have to heal his wounds. Then we can talk about everything else.[37]

Such a style not only resonates with gospel values of compassion but also appropriately accommodates the growing psychological consciousness of our era. Empirical clinical research, for instance, shows the central role trust and emotional bonding play in emotional healing; conversely, research demonstrates that fear-based rhetoric serves to reinforce the shame that obstructs lasting psychological and moral transformation. In their integration of these insights, our churches are growing in the capacity to see through all kinds of destructive behavior to their affective bases.

However, these affectively informed shifts in ecclesial consciousness have awakened a counterreaction. There are those in our churches who hold that such a shift in sensibility reflects a moral fuzziness, a lack of moral clarity, or softness in caving into cultural norms. They call for a church that ever more forcefully preaches repentance and ever more concertedly alerts people to their moral waywardness. Considering a holistic vision of conversion, it is especially difficult to accept this batch of analyses; it appears that such thinking skips a step—omits, in fact, an important realm of awareness. These judgments effectively bypass affective conversion and, on the way to a convicted moral stance, neglect the first-order issue of (ad)dressing wounds.[38] Even the typical stridency of moral appeal betrays ignorance, for we must detect in the attendant aura of indignation a species of the certitude that once made us so assured of our judgments about our destructive classmates. If the church softens and if the church opens, the imputation of a failure of moral nerve once again misses the mark, for it is not spinelessness but consciousness that identifies the emotional wound as prior to and as conditioning what was mistaken for solely a moral flaw.

Nevertheless, emotional attitudes have moral consequences that need to be faced: the proper identification of affective bases of emotional dysfunction does not dispense with the need for critical moral evaluation. As we have indicated, every psychological theory and approach contains moral presuppositions that may or may not be salutary. The negative tendency in therapy, for instance, has been to pull the individual human being out of relationship with either the potential guidance of the transcendent, the community, or both. Sociologist Philip Rieff's *The Triumph of the Therapeutic: Uses of Faith after Freud*, published in 1966, alleges that both of these tendencies have been borne out: a culture based on therapy has sprung up where a culture rooted in faith once oriented the life of the individual.[39] Absent a collective commitment to the transcendent, asserts Rieff, the culture has grown sick through a lack of direction, with the individual left preoccupied with their ultimately self-referential feelings.[40] Rieff's project is particularly polemical, and his cultural portrait is especially bleak.[41] Like Allan Bloom's 1987 *The Closing of the American Mind*, Rieff's book is the kind of vigorous agenda-setter that generates polarized camps.

We need not set ourselves up in one. Rather, we can apply his thesis heuristically as providing a necessary moral evaluation. According to our context, we must judge whether some variant of "therapeutic individualism" governs our paradigm of affective conversion, and, thus, whether our accepted models of healing license or rationalize moral self-centeredness. We may be on the far side of a revolution in psychological awareness (or perhaps still enmeshed within one), but we need not mistake psychotherapeutic models as the source of an autonomous and totalizing narrative of meaning for our time. As with nuclear weapons or artificial intelligence, moral responsibility demands that we do not allow our consciences to be dazzled into submission and instead prudently assess the consequences our ideas have on human freedom and dignity.

So, too, returning to the matter of the shift in mentality of our churches, any theological or spiritual attitude that negates the reality of sin undermines genuine human freedom and the moral responsibility that is central to Christian discipleship. Pope Francis's recommended sequence of action—"first heal the wounds, then talk about everything else"—leaves the work of moral conversion in place. His statement serves as a guideline for the proper discernment of the relationship between affective and moral conversion. The dialectic of affective and moral conversion finds here a basic shape: Although these two modes influence each other, affective conversion possesses a relative primacy in the holistic transformation of the human being. It is emotional healing that clears the way for true moral freedom. Moral conversion provides orientation to affective conversion, ensuring that the work of healing remains configured to genuine values.

Sociopolitical Conversion

As a differentiated mode of moral conversion, sociopolitical conversion *deprivatizes* the other forms of conversion through public involvement in causes of justice. Gelpi insists that no one can claim full sociopolitical conversion until they have committed themselves to participatory activism in support of the common good.[42] Sociopolitical conversion thus embodies Royce's principle of loyalty to a cause greater than one's own interests, or loyalty to loyalty. Whether through supporting workers in pursuit of a living wage, marching for civil rights, or fighting for environmental protections in warming cities, the abiding value of sociopolitical conversion is solidarity.[43] Today, as we confront the looming devastation of the environment, we are bid to imagine our solidarity as inclusive of all the living beings that suffer along with human beings. By extending ourselves in solidarity, we become capable of working toward change based on a common hope greater than ourselves, a change that would be impossible without collective effort. In so doing, we emerge from the fog of privatized living that, in the United States and throughout the world, shrouds us from the reality of our interconnectedness.

Sociopolitical Conversion and Personal Moral Conversion: A Classic Conflict

Gelpi arrived at the distinction between personal moral conversion and sociopolitical conversion in a quintessentially Peircean fashion: starting from a facet of experience that proved elusive to his understanding, he generated an abductive hypothesis, deduced the implications of the hypothesis, and then inductively validated his conclusions. His innovation began with his surprise that in his counseling work at the Jesuit School of Theology in Berkeley in the 1970s, many students were responsive to the good of individuals in their midst but, as he puts it, when faced with questions of institutional injustice, they "simply blinked."[44] Others showed just the opposite attitude. As Gelpi pondered the disconnect, he came to realize that public and private morality, conjoined though they are, represent two different realms of experience and refer to two different normative ends. Personal moral conversion hinges on responsibilities within one's circle, while sociopolitical conversion reaches outside to the public sphere. Personal moral conversion generally takes up norms of personal rights and duties, and sociopolitical conversion refers to the end of the common good. This hypothesis predicts that we should find many people showing a high degree of responsibility toward friends, family, neighbors, and colleagues (and thus converted personally) while remaining unmoved by systemic injustice and even contributing to its perpetuation (and thus unconverted sociopolitically), and vice versa. We should also expect to find misunderstandings between the two. Needless to say, Gelpi did not have to look far to verify this kind of division: the Berkeley of his time trembled all the more from the shocks and aftershocks that split the sociopolitically and privately oriented than from the activity of the San Andreas fault below.

In pointing to the conflicts and controversy that flared in Berkeley in the 1960s and thereafter, we do not mean to unduly diminish the historical complexity of the era but to give guidance to our imaginative understanding of these two modes of conversion. The sixties crystallized themes of conversion that remain significant, as we observe as well in the continued conversation around Rieff's 1966 book on the therapeutic culture. Throughout the sixties in Berkeley, students clashed with university officials and law enforcement as they protested against racial discrimination in hotel hiring practices, suppression of student political activity through bans of on-campus "tabling," and American involvement in the Vietnam War. California university president Clark Kerr and state governor Ronald Reagan deemed these students irresponsible in their defiance of university codes and their disruption of the peace of the city, heightening the conflict by calling upon the local police and the National Guard (in Reagan's case) to aggressively disperse students. The moral critics of the students reacted to their personal private excesses, especially recreational drug use and sexual promiscuity. The polarization here is instructive. By conceiving of the conflicting parties as types representing the emphasis upon one form of moral conversion while less adequately integrating the other, we can better understand the differentiation between sociopolitical and personal moral conversion.

The "longhaired revolutionaries," as the Polish poet Czeslaw Milosz dubbed them during his own stint as a visiting professor at UC Berkeley, evinced an intense sociopolitical determination as they opposed the social injustices of racial inequality, female inequality, predatory capitalism, and militarism.[45] The students' ideals included a wide scope of persons, focusing just as much on the children in Vietnam as on their parents back home in California. Their commitment to their causes through protests, marches, and sit-ins enacted their personal responsibility at risk to their own academic and physical security. At their very best, they collectively reflected the kind of empathy Simone de Beauvoir admired in French social activist and mystic Simone Weil when she said that Weil "had a heart capable of beating right across the world."[46] Yet, if the students' hearts beat with solicitude for the marginalized, they also tended to thump with rage at the perceived perpetrators of injustice. They plainly blamed not only national leadership but also their ordinary fellow citizens who enjoyed relative privilege, holding them accountable for maintaining the status quo through conformity to the structures in place and indifference to the suffering of those remote from them. For the indignant students, to fail to speak out, to adapt to the powers that be, and to carry on in pursuit of a fenced-off domestic life amounted to complicity in the machinery of racism, sexism, and war. Few preachers could match them in their zealous call for conversion.

To return to Milosz's assessment, it is fascinating to note that he judges, tongue somewhat in cheek, this protest of one America against another as taking the form of "hatred for virtue."[47] It is a kind of *private* virtue he means. Milosz identifies virtue with hard work, self-control, courage, and perseverance, along with, less favorably, unquestioning obedience and conformity to the established order. Ironically adopting the mentality of the "longhairs," he writes, "It is virtue which compels one to join the 'rat race,' to accept the given, to achieve, act, strive, to conform to the morals of one's neighbor."[48] Milosz confesses that he has more sympathy for the "virtuous," as he detects the seeds of destructiveness in the revolutionary mentality. As he writes mockingly of the longhaired philosophy, now spinning to take on the perspective of the virtuous: "To negate virtue, one must oppose industry with idleness, puritanical repression of urges with instant gratification, tomorrow with today, alcohol with marijuana, moderation in the display of emotion with shameless emotionality."[49] Here, then, is a glimpse of the equal and opposite contempt the virtuous reserve for the "longhairs," the sketch of a different kind of moral recklessness through self-indulgence.

We might sharpen the lines of Milosz's sketch to make out the moral impulses that demarcate sociopolitical and personal moral conversion. Stereotyped though these images may be, they reflect something of the underlying social reality. The animated student protester, willing to put him- or herself at risk for a higher dedication to humankind, reflects the public orientation to the common good in accordance with sociopolitical conversion. However, following Milosz's portrayal, the typical member of this group lacks private conversion, shirking the work ethic and self-discipline of the upright citizen. The virtuous display the ascetical capability of personal moral conversion, willing to dutifully deny themselves for the sake of those close to them. However, they leave much to be desired in terms of sociopolitical conversion: where their opponents are far-sighted, they are near-sighted, resisting taking a stand for structural change that impacts those beyond their immediate relationships. To lay out these two orientations side by side is not to say that reconciliation proves a simple step.[50]

The nerve struck in Milosz makes evident the deep, self-implicating emotional roots of the separation between the two sensibilities. As we see with Rieff too, in disagreements of this nature, we frequently find the commentator incapable of keeping at bay their own passionate identification. The moral battlegrounds they observe are quick to transmute as well into literal zones of violence, quick to escalate beyond the initial wishes of either party—a trajectory of which Milosz is weary in the association he makes between the "longhairs" and nineteenth-century European revolutionaries. Whether the confrontation emerges between the rising generation and the established generation, the rural and the urban, traditional and progressive social groups, or between comfortable and less settled classes, the clash of two moral-emotional sensibilities is a recurring historical reality. In these repeated conflicts across the world stage, when the kegs begin to explode, it may be a moral intuition that lights the fuse, but it is the load of affective powder that blows things into the air.[51]

Applying Depth Psychology to the Moral-Sociopolitical Conflict

Indeed, the pitched battle that often takes place across the lines of the two kinds of moral conversion touches upon an archetypal psychological tension. We witness something of the confrontation between the archetypal moral vision of the *senex* (Latin for old man) and the *puer* (youth). Senex-governed tradition, authority, and structure oppose *puer* innovation, egalitarianism, and idealism. Moral conversion, we should emphasize, depends upon the free commitment of the human being. But, speaking archetypally, the *impulses* of personal moral conversion "belong" to the disciplined *senex*, while the sociopolitical impulses belong to the *puer* of unbounded imagination. The fixed, unmitigated opposition between these archetypal stances invariably leads to the undermining of both. The starry-eyed *puer* turns violent; Robespierre begins as the emancipator and ends up as the executioner. The *senex*'s solidly crafted structures collapse, starting with the walls;

whether the threat comes from within or without, the chaos loosed proves worse than the disorder feared. As Royce pointed out of "dangerous pairs," every unmediated dyad is prone to tread a path of mutual destruction.

We can envision various reconciling thirds to overcome the opposing moral stances of the *senex* and *puer*. The Spirit's love may sweep away the mutual disdain that hangs in the air between them. The intellect may clarify the emerging moral contradictions of each and push toward deeper introspection. But just as we have identified the smoldering feelings that enflame the moral accusations, we can also suggest a source of affective mediation that has the power to cool: the development of empathy. Empathy may lead the virtuous *senex* to expand their range of responsibility, now including those they had previously feared or neglected. When personal morality does not reach beyond the perimeter of one's community, it is often because the personhood of those outside has been subtly dismissed. Through the power of empathy, the formerly demonized become humanized. By the same token, the *puer* may come to accept the selectivity of their moral attention, and, acknowledging their neglect of depth for breadth, learn to see better up close. The animating power of empathy—the extending of empathy and the deepening of empathy—becomes a source of reconciliation.

To pronounce the word *empathy* is to say something relevant, but it is also to say something intentionally vague. We cannot prescribe the mediating power that heals the rift between the *senex*, the deliberate builder and settler, and the *puer*, that angel-headed hipster for whom the *senex*'s structures appear as mere paper-mâché castles. James Hillman, in many ways William James's heir in American psychology, suggests paths of mediation, but he does not want to provide an over-specified solution either. When Hillman proposes the quelling of the *puer*'s restlessness through "the marriage between *puer* and *psyche*," he intimates one potential way forward.[52] The symbolic marriage entails the *puer*'s exploration of their reflective depths of feeling, which works to bring the *puer* down into the mess of existence and temper the tendency toward indignant absolutism. The subsequent recognition of the weight of relationships, both historical and personal, fosters a new sensitivity. Likewise, says Hillman, the *senex* overcomes their obstinacy by engaging in practices of "soul-making," through which they rediscover a denied complexity and learn to appreciate a lost musicality.[53] Thus, the *senex* begins to break up the interior hardness that manifests as closure to individuals and communities who challenge them. What Hillman reads in both cases as the development of interiority through the encounter with one's own complications, we can profitably connect with empathy. In the knowledge of one's own multiplicity and inconsistency, compassion becomes extended to others with whom one's own faults are shared. We should spotlight two crucial points in the discussion here: first, the by-now-familiar reminder of the affective factors involved in moral transformation; second, the perhaps surprising point that the solution for both "parties" is more similar than different.

Appropriately, then, Hillman sees the *senex* and *puer* as curious mirrors of one another. He names them as two split-off poles of a single united archetype.[54] No matter a person's age, to identify with one pole to the exclusion of the other not only generates conflict but also divides us against ourselves. In this view, individual and social growth depends on the integration of the other pole, on the reunion of *Senex-et-puer*, *puer-et-senex*. Their reunion constitutes a "union of sames," with the "two faces turned toward each other in dialogue."[55] In the realm of morality, this means the acceptance of moral claims outside of the preferred moral stances of *puer*-consciousness and *senex*-consciousness respectively. We should see these ideas from depth psychology as a unique validation of Gelpi's insight. Part of the integrity of Gelpi's account is his refusal to reduce morality to either the preferred moral stance of *senex*-consciousness or that of *puer*-consciousness.[56] Gelpi's distinction between personal and sociopolitical conversion illuminates two sides of a single unitive form, revealing both the necessary differentiation and underlying wholeness of the moral life.

Intellectual Conversion

Intellectual conversion pertains to the domain of the truth of beliefs, or the Peircean category of Thirdness: the intellectually converted person demonstrates a responsible approach to establishing their beliefs, including the willingness to revise their beliefs according to new evidence or frameworks. Like each form of conversion, intellectual conversion demands an openness to the limits of one's own perspective; and, like each form as well, it is only ever approached rather than entirely completed. The communal metaphysics we have outlined so far appropriately frames the process of intellectual conversion. We do not each stand independently related to the truth but rather approach reality through the communal mediation that precedes and conditions individual knowing. We overcome our own tendency to intellectual narrowness and inertia through constant openness to the dialogue through which emerges a more replete account of reality.

Peirce understands this communal turn as intimately connected to the habit (or virtue) of self-controlled inquiry, which leads to the establishment of true beliefs. In his own description of the social epistemology of a community of inquiry, Peirce uses the off-color example of a blind and deaf man who both witness a murder: "One hears a man declare he means to kill another, hears the report of the pistol, and hears the victim cry; the other sees the murder done."[57] Peirce notes that the two men experience entirely different sensations, but through discussion, they come to agree on a final shared opinion: "Their final conclusions, the thought remotest from sense, will be identical and free from the one-sidedness of their idiosyncrasies."[58] Effective inquiry depends upon our acknowledgment of our perspectival relationship to the truth: individually, we carry only a partial understanding, and even our communities look toward a fuller truth that lies ever in the future. This acknowledgment of our limitations constitutes a precondition of intellectual conversion: the recognition that we correct and widen one another in our thinking opens the way for the examination and eventual transformation of our beliefs in alignment with the truth. Peirce calls the attitude of maximal openness to transformation "contrite fallibleness," or *anti-cock-sure-ism*.[59]

For the tradition of pragmatism, recall, notions of truth emerge from actual experience and practice. In his 1877 essay, "The Fixation of Belief," Peirce draws a radical connection between our natural practices of inquiry and normative conceptions of the truth. For Peirce, attention to the path of inquiry we take in the course of life proves adequate to answer the question of how best to arrive at the truth. We only ever genuinely inquire into something, argues

Peirce, when we possess a genuine doubt. The preponderance of our beliefs are settled without provoking questions, but under certain circumstances (perhaps discovering evidence that contradicts a formerly settled belief, perhaps hearing the firm contrary opinion of a friend), the "irritation of doubt" besets us.[60] Dissatisfied by our real and living doubt, we seek to return once more to the calm state of settled belief. Given the close relationship of our beliefs to our behavior, such an unsettled state is not only uncomfortable but also inhibits our actions. Thus, we take up a given inquiry, the aim of which is the re-establishment of a firm belief, in order to regain our peace of mind and our resoluteness of action. Peirce provocatively asserts that a belief that is permanently settled in our mind is a true belief.[61]

When faced with doubt, we have several different methods to establish belief. We can will ourselves to believe despite the doubt, we can begin to investigate scrupulously, and much in between. Accordingly, the vital normative question for Peirce becomes the following: From amongst our ways of fixing belief, which method settles belief most effectively? Peirce compares four practical ways of settling belief: the method of tenacity, the method of authority, the a priori method, and the method of science. The method of tenacity is that of the ostrich who buries its head in the sand. Tenacity hangs on regardless of evidence or contrary opinion. Interestingly, for Peirce it is the "social impulse" that renders this method unstable—the influence of the different opinion of others that troubles the confidence of even the most unstinting adherent.[62] The second method, authority, is the regulation of opinion by political or religious power, enforced through punishment and intimidation.[63] The community now sets the belief rather than the individual, which more successfully secures the belief. However, the insight that different times and different places have held different beliefs—which begins with a few individuals and invariably spreads—eventually leads to broader doubts. The third method, the a priori method, seeks to settle belief outside of mere extrinsic designation, basing belief instead on what is "agreeable to reason."[64] The a priori method is the typical method of philosophers, sincere inquirers who are open to conversation and seek explanations in accordance with natural causes. Descartes's *Discourse on Method* epitomizes this approach. Even for philosophers, "agreeable to reason" ultimately means agreeable to *my* reason: it is not experience but inclination that finally sets belief. This dependence on taste means that what seems self-evident today often falls out of fashion in time; a priori beliefs are also susceptible to erosion.

The final method capable of addressing our doubts is the method of science. This method is compatible with Peirce's definition of realism, which you will recall from the previous chapter: the method of science presumes as its "fundamental hypothesis" that there are real entities, and inquiry remains independent of what you, or I, or any other person take the reality to be.[65] Peirce argues that the *method itself*, not only the beliefs set by it, cannot be genuinely doubted, for the course of investigation does not lead to the doubt that there are real entities, nor do people naturally hold such doubts. The success of the scientific method in settling opinion over the long haul also supports it over and above the other three.[66] The test of the method is its application, rather than, with each of the prior three, an immediate appeal to one's feelings and purposes. The method of science is the method eminently responsive to experience—the choice, as Peirce writes, for the one who wishes their "opinions to coincide with the facts."[67] Peirce does not assert his threefold method of inference in this article, but as he develops his thought, such a method proceeds according to the inferential logic of abduction, deduction, and induction. The consistent application of Peirce's method of science constitutes something of the supreme norm of intellectual conversion, offering an experience-based means of establishing belief maximally flexible to the reception of new evidence and evidentiary frameworks.[68]

At the close of "The Fixation of Belief," Peirce hints that, though the method of science may be vindicated by its efficacy, moral and esthetic considerations also guide the method's practice. In this way, he also intimates the relationship between the normative sciences, namely, how sound logic is configured to ethics and esthetics. The choice of one's method of inquiry stands for Peirce as a "ruling decision" of one's life, asking something of the whole person. He first points out that a moral attitude regulates inquiry: "Above all, let it be considered that what is more wholesome than any particular belief is *integrity* of belief, and that to avoid looking into the support of any belief from the fear that it may turn out rotten is quite as *immoral* as it is disadvantageous."[69] But even more fundamental for Peirce is an appeal to an esthetic end, to an end that the soul finds beautiful and worthy of devotion. Not only integrity (the fruit of moral conversion) but also ardor (the fruit of affective conversion) guides the quest for the truth: "The genius of a man's logical method should be *loved and reverenced* as his bride, whom he has chosen from all the world."[70] Once again, the grounding sequence of the normative sciences proves a guide to the interrelation of the modes of conversion.[71]

Animated by affective conversion and oriented by moral conversion, intellectual conversion in turn orders the other realms of experience through clarity and accuracy of thought. The intellectually converted better distinguishes between genuine concerns of justice and apparent claims, thus ensuring the coherence of sociopolitical action; more aptly clarifies personal duties and responsibilities, thus contributing to sound personal moral conversion; recognizes the connections between emotions and behavior in the realm of affective conversion; and identifies whether religious commitments are governed by adequate frames of reference.[72] Thus, intellectual conversion prevents the political malady of authoritarianism, the moral ill of hypocrisy, the affective sickness of emotional self-deceit, and the religious cramp of fundamentalism. Although mental pliability and openness to experience sound attractive, intellectual conversion remains a difficult virtue, requiring, as Peirce suggests, as much intestinal fortitude and heart as head. Three methods of fixing belief provide their own seductive comforts: tenacity, the comfort of the eternal same of one's present perspective; authority, the warmth of the like-minded herd; and the a priori method, the agreeability of sentiment. The fourth option, the method of science, by contrast, is the ascetical route, rewarding in line with its rigors.

PART II: CHRISTIAN CONVERSION

Christian Conversion

Natural conversion leads to the threshold of the divine, preparing the heart to receive God: the affectively healthy person perceives the beauty of the universe that hints at something more; the morally converted turns toward a deeper source of love undergirding their personally responsible action; the sociopolitically converted glimpses the universal community upheld beyond the plane of merely human inspiration; and the intellectually converted recognizes the uncanny and awe-inspiring harmony between the human mind and the structures and processes of reality. But this is not to say that one simply moves seamlessly from strength to strength in the spiritual life, for the hunger for God is not so much the hunger for the final course of a satisfying meal as the hunger of one starving. In the words of the Song of Songs, the human desire for God can best be likened to the "wound of love" that drives one to seek God with a lover's passion. To propose, then, a too-clean hypothetical: to be fully converted *solely according to the natural modes of experience* remains a condition of dissatisfaction and ultimate unfulfillment, seeing as the restless longing for the transcendent in the heart of the human being remains unquenched.

On this point, we return to Royce's portrayal of the spiritual journey in *Sources of Religious Insight*. The catalyst for the unfolding of religious insight is the experience of the need to be saved. Human beings cannot give themselves ultimate meaning, and communities—although they support the human being in the search for meaning—are also persons in need of salvation. In meeting the experience of betrayal beyond human powers of repair, and in the evils of suffering that no human intermediary can soothe, our limitations become even more evident. As Royce posits, only a Being who transcends the natural world has the power to impart meaning and to provide salvation from the human predicament. This salvation becomes open to all through the bridging, reconciling Spirit that grants experiential access to the divine.

The picture of religious experience that Royce deliberately leaves open-ended in *Sources* finds a form of realization in the Christian understanding of God's saving action, namely, through the incarnation and passion of Jesus Christ.[73] The atoning love of the betrayed Jesus imparts meaning to human suffering and extends forgiveness to human sinfulness. The Spirit that Jesus and the Father send forth gives each human being the means of access to God's saving power and establishes the community responsive to this offer of salvation. We can say, and indeed must, that the natural forms of conversion predispose the human being to be responsive to God's saving gift, but to grasp the gift's accomplishment, we enter a discourse about the mysteries of the Christian faith. In Christian conversion, one encounters this saving reality, reorienting one's life toward the presence of the triune God and the community that mediates God's presence.[74]

Christian Conversion in Relation to Natural Conversion

The breakthrough out of what Royce describes as the human being's paradoxical situation (desiring for oneself that which one cannot give oneself) and into faith in the saving God establishes a relationship between affective and moral conversion. In initial Christian conversion, the "love of God poured out into the heart through the Holy Spirit" (Rom 5:5) instills the attitude of repentance. Through the awareness and renunciation of emotional barriers to faith, repentance includes an affective dimension; in the commitment henceforth to live in the pattern of Jesus's life, repentance also includes a moral dimension. To put the matter differently: the healing of the heart that comes from deep experience of God not only enables the move beyond the repressed feelings of shame, guilt, anger, and fear that once held one back but also awakens the positive desire to transform one's personal moral conduct. For initial converts, this double movement instigates a kind of elation and a sense of fresh possibility. One feels oneself to be forgiven, or loved without condition, and, accordingly, even the recognition of the need for serious moral change becomes suffused with tenderness and appreciation. To hold one's spouse, children, or parents in the light cast by the experience of God's acceptance indeed stirs up regret at past deficits of love, but the interior healing simultaneously provides confidence and hope in the new departure point now available. In healing the heart's wounds, the experience of God removes obstacles to moral change. This dynamic of transformation describes, in short, how Christian conversion *mediates between* affective and moral conversion, drawing them into a new relationship.[75]

We might call the mediation between affective and moral conversion *the fruit of Christian awakening*: this mediation describes the kind of dramatic renewal attendant to the conversion experiences William James highlights. But as we have seen through James's analysis of conversion, Christian conversion has a total effect on human consciousness, leading to a new center of focus that pervades the personality. Change tends not to happen all at once but takes place both through the gradual assimilation of new perspectives and the signal moments that instigate new ways of thinking, feeling, and acting. Gelpi offers a technical way of speaking about this ongoing normative transformation in reference to multimodal conversion: the transvaluation of natural conversion. As Christian conversion solidifies, it *transvalues* the other modes of conversion, shifting the fundamental frames of reference of affectivity, morality, and intellect in light of Christian experience.[76]

Christian conversion transvalues affective balance and optimism by way of a transcendent hope that deepens resilience and joyfulness. It transvalues moral conversion through receptivity to the new moral outlook occasioned by God's love. With respect to personal moral conversion, Christian conversion elevates responsibility and care through fidelity to Christ's model and teachings. Sociopolitically, Christian conversion shapes commitments of justice and extends the scope of compassion into alignment with the norms of the Reign of God—in particular, alignment with God's concern for the poor and marginalized.[77] Christian conversion transvalues intellectual conversion by coordination of the fixation of belief with the truths of Christian faith. The transvaluation at play in intellectual conversion does not merely refer to belief in abstract doctrines, but just as much to the logical outworking of the practical consequences of faith. Rather than being conceived linearly, the new perspective that emerges from Christian conversion should be imagined as an organic model of reciprocity and multivalent change. On the communal plane, intentions and activities shift over time, growing through the interaction of various charismatic manifestations to create a new communal *gestalt*. When we notice local faith communities that change character over time—growing to become multidimensional hubs of activity—we observe the effects of sustained integral Christian conversion.

The transvaluation of affective conversion gives evidence of the organic character of change that emerges from Christian conversion. In the face of harsh circumstances, when emotional burdens increase to a breaking point and previous goals seem unrealizable, even the most resolute souls struggle with the erosion of natural optimism and the threat of emotional despair. In these circumstances, Christian faith provides inspiration that emanates from a different basis and shows forth a different horizon. Such was the experience of Martin Luther King Jr. at a low point in his own social activism. King received a midnight phone call on January 27, 1956: the voice on the other side threatened to blow up his home in Montgomery, Alabama, if he did not leave town within three days. Overwhelmed with fear for himself, his wife, and his young daughter, he said that the call set off in him a sense of "spiritual midnight."[78] After lying in bed in trepidation for hours, King got up and walked to the kitchen, where he prayed. He later told his Montgomery congregation what took place:

> Early on a sleepless morning, in January 1956, rationality left me....Almost out of nowhere I heard a voice that morning saying to me, "Preach the gospel, stand up for truth, stand up for righteousness." Since that morning, I can stand up without fear....If I had to die tomorrow morning I will die happy because I've been to the mountain top and I've seen the promised land and it's going to be here in Montgomery.[79]

The visitation did not allay King's immediate fears *at the level of his fears*. He was promised neither his own safety, nor the safety of his family, nor the concrete success of his work. Rather, he was gifted with a source of transcendent strength, guided to the sight of a horizon of hope that set his fears in a new perspective. We best understand the "promised land" to come in Montgomery as a foreshadowed eschatological reality—the ultimate transfiguration of the city in God's love—rather than as a prediction of the imminent end of racial conflict. Likewise, the affective fruit of Christian conversion is not the transformation of pessimism into its dialectical opposite, optimism, but the elevation into a greater field of hope in the Reign of God.[80]

We can see how this pivotal moment of King's ongoing conversion led past affective reanimation to transformation on multiple levels. King's experience of a divine message challenged him to the transvaluation of intellectual conversion through the deeper penetration of the promise of salvation into his beliefs about human destiny. The challenge on the personal moral level is perhaps easier to overlook. The midnight call, we can presume, came from within King's own Montgomery community, and reflects the mind of the enemies in his midst—the deep and dangerous hatred directed toward him. To resist giving back hatred in turn demands more than natural moral conversion. As Donald Gelpi insisted, the truest test of authentic Christian conversion is the ability to follow Jesus's command to love one's enemies. Jesus says in the Gospel of Matthew that loving those who love you or doing good to those who do good to you is not exceptional (Matt 5:46–47). To be like God, whole like the Father whose sun shines on the just and the unjust, you must love your enemies and be good to those who persecute you (Matt 5:48, 44). The imitation of Jesus's attitude of forgiving love, which King demonstrates in his abiding stance of nonviolence as he is threatened with violence, depends on a power greater than human strength alone, the very power that brought King from his spiritual midnight back into the daylight. In refusing to mirror the hatred that closed in around him, he becomes conformed to Jesus's most demanding ethical teachings and, most movingly, the self-donating pattern of Jesus's life.

Most saliently, the re-entrenchment that followed from King's kitchen prayer elevates his sociopolitical conversion, already shaped by the reign of God, to a new level of dedication. Through his willingness to die for the cause of justice rather than withdraw, King mirrors Jesus's fulfillment of his own mission on behalf of the reign of God. This turning point for King represents a leap, one of many he took, away from security and toward his eventual death. The word God gives him is a word of validation as it is a word of encouragement; a word that communicates that the institutions and practices King challenges indeed run counter to the purposes of God; a word that confirms that his higher cause indeed reflects God's cause. In King's graced hopes, biblical place and American place, biblical people and American people intermingle—as he conjoins Montgomery and Mount Zion, his fellow African Americans and the sojourning Israelites, the American nation and the pilgrim people of God. As his sociopolitical imaginary ever more sharply takes on the contours of God's promised restoration, his vision moves fluidly between and draws together the divine eschatological promise and the gritty temporal realities of injustice. Not only in the kitchen episode but throughout his life, King's ongoing Christian conversion grounds his call for public transformation. Only through this lens can we understand his rousing conviction and spine-chilling rhetorical power as he lifts up America's situation in the light of the narrative of God's salvation.

CONCLUSION: CONVERSION AND THE HOPE OF THE BELOVED COMMUNITY

King's life highlights the nexus point of sociopolitical and Christian conversion, the defining ground of spirituality in America. As King epitomizes, this intersection is both a national blind spot and, not incidentally, a site of outstanding prophetic inspiration. As much as American prophetic figures have faced patent hostility, they have challenged the willful ignorance of those who wish to remain unaware of their responsibility for collective suffering.

In this prophetic task, Trappist monk Thomas Merton is to be counted alongside King.[81] Merton not only exposes injustices but digs for their roots in the American psyche. As he points out in *Conjectures of a Guilty Bystander*, the American land has been driven from the time of discovery until the contemporary era by the myth of the "earthly paradise."[82] This melding of themes of religious longing and social progress has consolidated a certain durable American self-image. America, Merton asserts, was painted brightly as the land where the West could get off to "an entirely new start."[83] It was to be the exceptional land where one could escape from history and history's blight, effectively floating free from the gravitational field of original sin. Merton names the organizing symbol of the American mythos, appearing as a dominant motif in American literature and movies, as the symbol of "the frontier." As Merton puts it, "The frontier is not only the symbol of adventure but of clear-eyed innocence."[84] If we roam to the edge of one frontier, no matter the troubles encountered or caused there, the next frontier awaits. We start over each time innocent once again. Although Merton does not reference J. D. Salinger's famous novel, he depicts America as a kind of "catcher in the rye" society, ready to be caught at every stage and kept from a painful fall. Yet, as Merton announces, the sustaining national deceit, the children's tale of paradise preserved, must be parted with: "We have fallen into history like everyone else.…We are in the same mess as all the rest of them."[85]

Merton published these thoughts in 1965, the same year King led the Selma-to-Montgomery march—a breakthrough year in which the country's legacy of violence and subjugation, waged against those who were not considered neighbors but rather expendable others, was brought forcefully and painfully out into the open. Although the charge may be familiar today, the currents of resistance to honest self-appraisal remain. To acknowledge our guilt is to begin to be able to acknowledge our responsibility, and so to begin to be converted. Such a message represents the turning of the American mythos of innocence on its head, the deliberate dragging of the American shadow into the light. The shadow exposed includes the shadow of the prototypical figure that Czeslaw Milosz associated with "virtue": the hard-working, self-controlled, privately oriented citizen. With the application of a wider moral lens, the self-identified, socially reinforced "innocent one" is bracingly disclosed as guilty, for the closed circle of their interests has kept others suffering outside the gates.

The sharp declaration of guilt, however, represents the first wrenching step of the prophetic initiative, not the whole content of the message. For Merton—and no less for King—the foundational criticism remains connected with a spirit of idealism and genuine belief in the possibility of change that represents the best of the American spirit of optimism and solidarity. This very spirit is elevated in relation to absolute commitments of faith. Merton and King's purposes do not stop at castigating those deemed unjust. They are not about replacing the virtuous with the vindictive proponents of a new order—a wish Milosz perhaps rightly detected as tainting the actions of many of the zealous "longhairs." The purpose is not simply to dethrone the *senex* and crown the *puer* in his place. Rather, as with the biblical prophets, the repentance sought aims for the positive ideal of genuine unity and sincere reconciliation. Take the prophetic call given to Jeremiah, wherein God commands him to "root out and to tear down, to destroy and to overthrow," but finally, "*to build and to plant*" (Jer 1:10). Commitment to the reign of God takes in the whole of the verse. The prophetic initiative moves from the call to repentance to the hope (and the work) of transformation.

On the other end of the sharp pole of prophetic criticism, the end, that is, held close to the heart, an emblem of inspiration is stamped: the image of a community of charity that transcends divisions and hatred. Without collapsing into religious nationalism, the grand sociopolitical vision combines the dreams of the American *polis* and the hopes of the pilgrim people of faith. Merton's social criticism invoked American emancipatory ideals while being rooted in a Christian imagination sensitive to God's special love for the dispossessed, much in the way of King. Dorothy Day and Peter Maurin proclaimed the Catholic Worker as a project dedicated "to creating a society where it is easier to be good" while also stressing the underlying mission of sharing the poverty of the crucified Christ with the poor. Howard Thurman established the Church for the Fellowship of All Peoples in 1944 in San Francisco, bridging social solidarity and the Christian dedication to the reign of God. King's "I Have a Dream" speech in Washington, DC, appealed to national values of freedom and democratic participation while simultaneously evoking the biblical Exodus narrative.[86] This God-inspired vision for America's sociopolitical conversion pushes beyond the country's internal strife to embrace global responsibility. (Remember that each of these figures—aside from Maurin, who died in 1949—held the country responsible as an international aggressor in the Vietnam War.) Each prophet reveals the manifest distortion of "manifest destiny," through word or deed questioning the religiously rationalized selfishness that pulls God's cause down to the level of national fantasies. Their critique extends from responsibility for one's own to responsibility toward all—and their hope from internal to global reconciliation.

Each of these American prophets incarnates Royce's idea of an unbounded community of charity. Whether in the communities of service of Day and Maurin, the inspired rhetoric and ministry of King and Thurman, or the blistering critiques of Merton, the beloved community appears at the juncture of eschatological hope and social transformation. The summons to a faith-infused sociopolitical conversion represents an encounter with the American shadow as it draws on the brightest lights of its historical development. Just as the summons impels toward concrete commitments at home, it invariably draws the American imagination beyond America, to the sacred community without border. The commitment to a community of love demands the full fruits of integral conversion—including emotional honesty, moral probity, and clarity of thought. If, as we have discussed, religious experience is to be conceived as the form of insight that guides on to deepening conversion, then our insight points in a clear direction. In the prophetic call to authentic conversion, we discover the communal telos of religious experience, culminating in dedication to the arrival of the beloved community.

Chapter Six

THOMAS MERTON AND THE QUEST FOR THE BELOVED COMMUNITY

INTRODUCTION

WE STARTED THIS BOOK with the notion of the birth of the discipline of spirituality as a sign worth unfolding. The birth of Thomas Merton is also a sign of illuminating power. Thomas Merton opens *The Seven Storey Mountain* in an ostensibly conventional literary fashion, beginning with the day, context, and place of his birth: "On the last day of January 1915, under the sign of the Water Bearer, in a year of a great war, and down in the shadow of some French mountains on the borders of Spain, I came into the world."[1] Deeper knowledge of Merton makes apparent how much meaning is compressed into the traditional form of this opening sentence.

First, speaking of signs, the sign of the Water Bearer: Aquarius, the eleventh sign of the zodiac, is imaged by a man pouring out a jug of water, symbolizing the pure waters of higher wisdom flowing forth for the enrichment of humankind. Archetypally, Aquarius is the broadly oriented sign of forward-thinking humanitarianism, the sign of the underlying unity that breaks through the boundaries of the tenth highly structured sign of Capricorn. If the prototypical "Aquarian" is seen as the energetic visionary idealist, the Aquarian is likewise recognized as the frequently touchy, frustrated reformer, who laments that widespread prejudice and selfishness slow down the realization of their cherished dreams of universal solidarity. Merton fits the description: his stirring testimonies to humanity's irrevocable spiritual communion splintered the walls of supposed separateness, just as his stinging diatribes aimed at the recalcitrant spirit that sought to keep the walls in place.

Second, the coinciding of Merton's birth with World War I: like many of his generation, Merton's greatest sorrows were occasioned by the long shadows of the twentieth century's wars. Note that Merton writes that he was born in the year of "*a* great war." We may be justified in reading into the indefinite article a note of sadness, even of ironic pathos, for World War I was supposed to be *the* definitive war—named "The Great War" up until the dawning consciousness of the magnitude of World War II. He was impacted by this latter war not only as a searching thinker who decried the unconsciousness and brutality of the era's stunning violence but also as a man who lost a family member: Merton's brother's fighter plane crashed into the North Sea in April of 1943, and he did not survive. When Merton probed for the causes of war in the unacknowledged fear residing in the human heart, and when he railed against the senselessness of the political justification of nuclear armament as a "defensive strategy," he spoke bearing the wound opened by his brother's premature death. In his later phase, Merton's writings on peace and nonviolence targeted not so much the visible ravages of war as the psychospiritual ground of war's emergence, as he sought to expose the greed and self-deceit (in the United States as much as anywhere) that propelled the world to the edge of nuclear disaster.

Third, his description of his birthplace: he does not give a precise location, refraining from explicitly naming a town or even a region. Rather, he provides only vague descriptors: "*some* French mountains *on the borders* of Spain."[2] This choice is in keeping with Merton's self-understanding, especially at the time of the writing of *The Seven Storey Mountain*, published in 1948. Born in France to a father from New Zealand and an American mother, both artists,

Merton lived in New York City for much of his early boyhood. Both parents had passed away by the time he was sixteen, his mother of stomach cancer and his father of a brain tumor. When he made it to Columbia University in 1935, he had already lived in Queens and Long Island in the United States; Prades and Montauban in France; and Oakham, Surrey, and Cambridge in England. Once he arrived at Columbia, he resided in the United States thereafter, but he only became an American citizen in 1951 at thirty-six years old.

After he became a citizen, he acknowledged that growing to accept himself as an American stabilized his sense of self and purpose.[3] As contact with Merton's writings reveals, this evolution is not merely privately significant. At his best, Merton speaks from within the realm of influence of a spiritual vision appealing to the highest American ideals of spiritual freedom and openness, and, by the same token, his voice resonates most sharply when he addresses American hypocrisy, as if cauterizing the ailing American soul.[4] Nevertheless, it is no wonder that he intimates a vague sense of home. This too squares with Merton's eventual full belonging to the land that is forever setting out on an adventure and always struggling with the corresponding shadow of uprootedness. Ultimately, the borders are what fired Merton's imagination—in terms of his extended geographic wanderings, as well as his spiritual and literary vocation poised between the Gethsemani monastery that housed him and the turbid world outside that often occupied his attention.

Truly, in his youthful description of his birth, Thomas Merton's character shines through with special density—both who he was as a young man and who he came to be in maturity. His identification with the sign of the Water Bearer, his war-time entry into the world near the beginning of the century of horror, and his vaguely specified borderland birth each contribute in their own way to what Merton represents for so many today: the quest for a deep, universal ground of spiritual oneness beyond the reach of disintegrative discord, and the hope for an abiding community of love amidst a world embroiled in conflict.

In Josiah Royce, we find something of a spiritual ancestor of Merton. Royce anticipates Merton in the articulation of a spiritual vision of global unity emerging from a uniquely American context, especially in his 1913 *The Problem of Christianity*. Royce was himself a prototypical "American son." He was the child of an unsuccessful California gold prospector, and his philosophical talent and drive led him from Berkeley to Harvard. His journey reflects the expansiveness and sense of possibility characteristic of the American sensibility, while his thought simultaneously challenges the nation's tendencies to greed, self-absorption, and denial of collective moral responsibility. And, as we have discussed, his vision of the "Beloved Community" points promisingly to a way beyond the unrestrained individualism and fearful parochialism that stand in the way of authentic human solidarity.

The phrase "Beloved Community" became especially prominent through Martin Luther King Jr.'s adoption of it in the 1960s, but equally, it describes the horizon of Merton's life and work. M. Shawn Copeland associates King and Merton together with precisely this vision. She writes, "Each man so attuned himself to the Word of God as to recover and to exercise the biblical vocation of prophecy—to serve as a 'watchman,' to scrutinize the 'signs of the times,' to witness to God's care for the anguish of the world, to contribute to healing 'our body of broken bones' in light of a vision of 'beloved community.'"[5] As "watchmen," both King and Merton detected early the looming danger in the United States, grasping and forcefully naming the severity of the nation's social predicament. Beside this reality, both held up God's desire for the transformation of society according to divine designs of communion.[6]

Notably, Royce understood his own work as a kind of watchman's labor. In late December 1915, the year of Merton's birth and months before Royce's passing in September 1916, the American Philosophical Association honored Royce by dedicating the bulk of its fifteenth annual meeting to his lifetime philosophical contribution. At the end of the meeting, Royce thanked the participants and made a speech reviewing his career, stressing his most fundamental insight, "that we are saved by community."[7] He finished by reading the poem, "A Watch in the Night," by Algernon Charles Swinburne. The poem begins, "Watchman, what of the night?" as the speaker names the storms, the fears, and the haunted ruminations that bring terror in the nighttime, before closing: "Night, with the woes that it wore, / Night is over and done."[8] After reading Swinburne's poem, Royce said that it expressed "the spirit" for which he had been long working, and concluded, "May the light soon dawn. May the word of the poet and prophet soon come true. This is my closing greeting to you."[9]

Despite his stated hopes, all indications are that Royce was not confident of the imminent dawning of the light but rather dreading the prospect of a long darkness. By the time he addressed the APA, he had grimly faced the onset of World War I, the cresting of the first major wave of the rolling crises that came to dominate the twentieth century. When the war sparked, Royce at first struggled to clarify his sympathies, but following the sinking of the *Lusitania* in May of 1915, he spoke publicly and passionately against Germany's actions.[10] As Royce saw it, the nation's brazen attack on the civilian ocean liner struck out against the most fundamental conditions for human well-being, evincing "utter ignorance of human nature…utter contempt of everything which makes the common life of humanity tolerable or possible."[11] Doubtless, behind his anger lay the perception of the offense against the vision of an invisible community of loyalty that inspired his life's work. Inasmuch as Royce lived out the vocation of a watchman, he departed in anxiety over this storm of gathering strength.

In this chapter, we explore how Thomas Merton picked up Josiah Royce's watch, that is, how Merton grappled with and in many ways embodied the spiritual quest for the realization of the Beloved Community. Born a year before Royce's passing, Merton became as familiar with the challenges posed to this spiritual vision of human unity as Royce was at the end of his life. For both men, the quest travels through regions of human darkness and uncertainty—and even to the edge of personal despair. From start to finish, Merton's spiritual journey provides a compelling expression of the Beloved Community. We attend in what follows to but three slices of this spiritual journey: his service at the Friendship House in the summer of 1941, the early stages of his monastic vocation up until his ordination in 1948, and his later global, interreligious engagement epitomized by his open letter to Thich Nhat Hanh in 1966. In his time at the Friendship House, he not only internalized an attitude of concrete service in sight of an ideal, but he also grew in compassion toward the greater human family. As he became a monk, while still grappling with an attraction to a sectarian outlook, he cultivated an imagination receptive to the love that comes from above. And in his later years, as manifest in his plea for the support of Thich Nhat Hanh, he demonstrates a relentlessly committed spirit of universal solidarity.

We feature Merton's experiences—and thus meet the communal plane of reality through the individual—but one could just as well begin from an understanding of the respective communities Merton engages and work in reverse. Nevertheless, for Royce's philosophy, which holds that ideas are understood by their practical effects, Merton effectively explains the idea of the Beloved Community through his life. Even more, Merton acts as an interpreter of the Beloved Community, extending the understanding of Royce's formulation. The picture of continuity and development that emerges not only offers a rewarding prism through which to see Merton's life but also points toward the horizon of hope indicated by these two most prescient and inspired American spiritual figures.

REVIEWING THE BELOVED COMMUNITY IN THE THOUGHT OF JOSIAH ROYCE

It is appropriate that Royce originated the term *Beloved Community* in his final major work, for the idea represents the convergence of the principal strands of his thought. Just as we can unpack Merton's birth description according to three motifs, we might best grasp Royce's synoptic vision of the Beloved Community through the development and the coalescence of three pathways of Royce's thought: namely, his notion of loyalty, his account of religious experience, and his insight into the process of communal interpretation. In reviewing in conjunction these pathways that we have primarily elaborated separately, we can better see how Royce's notion of the Beloved Community caps his philosophical labor.

First, loyalty: Royce explored his recurring ethical keynote of loyalty in special depth in his 1908 *The Philosophy of Loyalty*. For Royce, loyalty most essentially entails the commitment to a cause greater than oneself, and thus the integration of an otherwise self-centered and splintered personality. *Loyalty* is a frequently misunderstood term in Royce's lexicon, especially given the deviations of loyalty that wreaked havoc in the twentieth century. In the Second World War in particular, the "blind loyalty" of members of the Nazi party in carrying out programmatic ethnic extermination is often held up as an example of the limits of such a virtue. Merton, for instance, looked upon Adolf Eichmann as a kind of monster of the age, one who sits uncomfortably close to many modern people in his bloodless bureaucratic spirit of cool and unquestioning execution of the tasks given to him.[12] One could suggest that Merton critiques Eichmann's loyalty. However, this is not the form of loyalty Royce has in mind. For Royce, loyalty runs much deeper than consistent obedience to human authorities.[13] Royce defines loyalty as "the will to manifest, so far as is possible, the Eternal, that is, the conscious and superhuman unity of life, in the form of the acts of an individual self."[14] Royce speaks here of a kind of loyalty beyond manipulation and thus not to be confused for its ersatz or distorted forms; Eichmann's loyalty is to Roycean loyalty what Augustinian *amor sui* (self-love) is to *amor Dei* (love of God). Loyalty, then, although it is attained through lived fidelity to a concrete cause, and thus grounded in particular human communities, reaches beyond ideology to embrace a higher aim.

Second, as we discussed in chapter 1, Royce investigated religious experience for decades, culminating in his 1912 *Sources of Religious Insight*.[15] Royce understands religious experience as beginning from the need of a human being who cannot live up to the ideal good that they recognize without the assistance of a power beyond their own capacities. The interaction of this experiential Need, the Ideal of absolute value that cannot finally be eschewed, and the action of the divine Deliverer together lead the person into increasing depths of religious experience.[16] Contrary to James, Royce understands religious experience according to seven different mutually implicating modalities, beginning with James's category of individual experience, which yields social experience, followed by the exercise of reason, leading through other intermediate stages, up until the culminating insight of the "unity of the spirit." For Royce, the Spirit guides the course, pulling the individual along to deeper communion and religious knowledge. The unity of spirit at the end of this human journey is what Royce calls "the spirit of the invisible church."[17] Not only does this picture provide intimations of his idea of the invisible communion of the Beloved Community to follow in *The Problem of Christianity*, but it remains consistent with his synthesis of concrete commitment and transcendent telos in *The Philosophy of Loyalty*. For Royce, religious experience may indeed come through exalted states of mystical consciousness, but just as well through the experience of love between human beings or through ordinary acts of service. The unifying action of the Spirit, the pull from above that leads ahead, gives even the most quotidian experiences their religious dimension and goal.

Royce's third major strand of thought—communal interpretation—emerges through the study of logic urged upon him by Charles Sanders Peirce. In Peirce's view, all human understanding arises through the process of the interpretation of signs. Through Peirce, Royce came to appreciate the role of interpretation in the growth of knowledge and the formation of human communities. As Royce develops Peirce's "triadic logic," every act of interpretation necessarily involves three parties: an interpreter, one whose actions are interpreted, and the one *to whom* the second's actions are interpreted. Any three parties of this nature constitute the most basic form of community, that is, a unit engaged in the active interpretation of reality.[18] A genuine community is grounded upon shared memories that mark its distinctive character and shared hopes that direct its processes of interpretation to a sought-after future. In engaging in the life of a community, a person participates in the memories that reach outside of their immediate experience and comes to make the hopes of the community their own. Through these acts of assimilation, the individual unites with the community, gaining the capability to participate in the community's ongoing processes of interpretation.[19]

From these three root concepts—loyalty, religious experience, and communal interpretation—Royce's synthesized philosophy offers an account of the human journey from alienation to communion. We can imagine the individual as standing in three potential existential positions with respect to human society (sometimes flitting among them): he or she can be consciously withdrawn and suffer from a sense of alienation; he or she can engage the social world for the purposes of personal gain; or the person can meet the world in a spirit of participatory service.[20] In either of the first two options, the individual remains a "detached individual."[21] The third way—the way of loyalty—is for Royce the only legitimate option for human growth. It is the path of integrity for each human being, as well as the basis for the attitude of collaboration and striving for the common good at the heart of the notion of genuine community. However, human experience teaches that the path of loyalty cannot be tread solely on the individual's own strength; only support from beyond one's powers guides the individual into the experienced reality of communion.

Royce's phenomenological inductive investigations thus lead him to the metaphysical suggestion of the Beloved Community. In getting beyond James's unduly individualistic account of religious experience, Royce's way of understanding the union between the human being and the divine also includes the union between the individual and the community. For Royce, every adequate explanation of human experience must appeal to this "sacred pair" of the individual and community. The Beloved Community emerges through the individual's coordination with the invisible community of love. Royce holds that both the individual and the community are metaphysically real: in its integrity of ideas, the community is itself a kind of person. The individual becomes oneself through entering the dialogue of community, contributing to the interpretation of reality, and living in fidelity to a communal cause.[22] Following Peirce, Royce understands the social world as made up of the vast interconnection of minds by way of a greater "community of interpretation" that has roots in divine reality. Through participation within immediate communities, one comes to contribute to the larger community of interpretation. The deepening configuration of the person with the life of the greater community, achieved through deeds of concrete loyalty and ongoing interpretation, is another way of naming the person's journey of spiritual transformation, a journey into alignment with the Beloved Community.

This journey of transformation, or conversion, depends upon divine love. For Royce, "love, when it comes, comes as from above."[23] As he writes, "I can be genuinely in love with the community [of all humankind] only in case *I have somehow fallen in love with the universe*. The problem of love is human. The solution of the problem, if it comes at all, will be, in its meaning, superhuman, and divine, if there be anything divine."[24] Thus, in *The Problem of Christianity*

Royce embraces a vision of the graced, Spirit-led emergence of the Beloved Community. The early Pauline churches, drawn together into a unity by the spirit of Christ, constitute the primordial expression of this reality. The Spirit works in each heart for the purpose of the body's greater unity, operating on both levels of the sacred pair. On the individual level, the Spirit overcomes isolation through guidance to the "transfiguring experience" of participation within the whole; on the social plane, the Spirit actively stitches together the Beloved Community.[25]

For Royce, the invisible Beloved Community is not defined by allegiance to a particular dogma or creed but rather formed decisively by the participation of people who express loyalty to the cause of love. Knowing well the historical divisions caused by sectarian strife, Royce emphasizes an essential axiom for participation within the Beloved Community: "Look forward to the human and visible triumph of no form of the Christian Church."[26] The Beloved Community can only ever be pluralistically and imperfectly instantiated. It remains a work to be accomplished in all times and places.[27] As Royce exhorts, "Since you cannot find the universal and beloved community, create it." "Act," he says, "so as to hasten its coming."[28]

MERTON AS MODEL OF THE QUEST FOR THE BELOVED COMMUNITY

Was Thomas Merton a Late "Convert" to the Beloved Community?

Told a certain way, the story of Thomas Merton's life from his ordination onward appears like the story of the triumph of the spirit of the Beloved Community over the precise sectarian attitude that Royce names as the chief obstacle to the community's development. In his public stance against the Vietnam War, his relationship with peace advocates such as Daniel Berrigan, his writings on racial injustice in America, and his growing interest in Zen Buddhism and other Eastern religions, Merton's clear breadth of compassion makes him an obvious candidate as a model citizen of the Beloved Community. However, he first needed to overcome within himself the resistance to this universality of heart. Merton's greatest danger of forsaking the Beloved Community came, ironically, at a high point in his spiritual enthusiasm—in his first flush of fervor leading up to Gethsemani and over his initial years there. First-time readers of *The Seven Storey Mountain* frequently bristle at Merton's Catholic triumphalism and his evident sense of the spiritual superiority of the Catholic monastic life.

Merton himself could hardly stand this version of himself in later life, describing himself when he set off for Gethsemani as the "stereotype of the world-denying contemplative—the man who spurned New York, spat on Chicago, and tromped on Louisville, heading for the woods with Thoreau in one pocket, John of the Cross in another, and holding the Bible open at the Apocalypse."[29] Looking back, he judges that during this first phase of his religious identity, from 1939 up until his ordination in 1948, he maintained "an arbitrary separation between God and the world."[30] Appealing to Merton's own testimony of having outgrown his triumphalist spirit, we might take ourselves to be licensed to speak of Merton's "conversion to the Beloved Community" through the expansion of his horizons during the 1950s and 1960s. According to this way of thinking, only once Merton opened himself beyond his exclusivist worldview could he embrace the community of all humankind.

His experience of a kind of mystical communion on a trip to Louisville in March of 1958, the famous "4th and Walnut experience," signals, then, a particularly decisive breakthrough into consciousness of unity. While standing on the corner of 4th and Walnut Street in downtown Louisville, as Merton looks in quiet, loving reverie at the faces of people "shining like the sun," the weight of separateness slides from his shoulders. In *Conjectures of a Guilty Bystander*, he frames the experience as a kind of epiphanic breaking of a spell: "It was like waking from a dream of separateness, of spurious self-isolation in a special world, the world of renunciation and supposed holiness....I have the immense joy of being man, a member of a race in which God Himself became incarnate."[31] His taste of mystical communion stands as a vital element in Merton's purported "turn to the world," alongside his growing sense of the monk's prophetic vocation, his own self-scrutiny, the liberalization of the Trappist order, and a host of other factors.[32]

The declaration of Merton's "turn to the Beloved Community" would qualify as a kind of modification of this storyline. There is something to be said regarding the impact of the 4th and Walnut experience and these other maturing factors on Merton's change in tone and focus throughout the late 1950s and 1960s. Decidedly, in this period, he progressed through a threshold in his orientation toward the non-Catholic, nonmonastic world, evincing a new spiritual freedom and a new resoluteness as a public voice. The flourishing of his social writings and his interreligious exploration indeed chart out fresh territory. However, a more thorough examination of Merton's life trajectory remains warranted. By considering his experiences at the Friendship House in New York City before he joined the monastery, as well as his formation as a Catholic monk, we can detect with greater insight the pervasive pull of the Beloved Community at each phase of his spiritual journey. In this light, Merton does not look like a surprise midlife convert to a universal community of love but a soul ongoingly guided toward its deepening expression.[33]

The Friendship House: *Contemptus Mundi* and Philadelphia in Harlem

In this movement toward the Beloved Community, Merton's experience at the Friendship House in Harlem represents a first major clarification of consciousness. Merton was led to the Catholic-Worker-Style Friendship House through his acquaintance with founder Catherine de Hueck (known as the Baroness), whom he met on her visit to St. Bonaventure University.[34] He took seriously her sharp charge that Catholics should be swarming Harlem, seeking to offer badly needed assistance to "the least of Christ's brethren" who populated the borough, yet their aesthetic disgust and excessive desire for comfort and security held them back.[35] Inspired and intrigued, Merton spent two weeks helping at the house during the summer of 1941.

Merton's time there awakened the engaged (and somewhat enraged) social conscience that the Baroness had all but anticipated during her visit to St. Bonaventure. The children's plays imitating out-of-reach white middle-class life stood for Merton as an indictment upon the whole of America. As he saw it, America's dominant superficial materialism only further crushed the poor who aspired to its hollow dreams. Merton writes, "Harlem is, in a sense, what God thinks of Hollywood, and Hollywood is all Harlem has, in its despair, to grasp at, by way of a surrogate heaven."[36] Recognizing Merton's draw to the Friendship House, on a later trip to St. Bonaventure the Baroness asked him whether he would join the House permanently. Merton was still unsure of his vocation, and he planned to leave St. Bonaventure to live and work at the Friendship House for an indefinite period. In a journal entry dated November 27, 1941, that reads like Hamlet's famous soliloquy, he anxiously tossed a future in Harlem and a future with the Trappists back and forth before settling on the Trappists because of the awe and desire with which the idea filled him.[37] When he at last chose to enter Gethsemani, he did so with a path of service at the Friendship House as the second horse in the race—and, most significantly, as an indelible touchstone of his moral and religious imagination.

Merton's stint at the Friendship House reveals an additional source of experience that made him "a world-denying contemplative," and perhaps not entirely according to the stereotype with which he later prodded himself. If we are to grasp Merton's appropriation of the principle of *contemptus mundi* (contempt of the world), we understand him as well through his response to Harlem as by any theological lesson he internalized at the monastery.[38] In "Aubade-Harlem," a poem he dedicates to the Baroness, he writes of the culpable gulf between well-off white New Yorkers and poor African Americans, bathing the comparison in the blood of Christ's passion:

> The white men's wives, like Pilate's,
> Cry in the peril of their frozen dreams:
> "Daylight has driven iron spikes,
> Into the flesh of Jesus' hands and feet:
> Four flowers of blood have nailed Him to the walls of
> Harlem."[39]

During his short period in Harlem, in his mixed disgust for America's grinding social machine and compassion for those ground down, we encounter the deep emotional wells that irrigate Merton's later social vision. Michael N. McGregor notes that in Merton's reflections upon Harlem, the themes of humility and authentic poverty, the oneness of humanity, and the value of the overlooked "other" are already present. McGregor writes, "Even a cursory look at books such as *Seeds of Destruction*, *Faith and Violence*, or his collected journals will show that these [already evident] understandings came to full flower in later life."[40]

As Merton entered Gethsemani, he may have yet had some spiritual growing up to do. However, we must not sever the roots of his sympathies in Harlem from the roots of his monastic quest: such a move would do a kind of violence to the integral character of his spiritual journey. Prior to arriving at Gethsemani shorn of his possessions, Merton had already lent his heart to a sacred community of the poor that took no monastic vows. If this meant contempt for the dynamics of greed and indifference that permeate the sinful "world," then the contempt sprang from a deeper love: his solicitude for the least of Christ's brothers whom he met in Harlem. In Merton's tortured sympathy for those he encountered while at the Friendship House, we find a source of his later explicit testimony of fidelity to the community of all humankind.

Turning to Gethsemani: Learning Loyalty and Sharing in a Common Hope

If we rightly notice in Merton's compassion for the poor in Harlem a sure sign of what Royce would call "falling in love with the universe," then in Merton's early monastic career, he began to cultivate the spirit of loyalty that unified his personality. When thinking about joining the Trappists, the consistency of Cistercian life—the rhythm of prayer and the ascetical regime—both terrified Merton and appealed to him.[41] He freely admitted that in his youth he had been prone to an unquenchable sense of alienation, wandering city streets in search of "unhealthy entertainments," losing sleep while gaining no tangible good.[42] He realized that his temperamental restlessness would be healthily challenged at Gethsemani, taming the rebelliousness he associated with sin, but he worried about stifling the creativity that meant so much to him. However, even his creative aspirations did not represent an undiluted good in his eyes. As he observed, tied to his motivation for literary accomplishment was a strong desire for fame—

not universal fame, but the approbation of a select, intelligent few. His confidence that he could not make a mistake in giving himself entirely to God ultimately secured his decision to join the monastery. If dedication to God could whittle away his anomie, and if God would turn his creativity to profit for the kingdom, why blunder down streets aimlessly or blunder into public squares seeking after vainglory?

The interior processes Merton describes resonate well with Royce's understanding of human integration as a communal process. For Royce, the attitude of the alienated human being is a despairing position, while the socially opportunistic attitude is diseased, as harmful to personal fulfillment as to society. The human being can only thrive through living for a cause beyond oneself. In Merton's late-night undirected restlessness, he wrestles with the alienation that leaves him outside of conscious participation within a human community. In his drilling down to detect his ambitions to receive the approbation of an elite set, he probes into the spiritual futility of engaging socially as a means of personal gain. As his desire for God deepened, his restlessness subdued and his hankering for personal glory lost its savor, just as both attitudes proved dead ends in Royce's view. In Merton's commitment to join the monastery in a spirit of self-surrender and willing service, he embodies the Roycean attitude of loyalty. While Royce speaks of the "will to manifest the Eternal," Merton broke through his deadlock in recognizing that whichever aspirations he entertained, he would be safe in entrusting himself *directly to* the Eternal. As he writes in *The Sign of Jonas*, published in 1953, "Coming to the monastery has been for me exactly the right kind of withdrawal. It has taught me how to live."[43] Lest we mistake his use of "withdrawal" for a form of self-centered cultivation, we can read on: "And now I owe everyone else in the world a share in that life…my first human act is the recognition of how much I owe everybody else."[44]

In being "taught how to live," Merton not only overcame the dual inclinations to dissipation and self-centeredness, but he also intellectually absorbed the Catholic tradition, emerging with a clarified eschatological imagination. The fruits of this perspective appear with special clarity in his later socially conscious writings.

In his "Letter to an Innocent Bystander," he speaks of the necessity of a pointedly Christian form of hope:

> There is a certain innocence in a kind of despair: but only if in despair we find salvation. I mean, despair of this world and what is in it. Despair of men and their plans, in order to hope for the impossible answer that lies beyond our earthly contradictions, and yet can burst into our world and solve them if only there are some who hope in spite of despair.[45]

By pointing to the need to eschew a worldly horizon of hope in favor of an orientation toward God, this passage provides additional insight into the spiritual foundations of the Christian principle of *contemptus mundi*. It also evinces a deepening of the growth he underwent in Harlem. The cultivation of hope that comes from above (to tweak Royce's phrase) is one description of the monastic task, one description of the aim of Merton's learning and living at Gethsemani.

According to this analysis, we can turn back once more to the question about Merton's "conversion to the Beloved Community" in light of Royce's axiom: "Look forward to the human and visible triumph of no form of the Christian Church." Insofar as Merton evinces an exclusive religious spirit, as he does in *The Seven Storey Mountain*, he violates this principle. As Merton reached beyond his triumphalism, he moved in step with the currents of the Second Vatican Council. In espousing an expanded notion of religious solidarity, he embodied the spirit of the Council so thoroughly that he eventually represented the vanguard of those opening to all that is best outside of the explicit Roman Catholic faith.[46] But this is not to say that he advanced by way of departure; rather, his spiritual position within the Catholic Church, solidified in his years as a novice and through his continued appropriation of the Catholic faith thereafter, provided the sustenance that made him a genuine participant in the broader human community.

We can recall especially the dialectic of the particular and the universal in Royce's thought on community. The individual flourishes through participation within the universal "community of interpretation," but this participation is necessarily forged through the mediation of concrete communities. These communities, nested within the larger invisible communion, are successful to the degree that they cultivate the spirit of loyalty and love that nourishes the whole. In the same breath, they are examples of unity and service at the local level. There is no place for impractical or ungrounded idealism in this way of thinking, no space for the attitude of the person, who, as the old saying goes, "loves humanity but cannot stand their neighbors." In this regard, Merton's Catholic training, albeit limited by a certain insularity and triumphalism, provides an indispensable foundation for his greatest contributions to the Beloved Community. By coming to live more resolutely from the shared memories of Christ's passion, death, and resurrection, and giving himself to the shared hope beyond all despair, he offers a portion of the beneficent life that, as he put in *The Sign of Jonas*, he "owes everybody else." Indeed, he shares best when he comes around to a more complete vision of the Catholic faith. As he writes in 1962, "The 'universality' and 'catholicity' which are essential to the Church necessarily imply an ability and a readiness to enter into dialogue with all that is pure, wise, profound, and humane in every kind of culture."[47] We may finally agree with the cringing mature Merton, embarrassed of his narrow outlook, that early on his heart still had to travel beyond the walls of Gethsemani, but like any sound-thinking friend, we must also offer the reminder that his final achievement depended upon what he learned there.

Beyond Gethsemani: The Bonds of a New Solidarity

The spirit of dedication to a universal human communion is not, as it turns out, a sudden accomplishment of the fabled later Merton who spoke out against the grain on racial injustice in the United States and who celebrated the likes of the Chinese sage Chuang Tzu as models of monastic wisdom. As a guest at the Friendship House in New York City, Merton was sensitized to the depths of human unity and the tragedy of its neglect; and in making his own the Cistercian monastic tradition and the Catholic intellectual and mystical heritage, he gained the eyes to see the greatness of Chuang Tzu. Nevertheless, we cannot resist the conclusion that his later years represent a special development, a uniquely radiant embodiment of the ethos of the Beloved Community. If this development reflects a ripening of contemplative wisdom, a synthesis of countervailing currents, or even an impatience upon feeling the chills of aging, his increasingly apparent wide embrace is most striking for his demonstration of creative courage.

His short open letter, "Nhat Hanh Is My Brother," first published in the magazine *Jubilee* in 1966, sums up much that is most remarkable in the attitude of the later Merton.[48] Merton's sympathy for Thich Nhat Hanh, the Buddhist monk, spiritual writer, and peace activist, emerged after a period of study of Zen Buddhism and epistolary exchanges with Zen scholars and practitioners. When the Vietnam War broke out, Merton grasped the crisis of the war with a unique sense of compassion. As Gordon Zahn writes, "He was able to view the conflict from a perspective closer to that of the Vietnamese themselves, not only in its political meanings and manifestations…but in its moral and philosophical overtones for those most directly involved."[49] Nhat Hanh came to the United States to appeal for a peaceful path out of the war, a course of action that put him at considerable risk of punishment from all sides upon his return to Vietnam. Merton was touched by his character and his witness, and he wrote "Nhat Hanh Is My Brother" to rally support for his protection. Merton offers all that he can in the letter, pleading to his readers: "If I mean something to you, then let me put it this way; do for Nhat Hanh whatever you would do for me if I were in his position. In many ways I wish I were."[50]

This profound gesture of identification with Nhat Hanh makes the letter's titular claim strongly: these are the kinds of aching words we hear from mothers, fathers, and siblings as they worry over the dreadful or dangerous situations in which family members find themselves. Merton sees Nhat Hanh as a brother for he recognizes something of his own spiritual center in him. He plainly ascertains his contemplative way of life and his own closely held values. They are brothers, Merton notes, in their condemnation of war and its justifications, in their refusal to be coopted by any worldly power, in their representation of the downtrodden, and in their unqualified responsibility for the welfare and genuine freedom of humankind. Merton's letter is worth quoting at length:

> I have said Nhat Hanh is my brother, and it is true....It is vitally important that such bonds be admitted. They are the bonds of a new solidarity and a new brotherhood which is beginning to be evident on all the five continents and which cuts across all political, religious, and cultural lines to unite young men and women in every country in something that is more concrete than an ideal and more alive than a program. This unity of the young is the only hope of the world.[51]

These words so aptly and movingly convey the vision of the Beloved Community that they should almost be left without comment. But if there is anything more to be said, it is to point out their affinity with Royce's characterizations in *The Problem of Christianity*. The "new solidarity" that cuts across all separative categories bespeaks the overcoming of human divisions that Royce ardently emphasizes, to the point that he demands the renunciation of exclusive missionary aspirations. The unity that is "more concrete than an ideal" encapsulates the Roycean attitude of loyalty in its unique power to bridge the particular and the universal: the Beloved Community is no mere kingdom of ideas but rather a reality brought about through tangible commitments. (In this manner, the pragmatist in Royce, that is, the sort of philosopher who holds that ideas can only be understood through their operational consequences, meets Merton, the contemplative in action.) If the unity Merton has in mind is also "more alive than a program," we might surmise that this is because it is a unity that emanates finally from beyond the plane of merely human inspiration. Only the Spirit that stitches together various formerly isolated individuals into one body of common concern can engender the community's authentic arrival. In a time of spiritual devastation, it is the young who remain open to the Spirit's promptings, the young in whom shared hope lodges.

Throughout his later writings, we find the sharpened Merton who is willing, as with the Thich Nhat Hanh piece, to put his neck on the line for the sake of an expanded sense of communion. This is necessarily a Merton who provokes, in no sense a made-to-order contemplative writer aiming to please every Catholic in the pews. In each of his principal final commitments, Merton unsettles the complacency of those comfortable with the boundaries established.[52] For those engaged actively in the deepening of divisions, Merton does more than unsettle; he exposes the greed, malice, selfishness, and fear that lie behind their dishonest self-justifying rhetoric. To those seeking to arm the United States for nuclear war, he names the cowardice driving the outward talk of strength, security, and peace.[53] To the so-called political moderates who ask to slow the pace of change in confronting racial injustice, he announces that they do not sincerely care about Black Americans but only about maintaining their privilege. He even tells white liberals that they are fair-weather friends to the oppressed—and that they have no right to complain about being mistrusted by African Americans.[54] He holds his fellow Christians to the standards of the gospel, the standards "not of this world," telling them that they may be surprised to realize that they bear resemblance to Adolf Eichmann in prizing efficiency and apparent rationality above courage and genuine humanity.[55] In calling for greater union, he calls out, as he must, the people and the forces that obstruct the way. In this final phase of his life, Merton proves himself worthy of the label M. Shawn Copeland gives him: he stands as prophet of the Beloved Community, taking on both the spirit and the burden of the office.

CONCLUSION

Josiah Royce's commitment to a philosophy of pragmatism demands that ideas be grasped through their concrete consequences. For Royce, ideas must be demonstrated in the course of life—must take on flesh, so to speak—in order to be understood at all. Thus, as an example of the ever-greater realization of human unity, Merton's life supplies a valuable outworking of the practical consequences of the idea of the Beloved Community. However, Merton at last proves to be more than the Beloved Community's evidentiary principle or even its paradigmatic proponent. Merton's singular prophetic witness renders him an interpreter, offering insight to enhance the understanding of the nature of the Beloved Community. Royce understands the Beloved Community precisely as an ongoing community of interpretation, and so we must imagine this as a development that Royce would welcome.[56] Merton's advance in the conversation proceeds along two tracks: one, the horizon of hope that lies beyond the world, and two, the contemplative or inward dimension of the attainment of spiritual unity.

Merton's first interpretive contribution is the appeal to a horizon of hope greater than the forward march of history, a source of hope that rests only upon divine action. Royce is fundamentally open to this mode of thought—notably through his appeal to the "love that comes as if from above"; the leading of the Spirit into greater communion; and the significance of the Pauline model of the Body of Christ. Nevertheless, Merton's eschatological vision makes more completely evident the perennial challenge that exists in the adoption of the attitude of loyalty to the cause of love. He provides a sound response to those interpreters like Charles Marsh who neglect to account for the transcendent dimension of Royce's communion, lumping Royce's Beloved Community in with unreconstructed progressive liberal Protestantism. As Marsh writes,

> Most of these [early] formulations [of the Beloved Community], however, had the effect of reducing transcendence to some mode or modulation of human experience, or of describing community as an inevitable historical achievement. The philosopher Josiah Royce...gave voice to the essence of Protestant ethical religion; the beloved community shimmers with liberal hopes of human progress and perfectibility. Most of what one needs to know of God is discovered in ethical religion, slightly adjusted for churchgoers in capitalist economies.[57]

We must resist defending Royce fully from Marsh's charges, remaining satisfied with the central role of vertical action in human spiritual transformation already described—and perhaps adding Royce's unmistakable communitarian challenge to the logic of "capitalist economies." Suffice it to say that Royce reads the Beloved Community in more of a spiritual than a strictly ethical key.

Rather, it is best to allow Merton to pick up Royce's watch, for the radical failure of shimmering hopes of human perfectibility that Marsh describes, although beginning to show through in

Royce's time, becomes irrefutable in Merton's. Merton takes the lesson to heart in his exposure of the folly of an all-too-human horizon of hope. This stance means recognizing, as he puts it in *Conjectures of a Guilty Bystander*, the "complete and systematic sham" that the world represents in its false approach to fulfillment.[58] Merton saw through this very sham character of "the world" at the Friendship House, and he deepened his coordination to the genuine good through his interiorization of the Catholic tradition at the Abbey of Gethsemani. His later work sheds the outworn skin of exclusivism, practically blazing with the awareness of the difference between the authentic and the merely seductive approach to the human world. He is clear, as for instance in his celebration of Thich Nhat Hanh, that many non-Christians provide the finest expression of this attitude of hope in that which lies beyond the human world.

For Merton, disengagement from the "sham world" begins with care for those who suffer most from its schemes. Thus, we encounter Merton's appropriately weighted *contemptus mundi* conjoined to the love of the poor. In Merton's hands, the love of the marginalized becomes the very door to the Beloved Community. A Mertonian epilogue to *The Problem of Christianity* might add to Royce's axiom, "Seek the success of no single sect," the exhortation, "Seek unity above all through solidarity with the disempowered."

Merton's second major interpretive contribution is his discovery of the Beloved Community in the practice of contemplation. As he develops, Merton expresses with increasing simplicity the idea that contemplation is directed to communion—not only with God but with all people. In *New Seeds of Contemplation*, he announces that the goal of withdrawal is doing good to others: "We do not go into the desert to escape people but to learn how to find them; we do not leave them in order to have nothing more to do with them, but to find out the way to do them the most good."[59] Merton's articulation of solitude as a means of the discernment of charity is laudable, but he reaches even further. In October of 1968, weeks before he died, Merton famously told an audience of Asian monks in Calcutta,

> The deepest level of communication is not communication but communion. It is wordless. It is beyond words, and it is beyond speech, and it is beyond concept. Not that we discover a new unity. We discover an older unity. My dear brothers, we are already one. But we imagine that we are not. And what we have to recover is our original unity. What we have to be is what we are.[60]

Throughout his life, and in various ways, Merton pointed to contemplation as a privileged means to recover this foundational unity. He reserves his purest testimony of brotherhood (including Nhat Hanh and the Dalai Lama) for those whose stance of commitment to the world emerges from the still point of contemplation.

Through his understanding of the contemplative grasp of authentic communion, Merton turns Royce's central dialectic inside out. Merton is no mystical individualist: he brings Royce's "sacred pair" of the individual and the community, which Royce insists upon as a metaphysical reality, to a fresh point of reconciliation. Merton discovers the community at the center of the human heart, the virginal point of absolute relationship. Thus, the metaphysical reality shines out from within. Given Merton's contemplative insight, the Beloved Community represents no mere external accomplishment—and certainly no pleasing fiction. Neither is the Beloved Community an overheated progressivist ideal, a rationalistic philosophical construct, or an ethical religion: it is a *mystical fact*.

Josiah Royce passed along his "night watch" striving for optimism but beset by anxiety, shaken by the questions flooding in at the outbreak of a great war. In the life of Thomas Merton, we find a worthy response, for Royce and for all disquieted by the horrific twentieth century and the fresh catastrophes of the twenty-first. Born into this first great war, under the sign of far-reaching human solidarity, along the borders he implored us to erase within, Thomas Merton, the global citizen, spoke too, spoke indeed most persuasively, as the American he belatedly took himself to be. His words of confrontation directed toward his own never failed to offer a deeper-lying assurance of an indefeasible unity. The

Beloved Community, he instructs still today, may be a hope, but it is not, in the end, a mere dream, for the only dream in truth is the dream of our separateness, the long slumber from which we must awake. Merton may have died too young, but he passed on having hastened the great community's coming, summoning each of us to the responsibility to do the same.

CONCLUSION

In Defense of Humanity

AS WE ROUND OUT our discussion, perhaps it is helpful to break with William James's fruits-rather-than-roots-maxim to gain a final perspective. After all, the pragmatist approach cannot long abide a dualism, and our conversation tends to want to return to the birth of the discipline of Christian spirituality, which brings parents and ancestors into the frame. As we circle back to the beginning, we recall that our first point is the usefulness of recognizing the discipline's foundation in the early 1990s as connected to—as in fact a kind of recurrence of—the turn to experience inaugurated by William James's *The Varieties of Religious Experience* in the early 1900s. Sandra Schneiders long played with refinements of her early definitions of the discipline, but, like James, she never broke faith with grounding her basic project in human experience.

If you ever have the privilege of participating in a conversation about the distinction between spirituality and theology, especially one involving theologians of a skeptical bent, you will likely reach a point of vexation where you feel as if entering the doomed second hour of a barroom debate. And if you find yourself on the underdog's side yet running out of arguments, it is advisable to let Sandra Schneiders do the talking. Let her speak through her articles in defense of the unique anthropological orientation of Christian spirituality. (Fittingly, *Sandra* means "protector of humanity.") Let her cut down and entangle the staid opponents as she lectures about the postmodern academic situation, about constitutive and problematic disciplines, and about the merits of the hermeneutical approach. But do not in so listening—or in entertaining rebuttals—lose track of what she first called for, and why such a call was necessary. The turn to experience does indeed have a defense of humanity at its heart—a defense of the many against the aristocratic pretense of arid intellectualism, a defense too of the dignity of the dispossessed against the powers incentivized to dismiss them as insignificant, and a defense at last of the universal human access to a relationship with the God of love. We could call this spirit democratic, in its expression of a liberative aspiration for which William James also deserves credit. Herein lies a dimension of spirituality's identity—her first experience that cannot be gainsaid at any juncture of debate.

In addition to the importance of fleshing out the Jamesian experiential imperative, our second related point is that, considering the state of self-sorting in which spirituality remains, it is worthwhile to attend closely to two other voices—those of Josiah Royce and Charles Sanders Peirce. As we have said, we do not through this inclusion seek to totally eclipse James. When we are too quick to pronounce against him, we forget that he has set the targets of inquiry that impart the distinctiveness and sense of direction to the field: the primacy of experience and the telos of conversion. Target setter that James is, it should be unsurprising that his work has become something like elementary target practice for students of religious experience. The criticisms of James are well-founded, and we have not hesitated to launch a few volleys of our own. Rather than continue to take aim at James, we advocate pausing to listen to his friends (who also made his most astute critics) as they provide constructive—and even breakthrough—proposals that inform our present work.

Their constructive contribution starts with a turn to community alongside the turn to experience: their interpretive approach invariably travels through the medium of the Spirit-led community of inquiry. Following Peirce and Royce, the idea of community must be handled just as carefully as the notion of experience: community may neither be nominalistically reduced to appear as a mere aggregate of individuals, nor undialectically elevated to swallow the freedom and autonomy of the individual. By understanding community as a third irreducible plane of reality in relationship with the human spirit and the Spirit of God, we draw our pivotal lesson from the dialogue. The Spirit, the individual, and the community are each involved in interpretation, and each with reference to one another. The Beloved Community may thus be seen in its multivalent reality: as the fruit of the individual's loyalty to a cause greater than oneself, which brings the ideal into being ever more fully; as the creative work of the Spirit, who leads each individual to greater degrees of self-donation in service to the whole; and as the final horizon of personal and shared religious experience, the hope that guides into the future.

Our particular community of inquiry, that of Christian spirituality, may be more in need of this approach than we first suppose. Peirce and Royce give explicitly philosophical proposals, and we tend to be uncertain when it comes to philosophy. In favoring an attitude of post-Heideggerian metaphysical defeatism, we in the Christian spirituality community have largely accustomed ourselves to giving up on philosophical sustenance; or, at times, forgetting our limits and throwing caution to the wind, to feasting obliviously on a smorgasbord of clashing philosophical flavors; or, snatching caution back and clutching it tightly, to measuring out our gains with analytic philosophy's coffee spoons. Usually, we simply go without. Accordingly, we are often much better at indicating which Enlightenment-era fallacies spirituality repudiates than we are at understanding how precisely the positions for which we advocate ultimately make sense. We know what a crime it is to be a Cartesian dualist. We know that the crime's punishment is a prisoner's thick-paned enforced distance from reality—a distance kept from our own embodied experience, from contact with the living face of creation, and from awareness of the Spirit's inbreaking spontaneities. Enemies of dualism we may be, yet we seldom rigorously contemplate the alternative of a triadic relational metaphysics. So, too, we resolutely pledge to fight against any conception of spiritual experience that classifies experience exclusively within a private, inner domain, holding instead to the invariably public and interpersonal character of spiritual life. And yet we are reluctant to take pains in our understanding of the pragmatist method through which beliefs and actions implicate one another in an unbreakable union.

Pragmatism's critique cuts both ways, from belief to action and action to belief: not only are we guilty of crying out for community without understanding what we intend by the word, but just as often we render our words meaningless through our actions, as we retreat from community's stringencies in favor of the soporific grooming of our virtual selves in our virtual worlds. Finally, we are zealous about opening ourselves to the whole of creation, as we impatiently and mightily push for prophetic redirection from our world's wayward course through the re-establishment of lost kinship. And yet we can be sluggish to entertain the semeiotics that grants and names the patterns of this broader communion. This litany is not meant to overwhelm, but rather to insist on the importance of grounding ourselves in frames of reference adequate to the reality we explore and the task we take up. We can despise the Cartesian hangover, and yet not quite wean ourselves from the poison. If there exists any solitary heroism in Peirce, and any admirable doggedness in Royce, it lies in their recognition and pursuit of just the kind of thoroughly alternative approach required to become well.

When it comes to these and related issues, we should be clear that this book states fundamental intuitions and commitments that can only be further developed within a dedicated community of inquiry. With respect to spirituality's questions about religious experience, the book endorses a socially mediated account grounded in the dynamics of conversion and tending toward the realization of the Beloved Community. Such an account emphasizes the mediating role of the Spirit best known by the effects of her charisms. The account resists mystical foundationalism without eschewing the process of mystical insight. With respect to the phenomenology (Peirce would say *phaneroscopy*) of "lived human experience"—growing out of thick descriptions and an inductive rather than deductive approach—we are committed to a triadic relational realism that includes possibility (Firstness), fact (Secondness), and generality (Thirdness). Thus, Bernard McGinn's rich study of historical fact remains as valid and essential as Sandra Schneiders's acknowledgment of general realities such as the conversion experience and human transformation. Further, where phenomenology shades into metaphysics, we are committed to a cosmologically inclusive sign-sending and sign-receiving system that begins from the connaturality between the human and the more-than-human world. Consistent application and development of this semeiotics should lead the contours of the Beloved Community to expand beyond Royce's initial anthropological model.

And lastly, in view of spirituality's "self-implicating" badge of honor, worn in defiance of the false opposition between disinterested research and merely extrinsic conduct, we hold to a pragmatic philosophy that unites theory and practice, wherein ideas can only be fully known by their operational consequences. This means that general and normative claims about spirituality need to have practical and concrete implications, leading not only to changing interpretations of a given reality but ultimately to acting in a way consistent with the new view of things. Peirce wrote that "verbal definitions are very inferior to the living definition that grows up in the habit," a way of communicating the living article that spirituality maintains to be the proper fruit of research.[1] In this way, spirituality and pragmatism establish themselves together at the revolving doors at the edge of the academy. They each open onto the realm of purposeful action, showing the way out of the familiar indoor hermetic circle of verbal interpretations feeding endlessly into verbal interpretations. They each affirm the integral relationship between theory and praxis, as well as their ongoing mutual refinement.

As this picture stands, we advance then, starting with James and continuing with his two friends, both a mild position and a strong position. The mild position holds that the work of these pragmatists proves a helpful aid for the development of Christian spirituality. It is the appropriative view—the view that we can bring out and dust off their philosophies like sturdy tools suited for spirituality's soil. According to the mild position, it is beneficial to get to know them. But we do want to say more. Our strong position, which we have been unable to resist, is the ancestry view, the entanglement of roots and fruits. This position reflects the crystallizing hunch that these philosophers of experience stand as descendants, among others, in the spirituality family tree. Paternity may not compel destiny, but it cannot help but exert an influence—an influence best dealt with consciously. According to the strong position, it would be a mistake to ignore these three.

The service rendered by this recognition is not only to our own self-identified projects but to the community of memory that James, Royce, and Peirce articulate and uphold. The strong position entails that work within the discipline of spirituality is crucial to the fulfillment of *their* philosophical aspirations, which outlive them and live on in the United States (yet not in the United States alone)—and that to appropriately carry on their work demands in one way or another carrying on the work of Christian spirituality. Where Royce's spiritual ideal of the Beloved Community, Peirce's replete account of signs and experience, and James's journey of conversion coalesce, we have found our way as well to spirituality's core dynamics. If the discipline of spirituality easily gets turned around without a philosophical compass to orient its understanding of experience, then the pragmatist experiential philosophy loses the fire of forward motion without spirituality, as lived and as theorized. Perhaps the relationship we outline represents a contemporary iteration of the ancient partnership between philosophy and theology—and do we not amuse ourselves a little when we say that Athens stands to Jerusalem as turn-of-the-century Boston stands to late twentieth-century Berkeley; or, to use an appropriately triadic form, that Royce, of Boston by way of Berkeley, mediates between James the Bostonian and Schneiders the Berkeleyite? Through relations such as these, we are inclined to believe, a rich possible future awaits the discipline of spirituality. Of course, in order to hasten this future's coming, one must act.

NOTES

INTRODUCTION

1. Evagrius Ponticus, *The Praktikos and Chapters on Prayer*, trans. John Eudes Bamberger (Kalamazoo, MI: Cistercian Publications, 1972), 60.

2. Hans Urs von Balthasar, "Spirituality and Theology," in *Explorations in Theology*, vol. 1, *The Word Made Flesh*, trans. A. V. Littledale and Alexander Dru (San Francisco: Ignatius Press, 1989), 213.

3. Von Balthasar, "Spirituality and Theology," 214.

4. Hans Urs von Balthasar, "Theology and Sanctity," in *Explorations in Theology*, 1:57.

5. Schneiders, "Theology and Spirituality: Strangers, Rivals, or Partners?," *Horizons* 13, no. 2 (1986): 258. https://doi.org/10.1017/S036096690003632X.

6. Ewart Cousins, ed., *World Spirituality: An Encyclopedic History of the Religious Quest* (New York: Crossroad, 1985).

7. Schneiders, "Theology and Spirituality," 264–65.

8. Kees Waaijman, "Spirituality: Forms, Foundations, Methods," *Studies in Spirituality Supplement* 8 (2002): 2.

9. "American pragmatism" makes reference to the cultural reality of the United States, specifically to the movement that emerged in the late nineteenth and early twentieth centuries therein. This moniker and subsequent references to "America" and "American" follow colloquial usage to refer to the United States. This usage is not intended to validate a harmful hegemonic understanding of the United States, nor to discount the rich body of

thought present within the broader region. For an excellent work that connects pragmatism to spirituality throughout the Américas, see Christopher D. Tirres, *Liberating Spiritualities: Reimagining Faith in the Américas* (New York: Fordham University Press, 2025).

10. "About the Society," The Society for the Study of Christian Spirituality. https://sscs.press.jhu.edu/about/About%20the%20Society.

11. Sandra M. Schneiders, "Spirituality in the Academy," *Theological Studies* 50, no. 4 (1989): 676–97.

12. Josiah Royce, *The Sources of Religious Insight* (1912; repr., Washington, DC: The Catholic University of America Press, 2001), 47–48, 63.

13. Josiah Royce, *The Problem of Christianity* (1913; repr., Washington DC: The Catholic University of America Press, 2001).

14. See Frank M. Oppenheim, *Reverence for the Relations of Life: Re-imagining Pragmatism via Josiah Royce's Interactions with Peirce, James, and Dewey* (Notre Dame, IN: University of Notre Dame Press, 2005), 43–63.

15. Royce, *The Problem of Christianity*, 278–82.

16. See Gabriel Marcel, *Royce's Metaphysics*, trans. Virginia and Gordon Ringer (Chicago: Henry Regnery Company, 1956), 121–23.

17. We follow Peirce's distinctive spelling here—*semeiosis* rather than *semiosis*.

18. Charles Sanders Peirce, "How to Make Our Ideas Clear," in *The Essential Peirce*, vol. 1, ed. Nathan Houser and Christian Kloesel (Bloomington: Indiana University Press, 1992), 139.

19. Marcel, *Royce's Metaphysics*, 123.

20. Royce, *Problem of Christianity*, 152, archaic English adapted.

21. Bernard McGinn, "The Letter and the Spirit: Spirituality as an Academic Discipline," in *Minding the Spirit: The Study of Christian Spirituality*, ed. Elizabeth A. Dreyer and Mark S. Burrows (Baltimore: The Johns Hopkins University Press, 2005), 31.

22. Bernard McGinn, "The Letter and the Spirit," 32.

23. See Bernard Lonergan, "The Transition from a Classical Worldview to Historical-Mindedness," in *A Second Collection:*

Papers by Bernard J. F. Lonergan, ed. William F.J. Ryan and Bernard J. Tyrell (Toronto: University of Toronto Press, 1974), 1–9.

24. McGinn, "The Letter and the Spirit," 33.

25. Sandra Schneiders, "A Hermeneutical Approach to Christian Spirituality," in Dreyer and Burrows, *Minding the Spirit*, 55.

26. Schneiders, "A Hermeneutical Approach to Christian Spirituality," 55.

27. In addition to the aforementioned article by Schneiders, see also, collected in the same volume, "The Study of Christian Spirituality: Contours and Dynamics of a Discipline," 6, originally printed in the *Christian Spirituality Bulletin 6* (1998): 3. For a summary of the conversation, see Waaijman, "Spirituality: Forms, Foundations, Methods," 309.

28. Schneiders, "A Hermeneutical Approach to Christian Spirituality," 56–57; Although Schneiders draws most explicitly on Paul Ricoeur and Hans-Georg Gadamer for her hermeneutical understanding, the hermeneutical approach for which she advocates provides an opening for the interpretive developments of Royce and Peirce. Through her dual emphases of hermeneutical rigor and the need for common objects of inquiry, Schneiders names the commitments that led Peirce and Royce to develop a semeiotic realism that overcomes nominalistic prejudices.

29. Schneiders, "A Hermeneutical Approach," 59.

30. Schneiders, "The Study of Christian Spirituality," in Dreyer and Burrows, *Minding the Spirit*, 8–10.

31. Schneiders, "A Hermeneutical Approach," 51.

32. Schneiders, "A Hermeneutical Approach," 51, emphasis added; the polar structure is also adopted by the *World Spirituality* series. See Waaijman's comment on the series in "Spirituality: Forms, Foundations, Methods," 4: "Spirituality is conceived as a polar structure: the relation of the human person (inner dimension, spirit, spiritual core, deepest center) to a transcendent dimension (ultimate reality, ultimate goal).

33. Schneiders's more recent articulations of the nature of the discipline do better to overcome the dipolar construct. In a 2022 paper, she wrote the following: "What we are studying is *a*, if not *the*, major reality of human life—namely, the relation of the individual in community with God as that project is mediated to us in Sacred Scripture and throughout history in the believing

communit(ies), in dialogue with the socio-historical realities of our life situations." Sandra M. Schneiders, "The Future of Christian Spirituality as an Academic Discipline," in *The Future of Christian Spirituality: In Our Lives, in Our Churches, and in the Academy: Essays in Honor of Fr. Ron Rolheiser*, ed. David Pocta and John J. Markey (New York: Crossroad, 2022), 134. The point remains that this communal mediation needs to be accounted for through a consistent metaphysics and method of interpretation. One of this book's central proposals is that Royce and Peirce provide the triadic philosophy to support a triadic basic definition.

CHAPTER 1

1. Pseudo-Dionysius, *The Mystical Theology*, in *Pseudo-Dionysius: The Complete Works*, ed. Colm Luibheid, Classics of Western Spirituality (Mahwah, NJ: Paulist Press, 1987), 997B.

2. Gregory of Nyssa, *Sermon XIII. Commentary on the Song of Songs*, trans. Casimir McCambley (Brookline, MA: Hellenic College Press, 1987).

3. Friedrich Schleiermacher, *On Religion: Speeches to Its Cultured Despisers*, ed. and trans. Richard Crouter. Cambridge Texts in the History of Philosophy (Cambridge: Cambridge University Press, 1996), 101.

4. The term *religious experience* has a short past, first noted in the *Oxford English Dictionary* in the title of the 1809 Quaker devotional work, *A Diary of the Religious Experience of Mary Waring*. Prior to the explicit usage of the term, going back to the sixteenth century, the idea was in the air in Puritan circles where confirmation of salvation was sought through interior signs. Talk of "religious experience" emerged with a focus upon the personal need for and process of conversion. This same Puritan tradition, brought to the United States and prominent in New England in the late nineteenth century, served as a seedbed for the emphases of William James (of Calvinist ancestral background) in *The Varieties of Religious Experience*. See David Hay, "Experience," in *The Blackwell Companion to Christian Spirituality*, ed. Arthur Holder (West Sussex, UK: Wiley-Blackwell, 2011), 420–21. On the

American movement, see also David Hay, "Experience, Religious," in *The New Westminster Dictionary of Christian Spirituality*, ed. Philip Sheldrake (Louisville, KY: Westminster John Knox Press, 2005), 296.

5. As Schleiermacher's thought developed, he became increasingly focused on questions of biblical and textual interpretation, lecturing widely on biblical hermeneutics and translating Plato for his German contemporaries. Schleiermacher's *Speeches*, revised in 1806 and 1821, became tied to these questions of the parameters for the interpretation of texts and experiences.

6. They may as well be understood to be dealing with "spiritual experience," in many ways a more suitable term for a paradigm in which religions follow second-order from the essential primary experience that is not necessarily dependent on any particular religious system. Such terminology is more available today. We will treat religious experience and spiritual experience as interchangeable in what follows.

7. As Steven Katz argues, the Jewish mystic has a markedly different experience in the encounter with the personal God of Judaism than the Buddhist practitioner who holds that there is no real self and no greater transcendent being either. Steven Katz, ed., *Mysticism and Philosophical Analysis* (New York: Oxford University Press), 1978.

8. Lash, it should be noted, is more favorable to Schleiermacher than most, understanding him to be a hermeneutical theologian, that is, relying on grammatical-theological principles rather than descriptions of states of consciousness as his foundation. For Lash, it is precisely the misunderstanding of succeeding generations that reduced his more rigorous hermeneutical thought to an overriding focus on empirical descriptions of states of consciousness. See Nicholas Lash, *Easter in Ordinary: Reflections on Human Experience and the Knowledge of God* (Notre Dame, IN: University of Notre Dame Press, 1988), 120–30.

9. See Denys Turner, *The Darkness of God: Negativity in Christian Mysticism* (Cambridge: Cambridge University Press, 1995). Bernard McGinn finds Turner's anti-experientialist thesis to be "at best only half-right." For McGinn, Turner is correct to point out that the great mystical theologians deconstruct naïve views of experience, especially concerning metaphors of ascent,

inwardness, light, darkness, and union. He also appropriately emphasizes the necessary mutual linkage between the cataphatic and apophatic linguistic moments. However, his treatment neglects the reality that the dimension of experience or, in McGinn's terms, "consciousness of God," invariably plays a role—and even shapes the central intentions—of mystical theology. Bernard McGinn, review of *The Darkness of God: Negativity in Christian Mysticism*, by Denys Turner, *The Journal of Religion* 77, no 2 (1997): 309–11.

10. William James, *The Varieties of Religious Experience: A Study in Human Nature*, ed. Martin E. Marty (New York: Penguin, 1982), 31. To use the term *divine* is to carry forward James's language of religious objects from *Varieties*. Royce speaks of the *supernatural* or *superhuman*, which can be treated as serving the same function in *Sources* as does James's *divine* in *Varieties*. However, scratching beneath the surface, distance opens up between them. James clarifies his term (somewhat) by explaining that the *divine* denotes "any object that is godlike, whether it be a concrete deity or not" (*Varieties*, 34). As James unfolds his account of conversion, he presents an understanding of the divine as something "More" beyond the plane of ordinary experience, and he argues for the mediation of this "More" through the subconscious mind. Royce disagrees with the idea of the chiefly subconscious mediation of religious realities. Still, even as Royce extends the potential modes of mediation, James's indication of a deeper field of consciousness interacting with the human mind abides in his explication of the terms *supernatural* and *superhuman* in *Sources*, 257–72. See Royce's basic statement of common intention with James in *Sources*, 27: "In portraying what he meant by 'the divine,' James emphasized, although in terms different from what I am using, the very features about the objects of religious experience which I have just been trying to characterize in my own way."

11. As he expresses in a letter to his friend Frances Morse, he seeks to show "experience against philosophy as the real backbone of the world's religious life—I mean prayer, guidance, and all that sort of thing immediately and privately felt, as against high and noble and general views of our destiny and the world's meaning." William James, *The Letters of William James*, ed. Henry James (Boston: Atlantic Monthly Press, 1920), 2:127.

12. When compared to subsequent depth psychology, James's subconscious remains a relatively primitive conception. He treats the subconscious as a hazy, porous marginal zone and he does not anatomize this zone precisely. James's subconscious is not, for instance, the subconscious of Freud with its drives and complexes, nor the subconscious of Jung as fount of "archetypes."

13. Charles Taylor observes that the "sick soul" can be characterized by three distinguishable forms of negative experience: religious melancholy, a kind of melancholy rooted in fearfulness, and an acute sense of personal sin. See Charles Taylor, *Varieties of Religion Today: William James Revisited* (Cambridge, MA: Harvard University Press, 2002), 34–35.

14. This portraiture so happens to be the area in which James is most in his element—the depiction of lasting states of mind as fashioned by the interaction of mobile, mutually entailing perceptions and emotions; the vivid dramatization of the inner life that blends detachment and sympathy, persuading the reader (or listener) not only *of* the gripping power of a state of mind but also *toward* a measure of identification with the subject's processes and convictions. In James's impressionistic portrayal of the anguished, bereft consciousness of the sick soul, he asks for his audience's validation of this angsty everyman's sense of alienation.

15. James dubs this more profound reading "the philosophic presumption of sick-mindedness" (James, *Varieties*, 131).

16. James, *Varieties*, 162.

17. James, *Varieties*, 172–73.

18. James, *Varieties*, 196.

19. James, *Varieties*, 248–49.

20. James, *Varieties*, 157.

21. To sketch their respective positions in their "Battle for the Absolute": James disagreed with Royce's absolute idealism, a conception of the universe in which individuals form a part of the greater whole of the All-Knowing Absolute Spirit. For James, Royce's picture failed to account for the relative autonomy of individuals, necessarily subsuming individuals into a "block universe." Royce worked to refute this charge; for his part, he confessed that he found James's pluralistic cosmos just short of a picture of total chaos, lacking the relations that could explain how things hang together.

22. See John Clendenning, *The Life and Thought of Josiah Royce*, rev. ed. (Nashville: Vanderbilt University Press, 1999), 268.

23. Josiah Royce, *The Sources of Religious Insight* (1912; repr., Washington, DC: The Catholic University of America Press, 2001), constitutes part of a larger project for Royce as he developed a religious philosophy of loyalty from 1900 to 1913. *Sources* synthesizes themes that he had previously taken up in isolation. Royce commented, "[*Sources*] contains the whole sense of me in a brief compass," in Clendenning, *Letters of Josiah Royce*, 570.

24. This speech, a celebration of James's life, was the Phi Beta Kappa Oration delivered by Royce in June 1911. He named James as the third great "representative American thinker," alongside Ralph Waldo Emerson and Jonathan Edwards. See Josiah Royce, "William James and the Philosophy of Life," in *William James and Other Essays on the Philosophy of Life* (New York: Macmillan, 1911).

25. Royce, "William James and the Philosophy of Life," 25. Royce pays the compliment that, in *Varieties*, "[America's] national religious life has found its manifold and characteristic expression."

26. Royce, *Sources*, 8–9.

27. If Royce follows James in his effort to provide empirical foundations capable of validation without prior assent to specific propositions of faith, he also strikes up a Jamesian posture. Though perhaps without the same inimitable Jamesian color, he adopts the style of the genial guide speaking unpretentiously to reasonable listeners. Royce encourages his audience to assess for themselves the legitimacy of his conclusions. In each of these major decisions—the choice for loose rather than precise definitions, the choice for an empirical-experiential approach, and the choice for broad accessibility of presentation—Royce intends the same goal as James. Both hope for the advance of a form of religious inquiry grounded upon human experience, possessed of the power to unify where previous methodologies only divided, and able to enliven the imagination of the contemporary listener. For Royce especially, there is something of an irony in the attempt to construct a broad and nonpolemical definition while still depending heavily on Christian paradigms of salvation. See Royce, *Sources*, 41, for the shared vision of the unity of religions.

28. Royce, *Sources*, 17.
29. Royce, *Sources*, 33, emphasis added.
30. Royce, *Sources*, 28, 47–48, 63.
31. Royce, *Sources*, 48.
32. Royce, *Sources*, 6.
33. Royce, *Sources*, 102.
34. Royce, *Sources*, 16; Heb 13:14.
35. Royce, *Sources*, 27.

36. See James, *Varieties*, 7. In his criticism of mainstream churches, James is not only concerned with religious inspiration. He also worries about darker realities, fearing the unreflective conformity that leads to a level of mass moral irresponsibility and degradation of which few individuals are capable on their own (338). As we will see in the next chapter, Royce's philosophy of community addresses these negative group realities as well.

37. Royce, *Sources*, 34. He argues nearly identically in *The Problem of Christianity* (Washington, DC: The Catholic University of America Press, 2001), 41, when he compares his view to James's: "All [religious] experience must be *at least* individual experience, but unless it is *also* social experience, and unless the whole religious community which is in question unites to share it, this experience is but as sounding brass, and as a tinkling cymbal."

38. Despite his language of the "invisible church," Royce does not limit participation within or comprehension of these realities to Christians. Nevertheless, his understanding does emerge from an inherently Christian paradigm, inspired by the early Pauline communities (cf. Royce, *Sources*, 278–80).

39. Royce, *Sources*, 297.

40. In *Problem*, in which Royce makes his metaphysics more explicit, he endorses a two-level understanding of reality—in which the alternation of the idea of the individual and the idea of the community, both of which constitute appropriate starting points for investigation—lend the richest interpretation of existence. As with *Sources*, the community emerges as the means of salvation. Here, the significance of the Pauline churches and the dynamic role of the Spirit therein (intentionally underdeveloped in *Sources* to support an interreligious understanding) becomes evident: "Man the community is the source of salvation....By man the community I mean man in the sense in which Paul conceived

Christ's beloved and universal Church to be a community,—man viewed as one conscious spiritual whole of life....And I say that this conscious spiritual community is the sole possessor of grace, and is the essential source of salvation of the individual" (Royce, *Problem*, 218–19).

41. Consider that Royce's socially alienated individual presents another face of James's "sick soul," translated from an interior to a social form of expression.

42. Royce, *Sources*, 75.

43. Cf. James, *Varieties*, 248.

44. Royce, *Sources*, 74.

45. James, *Varieties*, 203.

46. James, *Varieties*, 222.

47. James, *Varieties*, 224–25.

48. James, *Varieties*, 250.

49. This highly peripheral activity of additional actors may arouse our suspicions. Of course, we could propose one obvious reason for the deliberate marginalization of others from the story: in a climate of religious skepticism, the converted subject wishes to be certain (in their own mind and in the eyes of others) of divine mediation; an experience of utter aloneness provides a stronger basis to explain the event as emerging exclusively from divine action. If we indeed doubt that the solitary form of conversion is as predominant as the testimonies might suggest, we can raise plenty of other potential factors of bias. We can certainly point out that James has selected which documents appear in *Varieties*, and it would be no surprise if he were to choose reports consistent with his preconceived notions of religious experience. We can consider the prejudices introduced by the journaling method or by the leading questions of researchers. We can even reflect on the influence of the canon of popular texts of religious conversion in shaping reports; several subjects present variations on the "take and read" experience that stands as Augustine's turning point in *Confessions*. These indications are worth pursuing.

50. It makes little difference whether we consider these social influences to be unconsciously registered and later brought to light, or rather consciously received and yet willfully ignored: the conclusion remains that social mediation guides the process of conversion.

51. Taylor, *Sources of the Self*, 428.

52. See Thomas Merton's famous "Fourth and Walnut" experience for an example of the mystical-aesthetic appreciation of others: "In Louisville, at the corner of Fourth and Walnut, in the center of the shopping district, I was suddenly overwhelmed with the realization that I loved all those people, that they were mine and I theirs, that we could not be alien to one another even though we were total strangers. It was like waking from a dream of separateness, of spurious self-isolation in a special world, the world of renunciation and supposed holiness....I have the immense joy of being man, a member of a race in which God Himself became incarnate. As if the sorrows and stupidities of the human condition could overwhelm me, now that I realize what we all are. And if only everybody could realize this! But it cannot be explained. There is no way of telling people that they are all walking around shining like the sun." Thomas Merton, *Conjectures of a Guilty Bystander* (Garden City, NY: Doubleday, 1966), 153–54.

53. Royce, *Problem*, 40.

54. Part 2 of *Problem of Christianity* is devoted in large part to explaining the philosophical advantages of a Roycean social metaphysics.

CHAPTER 2

1. For the canonical treatment of radical individualism, see Robert N. Bellah, Richard Madsen, William M. Sullivan, Ann Swidler, and Steven M. Tipton, *Habits of the Heart: Individualism and Commitment in American Life* (Berkeley: University of California Press, 1985).

2. Josiah Royce, *The Sources of Religious Insight* (1912; repr., Washington, DC: The Catholic University of America Press, 2001), 9–10.

3. John Clendenning, *The Life and Thought of Josiah Royce*, rev. ed. (Nashville: Vanderbilt University Press, 1999), 343–44.

4. Note that this Roycean triad closely resembles our central triad of divine spirit, human spirit, and community. Although the third term (interpretation of signs) is not semantically identical to

"the human spirit," we can understand the interpretation of signs as the outworking of the creative activity of the human spirit, thus reinforcing the significance of the action of these three realities (divine spirit, human spirit, and community) as the essential dynamic of Christian spirituality.

5. See Royce on the importance of dialogue for the growth of individuals in *The World and the Individual*: "Our fellows are known to be real and have their own inner life, because they are for each of us the endless treasury of *more ideas*. They answer our questions; they tell us news; they make comments, they pass judgments; they express novel combinations of feelings; they relate to us stories, they argue with us, and they take counsel with us.... *Our fellows furnish us the constantly needed supplement to our own fragmentary meanings*." Josiah Royce, *The World and the Individual*, vol. 1 (New York: Macmillan, 1900), 260, italics original.

6. See Lonergan on progress and decline, expressing the communal-individual dialectic in another manner in Bernard Lonergan, *Insight*, vol. 3 CWL, ed. Frederick Crowe, SJ, and Robert Doran, SJ (Toronto: University of Toronto Press, 1992), 8–9.

7. For a fine example of the significance of the communal-individual dialectic in Orthodox thought, see John D. Zizioulas's *Being in Communion*. As he writes: "The ultimate ontological category which makes something really *be*, is neither an impersonal and incommunicable 'substance,' nor a structure of communion existing by itself or imposed by necessity, but rather the *person*.... True being comes only from the free person, from the person who loves freely—that is, who freely affirms his being, his identity, by means of an event of communion with other persons." John D. Zizioulas, *Being as Communion: Studies in Personhood and the Church* (Crestwood, NY: St. Vladimir's Seminary Press, 1985), 17–18.

8. *The Problem of Christianity* (Washington, DC: The Catholic University of America Press, 2001), 194.

9. Josiah Royce, "Letter to Mary Whiton Calkins, March 20, 1916," in *The Letters of Josiah Royce*, ed. John Clendenning (Chicago: University of Chicago, 1970), 646; compare Royce's view to that of James, for whom communities reflect not actual persons but the "compounding of consciousness." See Royce's evaluation in *The Problem of Christianity*, 240–42, wherein he quotes the

phrase from James's Oxford Hibbert lectures of 1908, later published under the title "The Pluralistic Universe."

10. Royce, *Problem of Christianity*, 80.

11. Royce, "Letter to Mary Whiton Calkins," 646.

12. Royce, *Problem of Christianity*, 236–38.

13. Likewise, given the reciprocal relationship between individuals and communities, communities become less clearly bounded and more complex in their make-up.

14. Royce, *Problem of Christianity*, 239–40.

15. Royce, *Problem of Christianity*, 243.

16. Royce, *Problem of Christianity*, 244.

17. Royce, *Problem of Christianity*, 248–49.

18. This process of reinterpretation in terms of a communal life finds an echo in the "narrative turn" in moral theology, which emerged especially in the late twentieth and early twenty-first century through the work of Stanley Hauerwas. The narrative-based hermeneutic emphasizes the personal recognition and appropriation of a community's stories as essential to moral formation. See Stanley Hauerwas, *A Community of Character: Toward a Constructive Christian Social Ethic* (Notre Dame, IN: University of Notre Dame Press, 1981).

19. Royce, *Problem of Christianity*, 253.

20. This notion of maximal inclusivity inspires the synodal process instituted by Pope Francis in the Catholic Church. Whether inclusivity has been satisfactorily achieved remains up for debate.

21. Royce, *Problem of Christianity*, 255–56.

22. Royce, *Problem of Christianity*, 256–57.

23. To return to an earlier example, the Olympic torch relay represents a secular example of *anamnesis*.

24. These active commemorations most fully unite the individual to the community: to begin to approach the analogy to America's founding, one would have to imagine not only the viewing of fireworks and other celebrations but also the present-day ritualized signing of the Declaration of Independence.

25. Royce, *Problem of Christianity*, 264.

26. Royce, *Problem of Christianity*, 265.

27. Randall E. Auxier, *Time, Will, and Purpose: Living Ideas from the Philosophy of Josiah Royce* (Chicago: Open Court Publishing, 2013), 48.

28. Royce, *Problem of Christianity*, 269.

29. Royce, *Problem of Christianity*, 270.

30. For discussion of the Interpreter Spirit, see Royce, *Problem of Christianity*, 318.

31. See Royce, *The World and the Individual*, 290: "Never in the present life do we find the Self as a given and realized fact. It is for us an ideal. Its true place is in the eternal world, where all plans are fulfilled. In God alone do we fully come to know ourselves. There alone do we know even as we are known."

32. Royce, *The Problem of Christianity*, 404–5.

33. Tommy J. Curry's *Another White Man's Burden: Josiah Royce's Quest for a Philosophy of White Racial Empire* (Albany: SUNY Press, 2018) critiques Josiah Royce's thought and certain facets of his notion of the Beloved Community. A full evaluation of the Beloved Community in light of Curry's work demands separate treatment, but it is necessary to offer an overview. Curry holds that while Royce rejected all forms of pseudo-scientific racism (and thus separated himself from many of his peers), he still purveyed a form of white supremacism that understood white, Western culture to be more advanced than the cultures of other peoples, including those of African origin and African American subcultures. Royce advocated for a degree of diversity through his plan for the preservation of provincial cultures but presupposed an Anglo-American shape within this diversity.

Clearly, Royce's colonialist-inflected ideas problematize his vision of the Beloved Community. Curry's criticisms reveal a significant deficit in Royce's understanding of diversity and pluralism. His Anglo-American prejudices demand to be revised in any future account of the Beloved Community. However, this need not mean throwing out the philosophical and spiritual bases that I have described here. We see in Martin Luther King Jr., Howard Thurman, and M. Shawn Copeland, among others, a healthy notion of the Beloved Community free of colonialist and racist biases. In fact, through their vision of human solidarity, white supremacist prejudices are brought sharply into question. As Dwayne Tunstall has pointed out, we can envision a committedly antiracist version of the Beloved Community. See Dwayne Tunstall, "The Good Royce and the Bad Royce: Or, Is Saving Royce from Himself Worth It?" *Pluralist* 16, no. 2 (2001): 22–29. In our judgment, dedication to Royce's principle of the "community of interpretation" is essential to this continuing examination. We must see the criticisms of Royce's work—and most especially the blistering ones (like Curry's)—as the continued effort of a community of interpreters to be loyal to the cause of truth. The best of this interpretive spirit remains open to the fallibility of hypotheses and accepts justified corrections. The orientation of the Beloved Community to the absolutes of truth, goodness, and justice leaves in the end no abiding space for culture-bound presuppositions regarding the ideal shape of community.

34. Barbara A. Holmes, *Joy Unspeakable: Contemplative Practices of the Black Church*, 2nd ed. (Minneapolis: Fortress Press, 2017); Barbara A. Holmes, *Crisis Contemplation: Healing the Wounded Village* (Albuquerque, NM: CAC Publishing, 2021).

35. Holmes, *Crisis Contemplation*, 21.

36. Holmes, *Crisis Contemplation*, 89.

37. Holmes, *Crisis Contemplation*, 26–27.

38. Recalled from memory of attendance at Hillman lectures by Ron Rolheiser, OMI.

CHAPTER 3

1. See, for instance, Raniero Cantalamessa's Lenten meditation delivered to the Roman curia on March 1, 2024: "Theology, above all in the West, has increasingly moved away from the power of the Spirit to rely on human wisdom." https://www.ncronline.org/vatican/vatican-news/papal-preacher-warns-rise-overly-academic-theology.

2. The connection between individualism and suppression of the Spirit is borne out in the consideration that much of the most remarkable theological reflection on the Holy Spirit in recent times has emerged from the context of the vibrant base communities of the Latin American churches. See Gustavo Gutierrez, *We Drink From Our Own Wells: The Journey of a People*, 20th anniversary ed.,

trans. Matthew J. O'Connell (Maryknoll, NY: Orbis, 2003), and Ignacio Ellacuría, "Christian Spirituality," in *Ignacio Ellacuría: Essays on History, Liberation, and Salvation*, ed. Michael E. Lee (Maryknoll, NY: Orbis, 2013).

3. See especially Catherine Lacugna, *God for Us: The Trinity and Catholic Life* (San Francisco: Harper, 1993); Yves Congar, *I Believe in the Holy Spirit*, trans. David Smith (New York: Crossroad, 1997); Karl Rahner, *The Trinity*, trans. Joseph Donceel (New York: Crossroad, 1997).

4. This principle that openness to the Spirit leads to greater, previously unimagined participation is precisely the trajectory at play in the Second Vatican Council of the Catholic Church. We can detect a thread from the words attributed to Pope John XXIII as the rationale for the council—"let the Spirit blow through the windows of the Church"—to the council's subsequent strengthening of the role of the laity and the newly receptive attitude toward other churches and the wider world.

5. The term *pneumatological imagination* comes from the work of Pentecostal theologian Amos Yong, for whom the idea represents a methodological way of doing theology. For our purposes, the "pneumatological imagination" reflects a practical understanding of how our spiritual lives are tied to the third person of the Trinity. See Amos Yong, *The Hermeneutical Spirit: Theological Interpretation and Scriptural Imagination for the 21st Century* (Eugene, OR: Cascade, 2017).

6. James, *Varieties*, 196.

7. See Congar, *I Believe in the Holy Spirit*, 3.

8. See especially the characterization in Wis 7:22–26: "For in her is a spirit intelligent, holy, unique, Manifold, subtle, agile, clear, unstained, certain, Never harmful, loving the good, keen, unhampered, beneficent, kindly, Firm, secure, tranquil, all-powerful, all-seeing, And pervading all spirits, though they be intelligent, pure and very subtle. For Wisdom is mobile beyond all motion, and she penetrates and pervades all things by reason of her purity. For she is a breath of the might of God and a pure emanation of the glory of the Almighty; therefore nothing defiled can enter into her. For she is the reflection of eternal light, the spotless mirror of the power of God, the image of his goodness" (NABRE).

9. See Prov 1:20–33; 3:13–20; 8:1–36; 9:1–12.

10. Likewise, 1 Cor 15 supports this picture of relationship and even identity. In response to doubts from members of the Corinthian community about the reality of Jesus's bodily resurrection, he remarks upon the relationship between Jesus and the Spirit. He makes what at first seems like an astonishing claim: through the resurrection, Jesus has "become a life-giving Spirit [*Pneuma*]" (1 Cor 15:45). In the first place, this claim implies that Jesus's personal transformation in the Spirit culminated in the resurrection because it transformed him totally, making his physical body into a pneumatic (spiritual) body capable of existing in an imperishable and heavenly mode of existence. Second, the claim reveals the vital and functional identity of life between the risen Christ and the Spirit of God—vital because the two share fully in the same divine life; and functional because both act in life-giving ways for people of faith.

11. In this manner, the scriptural account treats the communities of disciples as persons in the way that Royce describes—as possessing a single mind and integrity of purpose.

12. Instead of "hidebound," we could also say "frozen" or "sclerotic." Communities often become fixed in an attitude of resistance to change to the point that they block and even contravene the Spirit.

13. Nevertheless, the result of remaining in touch with the Spirit generally leads to more rather than less urgency in the rebalancing of the social and ecclesial order.

CHAPTER 4

1. Josiah Royce, *The Problem of Christianity* (1913; repr., Washington DC: The Catholic University of America Press, 2001), 41. To use Aristotelian terminology: although from the standpoint of final causality, the Spirit's action is the cause of the initiating individual experience, from the standpoint of efficient causality, the individual experience enacts the process of religious insight.

2. Royce began his study of logic in earnest in the early 1900s, after Peirce encouraged him to dedicate himself to logic in a letter that followed upon his reading of Royce's *The World and*

the Individual. (See Royce, *Problem of Christianity*, 276–77, for Royce's retelling.) The fruits of his studies are presented in their most polished and accessible form in *The Problem of Christianity*.

3. Richard Hocking and Frank Oppenheim, "Foreword," in *Josiah Royce: Metaphysics, His Philosophy 9 Course of 1915–16* (Albany: State University of New York Press, 1998), x.

4. Royce understood Peirce's work better than James, though both James and Royce admired Peirce's thought. James confessed on several occasions that he found Peirce's lectures and many of his papers impenetrable. The depth of their friendship, however, is evident by James's commitment to support Peirce financially, even in the waning years of his own life: from 1907 until his death in 1910, James wrote to his friends in Boston to request funds for the struggling Peirce, as he also bailed him out personally. In 1911, Peirce expressed both his differences from James as well as his deep appreciation of the man: "He so concrete, so living, I a mere table of contents, so abstract, a very snarl of twine. Yet all my life I found scarce any soul that seemed to comprehend, naturally, (not) my concepts, but the mainspring of my life better than he did." J. H. Cotton, *Royce on the Human Self* (Cambridge, MA: Harvard University Press, 1954), 204–5, quoted in Richardson, *William James: In the Maelstrom of American Modernism* (New York: Mariner, 2006), 138.

5. Charles Sanders Peirce, "Some Consequences of Four Incapacities," in *The Essential Peirce*, vol. 1, *(1867–1893)*, ed. Nathan Houser and Christian Kloesel (Bloomington: Indiana University Press, 1992), 28.

6. The static cast of substance metaphysics fails to adequately encompass the processes of change and development at the heart of an evolutionary worldview. Because the fundamental categories of substance metaphysics (form and matter, act and potency, and substance and accident) are posited a priori, they become empirically unrevisable, even when hypotheses demonstrate the necessity of adjustment.

7. *The Essential Peirce*, 1:88.

8. *The Essential Peirce*, 1:88.

9. Charles Sanders Peirce, *Collected Papers*, vol. 1, *Principles of Philosophy*, ed. Charles Hartshorne and Paul Weiss (Cambridge, MA: Harvard University Press, 1932), 19.

10. For insight into the mathematical basis of synechism, see Paniel Reyes Cárdenas, *Scholastic Realism: A Key to Understanding Peirce's Philosophy* (Oxford: Peter Lang, 2018), 153–60.

11. *Essential Peirce*, 1:89; See also, in his 1878 "How to Make Our Ideas Clear," *Essential Peirce*, 1:139: "The opinion which is fated to be ultimately agreed to by all who investigate is what we mean by the truth, and the object represented in this opinion is the real." For the most part, especially later in his career, Peirce steers clear of the language of finality to express the idea of the orientation to a future communal consensus. The notion of the "final end of inquiry" raises questions about how we know whether this end has been attained, or whether it might be attained at all. As Cheryl Misak points out, Peirce comes to favor versions of the following more solid articulation: "A true belief is such that it would withstand doubt, were we to inquire as far as we fruitfully could into the matter. A true belief is such that, no matter how much further we investigate and debate, it would not be overturned by recalcitrant experience and argument." Cheryl Misak, *The American Pragmatists* (Oxford: Oxford University Press, 2013), 37.

12. Charles Sanders Peirce, *Collected Papers*, vol. 5, *Pragmatism and Pragmaticism*, ed. Charles Hartshorne and Paul Weiss (Cambridge, MA: Harvard University Press, 1935), 354.

13. Donald L. Gelpi, *The Turn to Experience in Contemporary Theology* (Mahwah, NJ: Paulist Press, 1994), 3. See also Royce, *Problem of Christianity*, 277–81.

14. Interestingly, Gelpi began teaching at the Graduate Theological Union in Berkeley the same year that Sandra Schneiders joined the faculty (1986).

15. Peirce on the kind philosophy based upon dualistic constructs: "the philosophy which performs its analyses with an axe, leaving as the ultimate elements, unrelated chunks of being." Charles Sanders Peirce, *Collected Papers*, vol. 7, *Science and Philosophy*, ed. Arthur W. Burks (Cambridge, MA: Harvard University Press, 1958), 570.

16. For a good primer on Peirce's phaneroscopy (as well as his semeiotics), see Cornelis de Waal, *Peirce: A Guide for the Perplexed* (London: Bloomsbury, 2013), 33–46. De Waal's astute reading of Peirce has been invaluable in informing this chapter.

17. Peirce, *Collected Papers*, 1:284.

18. Charles Sanders Peirce, *The Essential Peirce*, vol. 2, *(1893–1913)*, ed. Nathan Houser et al. (Bloomington: Indiana University Press, 1998), 362.

19. Charles Sanders Peirce, *The New Elements of Mathematics*, vol. 3 (The Hague: Mouton Publishers, 1976), 384.

20. Peirce, "The Basis of Pragmaticism in Phaneroscopy," *Essential Peirce*, 2:362.

21. Richard Robin's *Annotated Catalogue of the Papers of Charles S. Peirce* (Amherst: University of Massachusetts Press, 1967), 477:10.

22. Charles Sanders Peirce, *The New Elements of Mathematics*, vol. 4, ed. Carolyn Eisele (The Hague: Mouton Publishers, 1976), 19.

23. Charles Sanders Peirce, "A Guess at the Riddle," *Essential Peirce*, vol. 1. The essay was originally written between 1887 and 1888.

24. "A Guess at the Riddle," *Essential Peirce*, 1:246, emphasis added.

25. Peirce, "A Guess at the Riddle," 247.

26. Peirce, "A Guess at the Riddle," 248.

27. In its openness and possibility, Firstness might be compared to the notion of being in the Western philosophical tradition. Compare Peirce's description of Firstness in "A Guess at the Riddle" to Bernard Lonergan's definition of *being* in his essay "The Subject," in *A Second Collection: Papers by Bernard J. F. Lonergan*, ed. William F.J. Ryan and Bernard J. Tyrell (Toronto: University of Toronto Press, 1974). Peirce: "[Firstness] precedes all synthesis and all differentiation: it has no unity and no parts. It cannot be articulately thought: assert it, and it has already lost its characteristic innocence....Stop to think of it, and it has flown! What the world was to Adam on the day he opened his eyes before it, before he had drawn any distinctions, or had become conscious of his own existence,—that is first, present, immediate, fresh, new, initiative, original, spontaneous, free, vivid, conscious, and evanescent. Only remember that every description of it must be false to it" (248). Lonergan: "The notion of being first appears in questioning. Being is the unknown that questioning intends to know, that answers partially reveal, that further questioning presses on to know more fully. The notion of being, then, is essentially dynamic, proleptic,

an anticipation of the entirety, the concreteness, the totality, that we ever intend, and since our knowledge is finite, never reach" (65). The insight is sustained in the likes of Gabriel Marcel and Martin Heidegger, who are apt to characterize being as what is not known fully and yet always present—as the immediate presentation of reality standing beyond all circumscription and intimating the mystery of existence.

28. Charles S. Peirce, "Pythagorics," *The Open Court* 263 (September 8, 1892): 3375–77, at 3376; though Chinese metaphysics likely was not in his purview, Peirce's triadic system echoes the Daoist cosmology of the Dao De Jing: "The Dao begot one. One begot two. Two begot three. And three begot the ten thousand things." In each case, three constitutes the metaphysical foundation; all that follows is multiplication and recombination.

29. Charles Sanders Peirce, *Collected Papers*, vol. 8, *Reviews, Correspondence, and Bibliography*, ed. Arthur W. Burks (Cambridge, MA: Harvard University Press, 1958), 330.

30. Peirce, "A Guess at the Riddle," 250.

31. As we will touch upon in the following chapter, the pragmatic consequences of mystical exclusivity include the failure to attend to the diverse forms of experience that lead to conversion, that is, to the fullness of Christian life.

32. In referring to "what we call mystical experience," we allude to the status of mystical experience as a modern category. *Mysticism* first became named uniquely as a mode of spiritual experience of its own by French scholars in the sixteenth and seventeenth centuries, not incidentally in the place and epoch in which the Cartesian method became established. See Michel de Certeau, *The Mystic Fable*, vol. 1, *The Sixteenth and Seventeenth Centuries*, trans. Michael B. Smith (Chicago: University of Chicago Press, 1992), 102–8. Additionally, as Bernard McGinn reports, *mystical experience* was not a term in use by mystics or students prior to the nineteenth century. "Mystical theology" is the traditional usage, invented by Dionysius the Areopagite around the fifth century CE. Bernard McGinn, "Mystical Consciousness: A Modest Proposal," *Spiritus: A Journal of Christian Spirituality* 8, no. 1 (2008): 44–63, at 44–45.

33. For Peirce, in any case, absolute Secondness stands as an empirical impossibility.

34. Bernard McGinn, *The Foundations of Mysticism: Origins to the Fifth Century*, vol. 1 of *The Presence of God: A History of Western Christian Mysticism* (New York: Crossroad, 1991), xv–xvi.

35. Even the experience of God's absence described by mystical authors centers on Secondness, for it stands in dialectical relationship to the Secondness of presence.

36. *The Life of Teresa of Jesus: The Autobiography of St. Teresa of Avila*, trans. and ed. E. Allison Peers (Garden City, NY: Doubleday Image Books, 1960), 1.10 (p. 119).

37. Bernard McGinn, *The Growth of Mysticism: Gregory the Great through the 12th Century*, vol. 2 of *The Presence of God: A History of Western Christian Mysticism* (New York: Crossroad, 1994), x–xi.

38. McGinn, "Mystical Consciousness: A Modest Proposal," 44.

39. We follow Peirce's preferred spelling of *semeiotics*.

40. Peirce, "Questions Concerning Certain Faculties Claimed for Man," *Essential Peirce*, 1:22–23.

41. Charles Sanders Peirce, *Collected Papers*, vol. 2, *Elements of Logic*, ed. Charles Hartshorne and Paul Weiss (Cambridge, MA: Harvard University Press, 1932), 228; since Peirce understands a sign as notion of pure logic, he eventually sought to tighten this definition to eliminate its vagueness and the psychological inferences necessary to unpack its meaning.

42. Saussure's semeiotics appears in his *Course of General Linguistics*, published posthumously in 1916. Ferdinand de Saussure, *Course in General Linguistics*, ed. Charles Bally and Albert Sechehaye, trans. Wade Baskin (New York: Philosophical Library, 1959).

43. Saussure, *Course of General Linguistics*, 68.

44. Cornelis de Waal, *Peirce: A Guide for the Perplexed* (London: Bloomsbury Academic, 2013), 75–76.

45. Peirce, *Collected Papers*, 5:421; Peirce calls a self a "being *in futuro*," living through the mediation of signs directed to a possible future (*Collected Papers*, 2:86).

46. All signs are inherently triadic, but Peirce notes that each respective type reflects one of the Categories *relatively*.

47. See Terrence W. Deacon, *The Symbolic Species: The Co-evolution of Language and the Brain* (New York: Norton, 1970), 76–77.

48. See Charles Sanders Peirce, *Collected Papers of Charles Sanders Peirce*, vol. 3, *Exact Logic*, ed. Charles Hartshorne and Paul Weiss (Cambridge, MA: Harvard University Press, 1933), 369.

49. For a magisterial application of Peircean semeiotics to the natural world, see Eduardo Kohn, *How Forests Think: Toward an Anthropology beyond the Human* (Berkeley: University of California Press, 2013).

50. Compare to Wittgenstein's statement that the task of philosophy is to "be rid of a certain kind of puzzlement. This 'philosophic' puzzlement is one of the intellect not of instinct." *Wittgenstein's Lectures: Cambridge 1930–1932*, ed. Desmond Lee (Oxford: Blackwell, 1980), 21.

51. Abduction operates according to a process akin to the "illative sense" proposed by John Henry Newman in *An Essay in Aid to A Grammar of Assent* (London: Longmans, Green, and Co., 1870), 343–83. For Newman, the illative sense is the form of synthetic, creative reasoning that leads to a unified judgment. The illative sense bears analogy to aesthetic taste in its simultaneous objectivity of judgment and subjectivity of flow, in its uncanny precision that nevertheless remains untranslatable by syllogism. The illative sense proceeds according to the sum of data rather than merely discretely according to separable rationally demonstrable truths. It takes the heft and lean of different pieces of information in balance, feeling toward a judgment through a play-like process that evades final, positivistic articulation. Eamon Duffy provides a helpful synopsis of the illative sense in his short book, *John Henry Newman: A Very Brief History* (London: SPCK Publishing, 2019), 41–50.

52. Peirce, *Annotated Catalogue of the Papers of Charles S. Peirce*, 754:3.

53. This idea of endless signification is latent in the adage of the theologians that when we say, "God is an incomprehensible mystery," we do not mean that God is utterly unknowable but rather that God is infinitely knowable. *Deus absconditus* (the hidden and unknowable God) is also *Deus revelatus* (the God who reveals Godself).

54. De Certeau, *Mystic Fable*, 1:99.

55. De Certeau, *Mystic Fable*, 1:299.

56. De Certeau, *Mystic Fable*, 1:98.

57. Plato, *Symposium*, trans. Alexander Nehamas and Paul Woodruff (Indianapolis: Hackett Publishing Company, 1989), 201D–212C.

58. Peirce, *Collected Papers*, 5:265.

59. Belden C. Lane, *The Great Conversation: Nature and the Care of the Soul* (New York: Oxford University Press, 2019), 4.

60. Pope Francis's *Laudato Si': On Care for Our Common Home* offers one striking "conversation starter." The line "everything is interconnected" appears as a mantra of sorts throughout the text: https://www.vatican.va/content/francesco/en/encyclicals/documents/papa-francesco_20150524_enciclica-laudato-si.html, nos. 70, 138, 240.

61. Website for the International Society for Biosemiotics Studies: https://www.biosemiotics.org/what-is/. For the significant relationship between Peirce's philosophy and biosemiotics, see Claudio Rodríguez Higuera "Charles Peirce's Philosophy and the Intersection between Biosemiotics and the Philosophy of Biology," *Biol Theory* 19 (2023). https://doi.org/10.1007/s13752-023-00445-1.

62. Mary Frohlich, "The 'New Animism': Implications for a Postmodern Christian Spirituality, *Spiritus: A Journal of Christian Spirituality* 24, no. 1 (2024): 5–23, at 20.

CHAPTER 5

1. Josiah Royce, *The Sources of Religious Insight* (1912; repr., Washington, DC: The Catholic University of America Press, 2001), 33.

2. For the influence of the rhetoric of conversion in American politics, see Sacvan Bercovitch, *The American Jeremiad* (Madison: University of Wisconsin Press, 1978). As compared to the flourishing of the theme in the United States, conversion has traditionally been neglected as a central concern in European theological circles.

3. In a letter to Carl Jung, Bill Wilson wrote that the goal of AA was to make "conversion experiences—nearly every variety reported by James—available on an almost wholesale basis." See Robert D. Richardson, *William James: In the Maelstrom of American Modernism* (New York: Mariner, 2006), 405.

4. Bernard Lonergan, *A Second Collection*, Collected Works of Bernard Lonergan 13, ed. Robert M. Doran and John D. Dadosky (Toronto: University of Toronto Press, 2016), 58. See also Bernard Lonergan, *Method in Theology*, Collected Works of Bernard Lonergan 14, ed. Robert M. Doran and John D. Dadosky (Toronto: University of Toronto Press, 2017), 125.

5. For two typical descriptions, see Lonergan, *Method in Theology*, 125, 223.

6. See Lonergan's outline of the dynamics of conversion in *Method in Theology*, 223–30.

7. Bernard Lonergan, "Natural Right and Historical Mindedness," in *A Third Collection*, ed. Robert M. Doran and John D. Dadosky, Collected Works of Bernard Lonergan 16 (University of Toronto Press, 2017), 163–76.

8. To be precise, Gelpi discerns that moral conversion comes in two forms that, because they do not necessarily coincide and, indeed, engage separate realms of experience, must be named separately. This distinction will be developed in greater depth in the subsequent section.

9. Gelpi, *Committed Worship: A Sacramental Theology for Converting Christians*, vol. 1 (Collegeville, MN: Liturgical Press), 19.

10. See Donald L. Gelpi, *The Gracing of Human Experience: Rethinking the Relationship between Nature and Grace* (Eugene, OR: Wipf & Stock, 2007), 292–93.

11. See especially Gelpi, *The Gracing of Human Experience*, 263–65; we must recall that, in discussing the modes of conversion in turn, we only prescind from their relational character; we address each separately rather than supposing that they ever function as uncoordinated processes.

12. Gelpi, *The Gracing of Human Experience*, 294.

13. In basing our understanding of conversion on human experience, faith marks the line of division between the natural and the supernatural. Faith is the indicator of graced experience

that brings the person into relationship with God's self-revelation. See Gelpi, *The Gracing of Human Experience*, 301.

14. Peirce, *Collected Papers*, 5:129.

15. Peirce, *Collected Papers*, 5:129. For an excellent synopsis of the normative sciences, see Cornelis de Waal, *Peirce: A Guide for the Perplexed* (London: Bloomsbury, 2013), 48–49.

16. Peirce, *Collected Papers*, 8:256.

17. Peirce, *Collected Papers*, 2:3.

18. Peirce, *Collected Papers*, 5:191; aesthetics, in turn, depends on phenomenology, as the study of phenomena without any motive, including the motive of identifying the admirable.

19. Although he orders the normative sciences, he does not appeal to a single foundational starting point in the way of the Cartesian method. There remains an interplay of impact in both directions across the levels of the normative sciences.

20. For Gelpi, Peirce's work on the normative sciences not only validates Lonergan's idea of the modes of conversion but also provides indications of the fruits of each mode of conversion as well as their interrelationship. To take affective conversion as an example: the increased capacity to perceive beauty stands as a sign of affective conversion; also, just as esthetics grounds the other two normative sciences, affective conversion suffuses each form of conversion with vitality.

21. Hans Urs von Balthasar, *The Glory of the Lord: A Theological Aesthetics*, vol. 1, *Seeing the Form*, trans. Erasmo Leiva-Merikakis, ed. Joseph Fessio and John Riches (San Francisco: Ignatius; New York: Crossroad, 2009), 18.

22. Richard Tarnas, *Cosmos and Psyche: Intimations of a New World View* (New York: Viking, 2006), 44.

23. C. G. Jung, letter of September 23, 1949, to Dorothy Thompson, in *C. G. Jung, Letters 1: 1906–1950*, ed. G. Adler, A. Jaffé, trans. R. F. C. Hull (London: Routledge & Kegan Paul, 1973), 537.

24. See Carl Gustav Jung, *Modern Man in Search of a Soul*, trans. W. S. Dell and Cary F. Baynes (New York: Harcourt, 1933), 122: "We moderns are faced with the necessity of rediscovering the life of the spirit; we must experience it anew for ourselves. It is the only way in which we can break the spell that binds us to the cycle of biological events."

25. See Richardson, *William James*, 514–15.

26. Deidre Bair, *Jung: A Biography* (Boston: Little Brown, 2003), 167–68.

27. Gelpi, *Committed Worship*, 1:33.

28. See L'Arche International, "Summary Report from L'Arche International," February 22, 2020, accessed October 6, 2024. https://www.larche.org/wp-content/uploads/documents/10181/2539004/Inquiry-Summary_Report-Final-2020_02_22-EN.pdf.

29. See James, *Varieties*, 16–21.

30. We might posit the principle of primary and secondary causality to support James's understanding of Teresa's experience. The divine action is a primary cause that works through secondary means.

31. Peirce's "scientifically" oriented community should not be mistaken for the community of practicing scientists. For Peirce, what is most crucial is the adoption of the *scientific* attitude, which is not exclusive to scientists. The attitude follows according to his first rule of reason: "In order to learn you must desire to learn and not be satisfied with what you are already inclined to think"; or, the corollary: "Do not block the road of inquiry." Clearly, many trained scientists do not possess a scientific attitude, while many who are not trained as scientists adhere to the attitude. For the two quotations, see Charles Sanders Peirce, *Reasoning and the Logic of Things: The Cambridge Conference Lectures of 1898*, ed. Kenneth L. Ketner (Cambridge, MA: Harvard University Press, 1992), 178.

32. Those who exemplify moral conversion often become leaders of the communities to which they belong. As Royce points out in *A Philosophy of Loyalty* (New York: Macmillan, 1908), leadership requires self-possession, which he distinguishes from self-reliance, and autonomy, which he distinguishes from mere individuality.

33. See Gelpi, *The Gracing of Human Experience*, 296; note that Christian conversion also provides an orientation to ultimate value through revealed moral teachings. We take up Christian conversion in relationship to moral conversion later in the chapter.

34. The discrepancy in moral conversion is the most obvious difference between the two groups of scientists. However, it is also worth asking whether the majority group was intellectually

converted, especially in consideration of Peirce's view. Were they dedicated to the truth, which lies ever in the future, if their scientific-technical project potentially contributed to the eventual destruction of the world? Would they not then be preventing the full unfolding of the truth over the long haul?

35. J. Robert Oppenheimer, "The Physicists Have Known Sin," lecture, Massachusetts Institute of Technology, Cambridge, MA, November 25, 1947.

36. This transition in thinking reflects a communal turn—from the nominalistic declaration that a person is something like an isolated "bad seed" to the contextualization of individual behavior within a complex social context.

37. "A Big Heart Open to God: An Interview with Pope Francis," *America*, Sept. 19, 2013. https://www.americamagazine.org/faith/2013/09/30/big-heart-open-god-interview-pope-francis.

38. This "skipped step" compromises moral conversion. Instead of righteousness, we observe the self-righteousness of moral superiority, which Jesus explicitly condemns (Matt 23:27–33). Beyond telling people whether they are right or wrong, the fullness of moral conversion involves creating the conditions for others to do good.

39. See Philip Rief, *The Triumph of the Therapeutic: Uses of Faith after Freud* (Chicago: University of Chicago Press, 1987), 1–54.

40. To pick up on Rieff's point, we can interpose our triad of the human spirit, the divine spirit, and the community. As we would affirm, the cultural banishment of the sacred and the neglect of the community leads to a hollowing and enervating spirit of individualism. However, not every kind of therapy informs this precise kind of deficient cultural ethos. It is noteworthy on this point that Rieff builds his account of therapeutic culture based on Freud. (Rieff had already published *Freud: The Mind of the Moralist* in 1959.) Jung's approach is not prone to the same rigid foreclosure of spiritual experience as Freud's (despite, from the traditional Christian perspective, Jung's heterodox postulates and gnostic tendencies, such as the imputation of a "shadow" to God and intimations of a kind of intrapsychic salvation). As Jung confessed, a personal relationship with the transcendent was central to the working out of his ideas: "I find that all my thoughts circle

around God like the planets around the sun, and are as irresistibly attracted by Him. I would feel it to be the grossest sin if I were to oppose any resistance to this force" (C. G. Jung, with Aniela Jaffe, *Memories, Dreams, Reflections*, trans. Richard and Clara Winston [1961; repr., New York: Random House, 1995], 13). Rather than the charge of spiritual impoverishment, the stronger judgment against Jung may be the attenuation of the link between the "sacred pair" of the individual and the community in his highly interiorizing vision of personal development, which he calls *individuation*. As von Balthasar astutely remarks, "The whole diaological plane, the realm of becoming-a-self in the context of one's fellow human beings, is something that Jung, while he does not simply ignore it, passes through to get to the totality of the 'self,' which alone really interests him" (*Theo-Drama: Theological Dramatic Theory*, vol. 1, *Prolegomena* [San Francisco: Ignatius Press, 1988], 518). For Jung, the community figures within human depths through the collective unconscious but not so much in the mediation of external deeds and exchanges in concrete communities. In short, although Jung's insights reward study, spirituality still awaits an appropriately balanced and robust depth psychology.

41. Rieff's book has since generated a kind of cottage industry of scholars who evaluate and develop his thesis. In *Ars Vitae: The Fate of Inwardness and the Return of the Ancient Art of Living*, Elisabeth Lasch-Quinn names members of this group who have developed the idea of the therapeutic sensibility, including Peter Berger, Tom Wolfe, Christopher Lasch, Christina Hoff Sommers, Sally Satel, and Wendy Kaminer. See her treatment of Rieff on pp. 14–19. Elisabeth Lasch-Quinn, *Ars Vitae: The Fate of Inwardness and the Return of the Ancient Art of Living* (Notre Dame, IN: University of Notre Dame Press, 2020).

42. Donald L. Gelpi, *Closer Walk: Confessions of a Jesuit Yat* (Lanham, MD: Hamilton Books, 2006), 295.

43. Gelpi also notes how the four additional forms of personal conversion *authenticate* sociopolitical conversion, providing the norms to discern between just and unjust systems and practices. The intellectually converted see through ideologies that conceal injustice; the affectively converted detect the impact of collective psychological pathologies on institutional frameworks; personal moral conversion makes more evident concrete abuses of human

dignity; and religious insight brings the scriptural and theological norms of the Reign of God to bear upon our society's current form. *The Gracing of Human Experience*, 299.

44. Gelpi, *A Closer Walk*, 290.

45. Czeslaw Milosz, *Visions from San Francisco Bay*, trans. Richard Lourie (New York: Farrar, Straus and Giroux, 1983), 158.

46. Simone de Beauvoir, *Memoirs of a Dutiful Daughter*, trans. James Kirkup (New York: Harper & Row, 1959), 268.

47. Milosz, *Visions from San Francisco Bay*, 154. Full essay, "On Virtue," 149–59.

48. Milosz, *Visions*, 154.

49. Milosz, *Visions*, 154–55.

50. In many cases, the impulses informing sociopolitical and moral conversion do not lead to genuine conversion even in the realm to which they refer. Reactionaries who are merely aggressively opposed to an opposite party lead to sociopolitical breakdown rather than to communal sociopolitical conversion. In these situations, the common good suffers, for most people who stand outside the direct conflict tend not to identify with either side, recognizing that each side suffers from related problems of moral reductionism. John Stuart Mill's observation, "In all intellectual debates, both sides tend to be correct in what they affirm, and wrong in what they deny," tends to be even more the case in moral debates. John Stuart Mill, *On Liberty*, ed. Elizabeth Rapaport (Indianapolis: Hackett Publishing, 1978), 53.

51. Again, we are speaking of two types of moral impulses rather than two cases of full moral or full sociopolitical conversion, respectively: the fully morally converted seek resolution to conflict rather than the inflammation of conflict.

52. See James Hillman, "Peaks and Vales," in *Senex and Puer*, Uniform Edition of the Writings of James Hillman, vol. 3, ed. Glen Slater (Putnam, CT: Spring Publications, 2005), 80–84.

53. Hillman, "Negative Senex and a Renaissance Solution," in *Senex and Puer*, 283–92.

54. Hillman, "An Aspect of the Historical and Psychological Present," in *Senex and Puer*, 57–65.

55. Hillman, "An Aspect of the Historical and Psychological Present," in *Senex and Puer*, 63.

56. For a contemporary example of a theologian whose work emphasizes integral moral conversion, see the works of Charles Camosy, especially *Resisting Throwaway Culture: How a Consistent Life Ethic Can Unite a Fractured People* (Hyde Park, NY: New City Press, 2019). Camosy celebrates the consistent life ethic championed by Cardinal Joseph Bernardin, an idea Bernardin first announced at a 1983 address at Fordham University.

57. Charles Sanders Peirce, *Writings of Charles S. Peirce: A Chronological Edition*, vol. 2, *1867–1871*, ed. Christian J. W. Kloesel (Bloomington: Indiana University Press, 1984), 468.

58. Peirce, *Writings*, 468.

59. Peirce, *Collected Papers* 5:13.

60. "The Fixation of Belief," *Essential Peirce* 1:115.

61. Again, Peirce's method runs contrary to the Cartesian method of systematic contrived doubt. Peirce emphasizes the place of real doubts in inquiry. As Peirce distinguishes his approach from that of Descartes: "Genuine doubt does not talk of beginning with doubting. The pragmatist knows that doubt is an art which has to be acquired with difficulty; and his genuine doubts will go much further than those of any Cartesian." Peirce, *Annotated Catalogue of the Papers of Charles S. Peirce*, 845:10.

62. *Essential Peirce* 1:116.

63. *Essential Peirce* 1:118.

64. *Essential Peirce*, 1:119.

65. "Fundamental" should not be read as providing the form of foundationalist epistemology that Peirce repudiated.

66. *Essential Peirce*, 1:120.

67. *Essential Peirce*, 1:122.

68. Again, we should be careful not to misread Peirce's method of science. This is his own coinage, not the ratification of everything that flies under the banner of science or is justified in the name of science. Peirce was adamant that *scientism*, which unduly restricts the categories of experience, does not align with the *method of science*.

69. *Essential Peirce*, 1:123, emphasis added.

70. *Essential Peirce*, 1:123, emphasis added.

71. We have here an anticipation of Peirce's later work on the normative sciences: the doctrine was not explicitly formulated at

this early stage, but we can nevertheless see evidence of the seeds of his insight.

72. Psychologically speaking, without intellectual conversion, one struggles to move past inertia. Morally, one may be plenty tenacious about one's principles, but, unaided by solid reasoning, cherished principles may amount to little more than social pieties.

73. To speak of Christian conversion is not to deny the authenticity of religious conversion outside of the Christian faith. Starting from an anthropological basis, we understand Christian conversion as one subset of religious conversion. Other forms of conversion will have analogous results. This observation raises a related point about the methodology of the discipline of Christian spirituality. From the foundation of the discipline, Sandra Schneiders recognizes Christian spirituality as one form of spirituality among many—Buddhist, Hindu, Daoist, and more—with each kind of spirituality reflecting "lived human experience" in relation to the paradigms of each given tradition.

74. Theologically speaking, not only the completion of Christian conversion but also the initial turn in openness to God is suffused with God's grace. The theological tradition refers to this notion as prevenient grace. Because the human being is created in the image of God, the potentiality for God is already rooted in human experience.

75. Gelpi, *The Gracing of Human Experience*, 325–26.

76. The term *transvaluation* captures the theological insight of St. Thomas Aquinas: grace does not destroy but heals, elevates, and perfects human nature. Thomas Aquinas, *Summa Theologiae*, trans. the Fathers of the English Dominican Province (New York: Benziger Brothers, 1947), I, q. 1, a. 8, ad 2.

77. Jesus proclaims the reign of God, which comes into being through his very person (Mark 1:14–15, Matt 4:17). According to the full scriptural understanding, the reign of God not only brings human beings but the myriad of existent beings into relationship with the Creator (Rom 8:20–22). The new heaven and new earth (Rev 21:1) that God fashions entails a cosmic communion that does not stop short at the communion of human souls.

78. Described by James H. Cone, *The Cross and the Lynching Tree* (Maryknoll, NY: Orbis Books, 2011), 77–78.

79. Martin Luther King Jr., *Stride Toward Freedom: The Montgomery Story* (New York: Harper & Brothers, 1958), 135, quoted in Cone, *The Cross and the Lynching Tree*, 80.

80. Notice how the transvaluation of affective conversion relates to the Jamesian discussion of the two pre-converted mentalities—the "sick soul" and the "healthy-minded." For James, the sick soul possesses a more penetrating view of reality. The experience of conversion *does not reflect* the transition of the "sick soul" to the natural optimism of "healthy-mindedness" but the birth of a new perspective that transcends both categories. The experience of affective peace emerges from a deeper source of assurance, the same source (we might posit) that granted King the strength to carry on as a result of his early morning prayer in his kitchen.

81. Merton admired King. See his letter to Coretta Scott King following King's assassination, dated April 5, 1968: "Let me only say how deeply I share your personal grief as well as the shock which pervades the whole nation. He has done the greatest thing anyone can do. In imitation of his Master he has laid down his life for his friends and enemies. He knew the nation was under judgement and he tried everything to stay the hand of God and man. He will go down in history as one of our greatest citizens." Thomas Merton, letter to Coretta Scott King, April 5, 1968, in *The Hidden Ground of Love: Letters*, ed. William H. Shannon (New York: Farrar, Straus and Giroux, 1985), 294–95.

82. Merton, *Conjectures of a Guilty Bystander*, 27.

83. Merton, *Conjectures of a Guilty Bystander*, 27.

84. Merton, *Conjectures of a Guilty Bystander*, 28.

85. Merton, *Conjectures of a Guilty Bystander*, 31.

86. Martin Luther King Jr., "I Have a Dream," speech, March on Washington for Jobs and Freedom, Washington, DC, August 28, 1963.

CHAPTER 6

1. Thomas Merton, *The Seven Storey Mountain* (New York: Harcourt, 1948), 1.

2. Emphasis added.

3. See David W. Givey, *The Social Thought of Thomas Merton: The Way of Nonviolence and Peace for the Future* (Winona, MN: Anselm Academic, 2009), 13: "Merton had written in his journal *The Sign of Jonas* that he had not really possessed a nationality for the first thirty-six years of his life and had always been proud of his freedom. As a naturalized citizen of the United States, however, he began to feel more like a citizen of the Kingdom of God begun on earth."

4. See Pope Francis's address to the United States Congress on September 24, 2015. Francis names Merton, Martin Luther King Jr., Dorothy Day, and Abraham Lincoln as "four great Americans" who "provide a way of seeing and interpreting reality." Pope Francis, "Visit to the Joint Session of the United States Congress: Address of the Holy Father," September 24, 2015, Washington, DC. https://www.vatican.va/content/francesco/en/speeches/2015/september/documents/papa-francesco_20150924_usa-us-congress.html.

5. M. Shawn Copeland, "The Watchmen and the Witnesses: Thomas Merton, Martin Luther King, Jr., and the Exercise of the Prophetic," *The Merton Annual* 30 (2017): 156.

6. For more on the term *watchman*, see Copeland, "The Watchmen and the Witnesses," 159. "Watchmen" is a term for a prophet that appears in Isaiah: "They call to me from Seir, 'Watchman, how much longer the night?'" (Isa 21:11). The phrase also appears throughout Ezek 33, wherein Ezekiel is understood to be the watchman.

7. John Clendenning, *The Life and Thought of Josiah Royce*, rev. ed. (Nashville: Vanderbilt University Press, 1999), 376.

8. Charles Algernon Swinburne, "A Watch in the Night," *The Atlantic Monthly*, December 1868. https://www.theatlantic.com/magazine/archive/1868/12/a-watch-in-the-night/.

9. Reported in Clendenning, *The Life and Thought of Josiah Royce*, 376.

10. Royce's reaction was made more complex by his personal history in Germany. He studied in Germany as a young man, from 1875 to 1876. He spent time in Heidelberg, Leipzig, and Göttingen.

11. Royce shares about his public address in *The Letters of Josiah Royce*, ed. John Clendenning (Chicago: University of Chicago Press, 1970), 627–31.

12. See Thomas Merton, "A Devout Meditation in Memory of Adolf Eichmann," in *Raids on the Unspeakable* (New York: New Directions, 1966), 45–49.

13. Although he does not make the explicit connection, we understand Royce best when we bear in mind the rich Hebrew word *emeth*, translated as "fidelity, firmness, or veracity." It is the word for God's steadfastness or the trustworthiness of God's law (cf. Ps 119:142, 160). In the biblical vision, humans are called to participate in God's faithfulness.

14. Josiah Royce, "The Philosophy of Loyalty," in *The Basic Writings of Josiah Royce*, vol. 2 (New York: Fordham University Press, 2005), 996.

15. *Sources of Religious Insight* was first delivered as the Boss Lectures in Illinois in 1911. Josiah Royce, *The Sources of Religious Insight* (1912; repr., Washington, DC: The Catholic University of America Press, 2001).

16. Royce routinely capitalizes these terms in *Sources.* I follow his convention here.

17. Royce, *Sources of Religious Insight*, 278–80.

18. Josiah Royce, *The Problem of Christianity* (1913; repr., Washington DC: The Catholic University of America Press, 2001), 314–15.

19. Royce, *The Problem of Christianity*, 246–49.

20. See Frank M. Oppenheim, *Reverence for the Relations of Life: Re-imagining Pragmatism via Josiah Royce's Interactions with Peirce, James, and Dewey* (Notre Dame, IN: University of Notre Dame Press, 2005), 196–97.

21. Royce, "The Philosophy of Loyalty," 869.

22. See John J. Markey, *Creating Communion: The Theology of the Constitutions of the Church* (Hyde Park, NY: New City Press, 2003), 129.

23. Royce, *The Problem of Christianity*, 270.

24. Royce, *The Problem of Christianity*, 269–70; emphasis added.

25. See Royce, *The Problem of Christianity*, 18.

26. Royce, *The Problem of Christianity*, 404.

27. See Kipton Jensen, "The Growing Edges of Beloved Community: From Royce to Thurman and King," in *Transaction of the Charles S. Peirce Society* 52, no. 2 (2016): 241.

28. Royce, *The Problem of Christianity*, 200.

29. Thomas Merton, *The Seven Storey Mountain* (New York: New American Library, 1963), 314.

30. Thomas Merton, "Letter to Sister J.M., June 17, 1968," *The School of Charity: The Letters of Thomas Merton on Religious Renewal and Spiritual Direction*, ed. Patrick Hart (New York: Farrar, Strauss & Giroux, 1990), 384–85.

31. Thomas Merton, *Conjectures of a Guilty Bystander* (Garden City, NY: Doubleday, 1966), 153–54.

32. See Givey, *The Social Thought of Thomas Merton*, 8–14, for an exploration of the factors at play in this shift. James Thomas Baker takes a much more schematic, dualistic approach to Merton's two major phases, placing the vital turn in 1958, as the contemplative Merton turns into the active Merton and the Merton of prayer transforms into the Merton of social action. See his analysis in James Thomas Baker, "The World & Thomas Merton," in *Thomas Merton: Social Critic* (Lexington: University Press of Kentucky, 1971), 27–43.

33. Credit to Daniel P. Horan for his comments on the appropriateness of a more holistic vision of Merton's spiritual development. I am indebted to his line of thought in my evaluation of Merton's "conversion to the Beloved Community."

34. The Baroness received advice from Dorothy Day when she started the first Friendship House in Toronto. The Harlem House was the second to be founded.

35. Merton, *The Seven Storey Mountain*, 373–75.

36. Merton, *The Seven Storey Mountain*, 379.

37. Thomas Merton, *Run to the Mountain: The Story of a Vocation, The Journals of Thomas Merton*, vol. 1, *1939–41*, ed. Patrick Hart, OCSO (San Francisco: Harper Collins, 1995), 455–56.

38. Merton writes at length on *contemptus mundi*, especially in his assorted reflections in *Conjectures of a Guilty Bystander*. See 6–7, 40, 47, 90, 121–22, 203, 319–20, 328, 343, 352. The principle is a Christian notion developed from Neoplatonism and Stoicism. Merton's interpretation of *contemptus mundi* highlights the futility and lostness of the world when cut off from the salvific presence of grace and thus absorbed within the psychospiritual mechanisms of death. For an exemplary source from Merton's extended Benedictine family, see Bernard of Cluny, *Scorn for the World: Bernard*

of Cluny's De Contemptu Mundi, intro. by Ronald E. Pepin (East Lansing, MI: Colleagues Press, 1991).

39. The poem was published in Thomas Merton, *A Man in the Divided Sea* (New York: New Directions, 1946), 42. Merton wrote the poem well before the year of publication, however. The first half of the poems in this collection were written before Merton joined the monastery.

40. Michael N. McGregor, "The Persistence of Harlem in the Life and Legacy of Thomas Merton," in *The Merton Annual* 29 (2016): 97.

41. See Merton, *Run to the Mountain*, 462; *The Seven Storey Mountain*, 286–89.

42. Merton, *The Seven Storey Mountain*, 287.

43. Thomas Merton, *The Sign of Jonas* (New York: Harcourt, 1953), 322–23.

44. Merton, *The Sign of Jonas*, 323.

45. Merton, *Raids on the Unspeakable*, 60–61.

46. The opening lines of the Second Vatican Council's Pastoral Constitution on the Church in the Modern World, *Gaudium et Spes*, promulgated in December 1965, ring out as especially well fulfilled by Merton's late work on peace, race, and culture: "The joys and the hopes, the griefs and the anxieties of the men of this age, especially those who are poor or in any way afflicted, these are the joys and hopes, the griefs and anxieties of the followers of Christ. Indeed, nothing genuinely human fails to raise an echo in their hearts." Vatican Council II, *Gaudium et Spes: Pastoral Constitution on the Church in the Modern World*, December 7, 1965, in *Vatican Council II: The Conciliar and Post Conciliar Documents*, ed. Austin Flannery, 903–1001 (New York: Costello Publishing Company, 1984), par. 1.

47. Thomas Merton, "Christian Culture Needs Oriental Wisdom," in *Thomas Merton: Selected Essays*, ed. Patrick F. O'Connell (Maryknoll, NY: Orbis), 112.

48. I quote from the letter as republished in Thomas Merton, *Faith and Violence: Christian Teaching and Christian Practice* (Notre Dame, IN: University of Notre Dame Press, 1968), 106–8.

49. Gordon Zahn, "Thomas Merton: Reluctant Pacifist," in *Thomas Merton: Prophet in the Belly of a Paradox*, ed. Gerald Twomey (Mahwah, NJ: Paulist Press, 1978), 65.

50. Merton, *Faith and Violence*, 108.

51. Merton, *Faith and Violence*, 108.

52. See Daniel P. Horan, "What Thomas Merton Tells Us about the Gospel's Logic vs. Our Society's," *National Catholic Reporter*, August 10, 2022. https://www.ncronline.org/news/opinion/what-thomas-merton-tells-us-about-gospels-logic-vs-our-societys.

53. See Thomas Merton, "The Root of War Is Fear," in *New Seeds of Contemplation* (New York: New Directions, 1960), 112–222.

54. See Thomas Merton, "Letters to a White Liberal," in *Seeds of Destruction* (New York: Farrar, Straus, and Giroux, 1980), 3–71.

55. See Merton, "A Devout Meditation in Memory of Adolf Eichmann," in *Raids on the Unspeakable*, 45–49.

56. A hint toward a further path: I suggest that we continue this work of interpretation, extending the understanding of the Beloved Community to include all of creation. This is an important development to take up elsewhere.

57. Charles Marsh, *The Beloved Community: How Faith Shapes Social Justice from the Civil Rights Movement to Today* (New York: Basic Books, 2005), 49.

58. Merton, *Conjectures*, 343.

59. Thomas Merton, *New Seeds of Contemplation* (New York: New Directions, 1972), 80.

60. Thomas Merton, Address to International Summit of Monks, Calcutta, India (October 19–27, 1968), published in *The Asian Journals of Thomas Merton* (New York: New Directions: 1975), 51.

CONCLUSION

1. Charles Sanders Peirce, "Manuscript 318," unpublished manuscript, Peirce Edition Project, Indiana University–Purdue, Indianapolis.

INDEX